RESOLVING CONFLICTS AT WORK

Also by Kenneth Cloke

Conflict Revolution: Mediating Evil, War, Injustice and Terrorism

The Crossroads of Conflict: A Journey into the Heart of Dispute Resolution

Mediating Dangerously: The Frontiers of Conflict Resolution

Mediation: Revenge and the Magic of Forgiveness

Also by Joan Goldsmith (with Warren Bennis)

Learning to Lead: A Workbook on Becoming a Leader

Also by Kenneth Cloke and Joan Goldsmith

The Art of Waking People Up: Cultivating Awareness and Authenticity at Work

The End of Management and the Rise of Organizational Democracy

Resolving Personal and Organizational Conflicts: Stories of Transformation and Forgiveness

Resolving Conflicts at Work: A Complete Guide for Everyone on the Job

Thank God It's Monday: 14 Values We Need to Humanize the Way We Work

THIRD EDITION

RESOLVING CONFLICTS AT WORK

TEN STRATEGIES FOR EVERYONE ON THE JOB

KENNETH CLOKE • JOAN GOLDSMITH

Foreword by Warren Bennis

JOSSEY-BASS
A Wiley Imprint
www.josseybass.com

Published by Jossey-Bass
A Wiley Imprint
989 Market Street, San Francisco, CA 94103-1741—www.josseybass.com

Jossey-Bass books and products are available through most bookstores. To contact Jossey-Bass directly call our Customer Care Department within the U.S. at 800-956-7739, outside the U.S. at 317-572-3986, or fax 317-572-4002.

Jossey-Bass also publishes its books in a variety of electronic formats. Some content that appears in print may not be available in electronic books.

Credits appear after the Index.

Library of Congress Cataloging-in-Publication Data

Cloke, Kenneth, date.
Resolving conflicts at work : ten strategies for everyone on the job / Kenneth Cloke, Joan Goldsmith ; foreword by Warren Bennis. – Third edition.
p. cm
Includes bibliographical references and index.
ISBN 978-0-470-92224-8 (pbk.); ISBN 978-1-118-01062-4 (ebk.);
ISBN 978-1-118-01081-5 (ebk.); ISBN 978-1-118-01082-2 (ebk.)
1. Conflict management. 2. Interpersonal relations. 3. Personnel management–Psychological aspects. 4. Psychology, Industrial. I. Goldsmith, Joan, date. II. Title.
HD42.C56 2011
650.1′3–dc22

2010048701

Printed in the United States of America
THIRD EDITION
PB Printing 10 9 8

CONTENTS

FOREWORD

CONFLICT: AN OPPORTUNITY FOR LEADERSHIP

In the midst of the recent financial crisis, it is clear that leadership has never mattered more. We are in dire need of leaders who can courageously confront and resolve the many conflicts that plague our organizations and threaten our well-being, who can address and resolve the conflicts that damage the very fabric of society, and who can openly and skillfully resolve conflicts that have an adverse impact on our daily lives.

We need organizational leaders who can release us from unrelenting conflicts and do not merely paper over disagreements and disputes. We have to resist the temptation to follow leaders with perverse agendas that undermine or distort the authentic resolution of recurring conflicts. Instead, we need to develop organizational leaders who are skilled in resolving conflicts, who seek solutions that address underlying causes, and who serve the interests of all involved.

If we look to one of the leaders of our early Republic, Abigail Adams, we see that she had it right when she counseled her son John Quincy that hard times are the crucible in which character and leadership are forged. "It is not in the still calm of life or the repose of a pacific station that great characters are formed," she wrote to him in 1780. "The habits of a vigorous mind are formed in contending with difficulty. Great necessities call out great virtues." The spirit of this wife and mother of two founding presidents inspires us to consider our own era as a time when leaders can imaginatively create environments in which conflict resolution strategies generate a viable, collaborative new future. This future will be created by leaders who can cope with rapid, uncertain change and address social strains, psychological tensions, and chronic conflicts in cultures that foster collaboration, open and honest communication, and conflict resolution.

The first skill of these leaders is a capacity to exercise good judgment by making the right decisions in the midst of confusing and frightening conflicts based on knowledge, wisdom, and an ability to remain true to overriding values.

A second skill of these leaders is the ability to enlist others and motivate them to seek resolution to seemingly insurmountable conflicts. This skill flows from what the psychologist Daniel Goleman calls "emotional intelligence," the capacity to understand and connect with the hopes and fears of those who are in conflict and to find common ground in the values they share.

A third skill of these leaders is respect. Respect to those in conflict signifies that they have been seen and valued for who they are; disrespect signifies that they are invisible and do not matter. People in conflict often engage in destructive habits in order to gain respect. The debilitating dispute that seems unbearable and never-ending can evaporate when a leader affords respect to all involved and enables each person to experience being valued and included.

This new breed of leader creates respectful, ethical, innovative, and productive work environments where everyone is encouraged to invent solutions to ongoing conflicts. The characteristics of these leaders include widespread *alignment* based on a commitment to deal with conflict in a straightforward manner; *empowerment* of all parties to identify and resolve the conflicts they encounter; and *transparency* that allows conflict to be viewed openly and honestly so that inquiry, integrity, and reflection are generated and prized.

Alignment

Leaders align those who work on all levels of their organizations to perceive and accept common understandings of the causes of organizational conflicts. They inspire a commitment to resolve disputes by articulating shared values and goals. This alignment has a great deal to do with spirit and a team atmosphere. A shared understanding of the sources of conflict in the everyday organizational life aligns everyone to achieve a higher purpose and uplifts and harmonizes their aspirations. Each person is then able to view conflict as an opportunity to learn and one that can lead to improvement in work, in products, and in a shared future.

Empowerment

Empowerment means that everyone believes they are at the center of the organization rather than at the periphery, and they make a difference to the success of the overall effort. Empowered individuals take the risk of acknowledging the conflicts they generate or encounter. They *know* that what they do has significance and they take responsibility for surfacing conflicts, learning from them, and achieving lasting resolutions. They exercise discretion and responsibility and create a culture of respect in which everyone is encouraged to openly confront disputes and disagreements and to develop methods to resolve them, without having to check through five levels of the hierarchy for permission to take on contentious issues. Leaders who empower their organizations generate and sustain trust and encourage systemwide effective communication.

Transparency

When inquiry-based reflection and transparency are at the heart of organizational culture, learning opportunities and useful information flow unhampered. In these cultures people are open to problem *finding*, not merely problem solving. In these adaptive, values-based learning organizations, staff on all levels find, identify, and resolve conflicts before they generate crises. Leaders encourage the free discovery of ideas and the sharing of information to solve problems. They are not afraid to test their ideas, even if full disclosure threatens to reveal deeper conflicts. A learning and inquiring organization, in which transparent exchanges of information are a matter of course, allows everyone to reflect on and honestly evaluate their actions and decisions.

Thus, postbureaucratic organizations generate leaders who value meaningful interactions, healthy conflicts, and active dissent; who are not averse to risk taking; who support learning from their mistakes, rather than blaming others for them. They develop informal leadership in cross-functional teams and they actively listen to the ideas of colleagues and support the talents of others. They create organizations that are decentralized into autonomous units in which decision making is shared. They demand self-discipline and emphasize individual responsibility, collaborative relationships, widespread ethics, and open communication that resolves conflicts when they emerge.

This subtle yet profound and perceptible change taking place in our philosophy of leadership creates organizational cultures that encourage the honest expression of conflict and candid discussion of differences. These changes include

- A new concept of humanity, based on an increased understanding of our complex and shifting needs, that is replacing an oversimplified, mechanical idea of who we are
- A new concept of power, based on collaboration, reason, and synergy, that is replacing a failed model of power based on coercion and threats
- A new concept of values, based on humanistic-democratic ideals, that is replacing a rigid bureaucratic system that regards property and rules as more important than people and relationships

I now add a fourth change reflected in the central argument that Cloke and Goldsmith make in the pages that follow:

- A new concept of conflict, based on personal leadership and organizational learning, creative problem solving, collaborative negotiation, satisfaction of interests, and a view of conflict that can promote personal and organizational transformation. This creative model is replacing a limited approach to conflict that seeks to suppress, avoid, or compromise issues rather than resolve the underlying reasons that gave rise to them.

With this book, the authors offer wisdom, food for thought, and tools for those of us who seek to improve our abilities to address conflict and to create organizational cultures in which conflicts are openly and candidly addressed. Cloke and Goldsmith provide multiple strategies for addressing, resolving, transforming, and learning from conflicts. They challenge us to learn to live with ambiguity, to communicate more openly, to participate in conflicts with integrity, making a virtue of contingency, and finding unity in the issues that divide us. In doing so, they make a significant contribution to creating healthy organizations by providing methods for resolving the destructive conflicts to be found in this contentious era. I welcome the sound advice that follows.

WARREN BENNIS
Distinguished Professor of Business Administration
University of Southern California

This book is dedicated with love
to our grandchildren,
Orrin, Thacher, and Tallulah,
in hopes they will gain
wisdom from the lessons their conflicts
can teach them.

ACKNOWLEDGMENTS

Every effort to reach out to those with whom we disagree brings us all closer together, and this book could not have been written without the extraordinary courage and dedication of mediators and conflict resolvers who have joined us for over thirty years in improving our understanding of how to move from impasse to resolution in deeply entrenched conflicts, and how to create successful workplace collaborations.

We thank all of you for your unfailing support, your honest feedback, and your deep understanding.

We also thank the many courageous leaders who have joined us in experimenting, discovering, implementing, and improving the ideas we present here. It is only because of their courage and willingness to try something new that we were able to "field-test" our ideas, learn from our mistakes, and tell you their stories.

We especially want to acknowledge the many members and leaders of Mediators Beyond Borders (www.mediatorsbeyondborders.org) whose unflagging commitment to promoting peace and reconciliation around the world encourages hope and inspiration.

A special thanks goes to Warren Bennis for believing in us and supporting this book, and to our children and grandchildren, who have been our greatest teachers. We thank our editors, Alan Rinzler and Seth Schwartz, our talented indexer and friend, Carolyn Thibault, and our extraordinary assistant, Solange Raro.

KENNETH CLOKE AND JOAN GOLDSMITH

Center for Dispute Resolution, Santa Monica, California

We have thought of peace as passive
and war as the active way of living.
The opposite is true.
War is not the most strenuous life.
It is a kind of rest cure compared
to the task of reconciling our differences.
From War to Peace is not from the strenuous
to the easy existence.
It is from the futile to the effective,
from the stagnant to the active,
from the destructive to the creative way of life.
The world will be regenerated by the people
who rise above these passive ways
and heroically seek by whatever hardship,
by whatever toil
the methods by which people can agree.

—Mary Parker Follett

INTRODUCTION

TEN STRATEGIES FOR EVERYONE ON THE JOB

> The rules of the game: learn everything, read everything, inquire into everything.... When two texts, or two assertions, or perhaps two ideas, are in contradiction, be ready to reconcile them rather than cancel one by the other; regard them as two different facets, or two successive stages of the same reality, a reality convincingly human just because it is complex.
>
> — MARGUERITE YOURCENAR

It is nearly impossible to grow up in a family, live in a neighborhood, attend a school, work on a job, have an intimate relationship, raise children, or actively participate as a citizen in the world without experiencing a wide variety of disagreements, arguments, disputes, hostilities, and conflicts.

Much of our childhood is spent in conflict with those we love, with our parents, siblings, and playmates, who teach us the first and most difficult lessons of life, including how to respond to intense emotions and handle behaviors we find difficult to understand or accept. Our schools teach us hard lessons about rejection and compromise, about how to succeed and fail in a hierarchy, how to manage disputes with teachers and peers, and how to overcome shame, rage, and fear.

As adults, our most intimate family relationships are immersed in and deeply influenced by conflict. We learn how to respond to conflicts at work; in interactions with government agencies, schools, and companies; and in the neighborhoods and communities where we live. We learn different skills in response to conflicts with our spouses, partners, children, neighbors, and coworkers over miscommunications, false expectations and assumptions, unclear roles and responsibilities, disagreements and rejections, changes and losses.

Our diverse societies and multiethnic, religious, and social cultures seem saturated with conflicts that scream at us from headlines, ads, and movies that, in their intensity, subtly shape our psyches and perceptions. Our communities have been deeply divided by racial prejudice, hatred of dissenters and those who are different, and conflicts over competition regarding the use of scarce resources to satisfy disparate needs and expectations.

Our workplaces and organizations are profoundly shaped by conflicts between workers and supervisors, unions and management, competing departments, and stressed coworkers. Our competitive economy, status-conscious society, and politicized government agencies reverberate with chronic disputes between ins and outs, haves and have-nots, us and them, powerful and powerless—all battling over the distribution of power, status, goods, and resources.

When we lack effective skills, our first response is often to avoid or suppress conflict, or try to make it go away, causing us to miss its underlying meaning. As a result, we cheat ourselves, our opponents, and our organizations out of learning, making it impossible to correct what led to the problem in the first place, prevent future conflicts, and discover how to improve our overall ability to resolve and transcend our disputes.

Yet, the pain, loss, and irretrievable damage that are suffered by individuals, families, organizations, and communities in conflict can also create miracles of transformation when people find new solutions, are moved to forgiveness and reconciliation, and are able to reclaim peaceful lives, relationships, and organizations. These are the two faces of conflict, the destructive and the creative, the stagnant and the active, the aggressive and the transformative. Between them lies a set of strategies, techniques, and approaches for turning one into the other. It is these strategies that are the subject matter of this book.

Everyone is capable of seeing both these faces, though most of us, when we are in conflict, focus on the first rather than on the second. We have all learned how to fight and how to collaborate, how to run away and how to stand up for what we believe in, how to hide what we think and how to say what we really mean, how to resist change and how to embrace it, how to live as though no one else mattered and how to collaborate closely with others, how to get stuck in impasse and how to improve our lives and our relationships with those we love or respect.

In short, each of us has learned destructive as well as creative ways of responding to conflict. Yet in order to shift from the destructive to the creative, from the stagnant to the active, from aggression to transformation, we need to search within *ourselves* for the true meaning of our conflicts, and for the skills we need to turn one into the other. If we can become more aware of what we are contributing to our conflicts and start to listen and learn from our opponents, we can work together to improve the organizational structures, systems, processes, and relationships that generate *chronic* conflicts, and overcome the tendency to slip into negative or destructive responses.

Conflicts at Work

Most executives, managers, and employees face conflicts on a daily or weekly basis, spending from 20 percent to as much as 80 percent of their working hours trying to resolve or contain them. If we simply quantify the time spent by the average executive, manager, and employee on unresolved conflict and multiply it times their salary, the result would far exceed the cost of in-depth training in conflict resolution skills.

Yet, with the right approach, most of these conflicts are entirely avoidable, unnecessary, or easily resolvable. Many workplace disputes arise from simple miscommunications, misunderstandings, seemingly irrelevant differences, poor choices of language, ineffective management styles, unclear roles and responsibilities, false expectations, and poor leadership that can easily be corrected through listening, informal problem solving, dialogue, collaborative negotiation, and mediation.

Unfortunately, few of us have been trained in how to resolve the many conflicts that come our way. Few schools teach it, and few corporations, nonprofits, or government agencies offer conflict prevention programs. They rarely train managers and supervisors in dispute resolution, or orient employees to collaborative negotiation, creative problem solving, peer-based mediation, and other conflict resolution methodologies.

When organizations *do* try to train their executives, managers, and employees in conflict resolution techniques, these classes are often far too brief and oriented toward elementary skills, or toward suppressing or merely settling conflicts and trying to make them go away. They rarely take the approach that conflicts point to issues, problems, or difficulties that can provide unique learning opportunities and lead to significant improvements.

Thus, we pay a heavy price for conflict—not only individually and relationally, but organizationally and socially—through litigation, strikes, reduced productivity, poor morale, wasted time and resources, unnecessary resignations and terminations, lost customers, dysfunctional relationships with colleagues, destructive battles with competing departments, stifling rules and regulations, gossip and rumors, and reduced opportunities for teamwork, synergy, learning, and change.

Chronic Conflicts at Work

The deeper sources of conflict at work are *chronic* disputes that repeat themselves in various guises, but never fully disappear. The causes of these disputes often have little or nothing to do with the petty, superficial issues people commonly fight over, but go much deeper into the structures, systems, processes, and relationships in the workplace; the nature of conflict, the culture of conflict within organizations; and the ways work is organized, compensated, processed, and acknowledged.

Chronic conflicts can often be distinguished by the repetitiveness of their allegations, issues, and accusations; by their acceptance and tolerance for disrespectful and adversarial behaviors; by their low level of resolution, reescalation and renewal of hostilities; and by the seeming irrationality and incongruity between high levels of emotion and the apparently trivial issues over which people are fighting. For this reason, chronic conflicts are commonly mistaken for miscommunications, personality clashes, or accidental misunderstandings, yet on analysis reveal strong underlying similarities.

Simply defined, chronic conflicts are those that nations, societies, organizations, families, or individuals

1. Have not fully resolved
2. Need to resolve in order to grow and evolve
3. Are capable of resolving
4. Can only resolve by abandoning old approaches and adopting new ones
5. Are resistant to resolving because they are frightened, dissatisfied, insecure, uncertain, angry, or unwilling to change

How, then, do we resolve chronic conflicts at work? We can begin by recognizing that every chronic conflict contains at least two fundamental truths: the truth of impasse, that people are stuck with a problem from which they would like to escape and cannot; and the truth of resolution, that it is possible for them to become unstuck and move to a higher order of resolution or relationship. They can do this by understanding, at a deep level, that whatever it was that caused them to get stuck in the first place can also enable them, when they use the right skills, to transform the way they think, feel, and act about it.

We can also recognize that every organization, whether it is a corporation, school, nonprofit, or government agency, generates chronic conflicts. Each of these conflicts poses a challenge to the organization that it has not faced directly or in its entirety. Each chronic conflict thereby reveals a paradigm that has begun to shift, a problem that has yet to be solved, or an opportunity for improvement that has not been understood, seized upon, or implemented.

Indeed, every chronic conflict presents us with a unique opportunity to significantly enhance our personal lives, deepen our relationships, improve our processes, expand the effectiveness of our organizations, increase our work satisfaction, and release us from impasse. To reach these transformational outcomes, it is necessary to understand how and why we get stuck, and develop the strategies and skills that make resolution and transformation possible.

The Dark Side of Emotion in Conflict

When we are in conflict, we say things we do not mean and mean things we do not say. Only rarely do we communicate at a deep level what we really, honestly think and feel, or do so in ways that are empathetic. We seldom speak from our hearts or expose our vulnerability in ways our opponent can hear. Why do we fall into these traps? Why is it so difficult to do what we know is right?

Our conflicts have the capacity to confuse and hypnotize us, to make us genuinely believe there is no way out other than through combat. Conflict possesses dark, hypnotic, destructive powers: the power of attachment when it is time to leave, the power of demonization when it is time to forgive, the power of articulate speech when it is time to listen. Conflict alternately strokes and crushes our egos, fuels and exhausts our will, energizes and freezes us in fear. It speaks to a deep, ancient part of our soul that thirsts for power and delights in revenge.

When we are engaged in conflict, our emotions seem enormously powerful and overwhelming. When we are in the grip of strong emotions, they feel limitless and unstoppable, irresistible and all defining. Part of the seduction of strong emotions is that they allow us to present who we are and what we want in absolute terms. They force us to identify with the seemingly infinite power of our feelings and to surrender control to something larger than ourselves.

We have all experienced times in our lives when we lacked the skills we needed to communicate honestly and empathetically with others. We have all been aggressive, judgmental, and hypercritical, or passive, apathetic, and defensive. Our efforts at honesty have been misinterpreted as aggression and our empathy as weakness. We have not known how to temper our anger with compassion, how to listen to our opponent's pain when we were being criticized, how to discover what caused our opponents to act as they did, or how to take responsibility for our own miscommunications and conflicts. We have failed to find ways of working collaboratively with our opponents and find solutions to our problems. As a result, we have felt trapped in our conflicts, sensing or believing that there was no exit, no way out.

In addition, we have all resisted apologizing for our behaviors, acknowledging our miscommunications, or recognizing that our deepest, most destructive emotions originate *inside us,* having little or nothing to do with our opponents. We have become lost in self-aggrandizement or self-denial, sometimes simply by focusing exclusively on what our opponent did or said. We have engaged in conflict because we were unhappy with our lives, needed attention, felt rejected, lacked the courage to stand up for ourselves, felt insecure or upset by criticism, were ashamed of our own cowardice or grief, or did not have the skill to respond effectively to someone else's behavior. And our opponents have behaved exactly the same way for the same reasons.

Instead of facing these internal reasons for being upset and gaining insight into our deeper motivations, we have become angry with others and claimed our cause was noble, just, true, and right. We have described our opponents as evil, unjust, unfair, harassing, aggressive, dishonest, disloyal, and insane, as opposed to describing our own pain, or why our relationship with them is important to us, or searching for the misunderstandings, false expectations, miscommunications, and petty incidents that we have both blown out of proportion.

In the process, we have missed the truth: that these petty concerns can be transcended *only* by expanding our awareness of the deeper reasons that gave rise to them. We can escape them only by being honest with ourselves, our opponents, and our colleagues about what is really bothering us, by genuinely listening to those with whom we disagree, and by discovering that we have much to learn from them. Once we let go of our emotional investment in being right, we can begin to collaborate in the discovery and implementation of creative solutions.

Settlement Versus Resolution

In many organizations, executives, managers, and employees have learned to sweep conflicts under the rug in hopes that they will go away. As a result, organizations have developed cultures that encourage people to avoid discussing difficult issues, *not* fully communicate what they really want, and settle for partial solutions or no solution at all. In doing so, they cheat themselves and others in the workplace out of learning from their conflicts and discovering more skillful ways of resolving disputes.

Denying the existence of conflict does not make it disappear, but simply increases its covert power. Organizations that encourage people to avoid or suppress disagreements, or reward them for being "good employees," inevitably develop systems and cultures that sacrifice honesty, integrity, creativity, and peace of mind for a superficial, fragile, temporary, and false facade of agreement and civility.

In many workplaces, employees have learned to accept a level of humiliation, abuse, superficiality, and unresolved conflict simply in order to keep their jobs. Consider, for example, how much humiliation, abuse, and conflict you and others you know have accepted. Here are some questions to ask yourself and others at work:

- Do people in my organization embrace and try to learn from conflicts, or do they avoid them and try to sweep them under the rug?
- What price have my colleagues and I paid as a result?
- What price have I and others in conflict paid for being unable to resolve our disputes, or for having to dissemble and pretend they do not exist?
- How often do we carry our conflict with us for years?
- What price has the organization paid for unresolved conflict?

There is an enormous difference between communicating superficially to *settle* your conflicts and communicating deeply to *resolve* them, between *compromising* over issues and *transforming* your conflicts by learning from them. We try to settle our conflicts when we are uncomfortable with them, feel frightened by them or by what we imagine their resolution will entail, and wish to avoid or suppress them, or to pacify our opponents. We compromise and try to make them go away because we experience them as stressful, uncontrollable, violent, frightening, and irrational, because we lack the skill to handle our own intense emotions, or because we do not know how to respond safely to the intense emotions of others. Often, we see our conflicts as failures, or do not think they are important or useful. Sometimes we are simply afraid of hurting other people's feelings by addressing them directly.

Unfortunately, when we avoid, suppress, or compromise our conflicts, we often miss the chance to reveal their underlying sources, correct them, learn from them, or break through to the other side. If this is our approach, we will seek settlement for settlement's sake and cheat ourselves out of opportunities for resolution, learning, and transformation.

It may come as a shock to you that we do not advocate peace for its own sake, or believe that settlement and compromise are always better than conflict. As we see it, peace without justice soon becomes oppressive. Superficial settlements often lead to silence, sullen acceptance, distrust, and renewed hostilities. By contrast, resolution leads to learning, change, partnership, community, innovation, increased trust, and forgiveness. All these positive outcomes are lost when we "trade justice for harmony" or commit to "peace at any price." Peace, in this sense, does not mean the absence of conflict, but the skill and ability to engage in it collaboratively and constructively.

Into the Eye of the Storm

When we seek resolution, we are drawn toward the center of our disputes, into "the eye of the storm." While this may sound irrational and even dangerous, it is nonetheless true that by moving *toward* our adversaries rather than away from them, we more quickly discover what lies beneath the surface of our disputes, and begin to see how we can listen empathetically even to those who oppose us. We can then acknowledge what we have in common, clarify and resolve the issues that are dividing us, devise creative solutions, collaboratively negotiate differences, identify and resolve the underlying reasons for the dispute, learn from each other and the conflict, and strengthen and revitalize our relationships.

At the center, heart, or eye of every storm of conflict is a calm, peaceful place where opposition and antagonism are united, transformed, and transcended, where learning, dialogue, and insight take place. Journeying into the eye of the storm is, for this reason, a core, or meta-strategy for moving from impasse to resolution and transformation.

To move toward the center of our conflicts, we need to change the way we think about our disagreements, and how we behave in their presence. We cannot succeed in the long run by avoiding confrontation, or by simply ceasing to communicate with our opponents—these responses will not resolve anything. Instead, if we recognize that every conflict contains hidden lessons that can fuel our growth, change, learning, awareness, intimacy, effectiveness, and successful relationships, we will not be frightened of moving toward their center. As we do so, we may be able to see, hidden deep in our conflict, signs of the emergence of a new paradigm, indications of a desire for a better working relationship, a detailed guide to what is not working for one or both of us, and an implicit request that we work together to make things better.

Paradoxically, we may engage in conflict because we do not believe it is possible to resolve our disputes, and therefore become *more* aggressive in order to avoid feeling defeated. Sometimes we fight because we need to express strong feelings or beliefs about an issue, or we are trying to remedy an injustice. Perhaps the other side has refused to listen or negotiate, and conflict seems to offer a welcome antidote to stagnation and apathy. Being aggressive is sometimes the only way we believe we can spark communication and honest dialogue—not because it is right, but because we feel it is the only way we can get the other person or the organization to listen. Yet hidden in the allure of our principled opposition is the price we pay for having an enemy.

Lasting change happens when we use higher-level skills to move *through* our conflicts to achieve deeper levels of resolution, allowing us to shift from divergence to convergence, from antagonism to unity, and from impasse to transcendence. In this way, conflict resolution is an expression of the *highest* personal, organizational, social, and political responsibility. It is an antidote to unfairness and injustice, a more effective way of bringing about social change, and sometimes the only way of successfully communicating our opposition to policies and practices we do not like. In each of these cases, it is not *conflict* that is the problem, but the destructive, adversarial ways we engage in it.

How Far Apart Are People Who Are in Conflict?

Our greatest sources of inspiration and personal satisfaction come from love rather than hate, from moments of connection rather than moments of aggression and hostility. Yet even while we are searching for insight and transformation or trying to rise above the fray, we find ourselves mired in petty squabbles that make our efforts to avoid or ignore them seem almost laughable.

Every conflict we face in life is rich with positive and negative potential. Every dispute can be a source of inspiration, enlightenment, learning, transformation, and growth—or of rage, fear, shame, impasse, and resistance. The choice is fundamentally not up to our opponents, but to us, and depends on our willingness to face them by engaging directly, constructively, and collaboratively with our opponents.

For example, consider this question: How far apart are people who are in conflict? We believe there are three correct answers:

1. They are an infinite distance apart because they cannot communicate at all.
2. They are no distance whatsoever because their conflict makes them inseparable.
3. They are exactly *one step* apart because either of them can reach out and touch the other at any moment.

If these answers are correct, where are these conflicts actually located? Again, there are three correct answers:

1. They are located in the mind and heart of each party because their perceptions, attitudes, ideas, emotions, and intentions are indispensable to the continuation of the dispute.
2. They are located between them because every conflict is a relationship.
3. They are located in the surrounding context because all conflicts take place within a system, culture, or environment that influences how they are conducted.

The third location is especially important in workplace conflicts, which are always located at least partly in the organizational systems, structures, processes, and cultures that inform everyone's choices about how to respond.

The answers to these questions suggest that you can improve your ability to resolve conflicts not only by taking the one step that separates you from your opponent, but also by changing the way you think and act in their presence, by working to improve your relationship with them, and by redesigning and shifting the organizational systems, structures, processes, and cultures in the workplace in which they occur.

The German philosopher Nietzsche wrote, "When you look into the abyss, the abyss also looks into you." Looking into your conflicts means surrendering your illusions, no longer seeing yourself as a powerless victim, or your opponents as evil enemies. It means giving up your fear of engaging in honest communication with someone you may distrust or even dislike, and taking responsibility for the attitudes and behaviors that *you* bring to the conflict.

The Transformational Power of Conflict

When we choose to face the dark side of our participation in conflict, we begin to recognize its extraordinary capacity to transform our lives by shifting the way we understand ourselves, experience others, conduct our relationships, relate to our organizations, and learn and grow. This hidden, transformative power of each and every conflict lies in the potential for its resolution in a way that leads to a discovery of a better way of being, working, and living *simultaneously*.

If this proposition seems surprising to you, think of a time when your life shifted dramatically and your relationship to the world around you was transformed. Was your transformation connected in any way to a conflict? Did you achieve a flash of realization while in the midst of a dispute? Did you change as a result of loss, confrontation, criticism, divorce, or the death of someone you loved? Did it occur as a result of negative feedback, discipline, or termination? Before you achieved clarity, did you feel torn between conflicting alternatives? If so, you are not alone. As you consider these questions, we invite you to begin your own transformation by consciously and skillfully engaging in your conflicts, experiencing them completely, turning them into learning experiences and opportunities to practice new skills, and working to reach genuine closure.

By transformation, we mean significant, all-encompassing, lasting change. Transformation is not minor, incremental, small-scale, linear, temporary, or transitory. It is a change in the *form* of the conflict that leaves it, us, and them different from the way we were before. It alters our sense of reality, of identity, and of possibility. Transformation occurs when we let go of what happened and allow what is stuck in the past to die so our present and future can live. It occurs when we discover that what we *most* needed to resolve in our conflict was inside us all the time.

By using the strategies we describe in this book, we hope you will be able to find or create a new sense of yourself and your organization, a new direction in your life, a new understanding of any opponent, and a new approach to resolving future miscommunications, misunderstandings, and conflicts. We hope you will be able to redirect the energy, focus, and time that constitute your personal *investment* in conflict to fuel your personal and organizational growth, learning, and effectiveness. These transformational opportunities are open to each of us at every moment in every conflict.

Surprisingly, large-scale transformations often take place through very simple actions, such as listening, asking questions, and making commitments. To achieve transformational results in your conflicts, we ask you to make two commitments. First, we ask that you pay attention to the way you *are* when you are in conflict, and that you choose to listen and learn—both internally to your own voice and sense of truth, and externally to the voice of your adversary or opponent. Second, we ask that you alter the way you *act,* by exploring options without biases, separating problems from people and interests from positions, exploring the reasons for your own resistance, and that you decide to be a *leader* in your own conflicts and do so, as best you can, with courage and commitment.

Within these twin spheres of being and acting, there are innumerable techniques, methods, approaches, questions, interventions, and processes that can give birth to transformation. Each of these will be different for each person, organization, and situation. Not every method will work for every person, every conflict, or at all times. What matters is that you search for what works best for you, one opponent and one conflict at a time. The strategies we offer are not magic wands. The magic arises from your ability to select the right approach at the right time with the right person.

About This Book

Philosophers have written that the universe can be found in a single grain of sand. This book is our effort to describe the universe we have found in the sands of conflict, which we have studied, sifted, and shaped professionally over the last thirty years. In the process, we have helped thousands of people in workplaces in the United States and around the world resolve their disputes.

We wrote this book to assist everyone who works—employees, leaders, managers, teachers, principals, union representatives, and workers in corporations, nonprofits, schools, and government agencies—in learning from their conflicts. *Everyone* can increase their skills, not merely in making conflicts disappear, but in discovering their deeper underlying truths, resolving the reasons that gave rise to them, preventing future conflicts, and seeing them as drivers to personal and organizational transformation.

To assist you in discovering these truths for yourself, we present ten strategies for resolution. These strategies are a diverse set of tools you can use to improve your skills and resolve your conflicts—not just hammers and wrenches, but mirrors and scalpels, and meta-tools that will help you design your own special tools for each new situation. The mirrors are to help you reflect on what *you* are doing to sustain or encourage the conflict. The scalpels are to assist you in eliminating unproductive, destructive, and unwanted behavior patterns and free you to approach your conflicts in a more constructive, collaborative, and strategic manner. The meta-tools are to help you when the other tools don't seem to work. Our object in offering them is not to tell you what to do or how to do it, but to provide you with insights that will lead you to your own useful methods and important truths, as we have been led to ours.

The Ten Strategies

Each of the ten chapters that follow offers a core strategy that can lead you from impasse to resolution, and possibly to personal and organizational transformation. By working with each strategy, you will be able to improve your ability to confront, embrace, struggle with, and resolve disputes in your own way. As you investigate each strategy, we provide you with detailed suggestions on how to think about, practice, and redesign it to meet your needs.

While you may prefer a simple step-by-step guide guaranteed to help you navigate life's difficulties, we have found the recipe approach to dispute resolution hopelessly inadequate. Simplistic approaches to conflict cannot anticipate the unexpected, respond to complex issues and emotions, or account for individual or organizational uniqueness. They cannot appreciate the wholeness of conflict, which cannot be recognized by slicing it into smaller pieces. Instead, we offer a series of somewhat circular, iterative, intersecting strategies that will lead you to the center of your disputes and reveal their hidden transformational potential.

We refer to "strategies" in order to differentiate a strategic approach to conflict resolution from the more common tactical one that consists of a series of linear steps leading closer and closer to resolution. In our experience, transformation requires the introduction of something new, which requires more than tactical thinking, and resolution is rarely a linear process.

Rather, the search for resolution and transformation reflects a state of mind, an *intention* that cannot be located by following a previously crafted blueprint or map, but must be discovered for yourself. There is no guaranteed technique or tactic that can lead you there, yet *every* conflict resolution technique has the potential to open your eyes to hidden truths and reveal a path forward. In fact, it is likely that you already know the value of every strategy we suggest, and understand deep inside that successfully implementing any strategy requires you to first look inward to find the place where *you* get stuck.

The word *strategy* implies planning, but it also suggests a journey to a place that is, to some extent, unimaginable and indescribable before you arrive. For this reason, we ask you to adopt an attitude of openness, possibility, adventure, and curiosity, and to bring a commitment and desire for resolution to the process. We know from experience that if you pursue any of these strategies, opportunities for transformation will automatically begin to open for you. We invite you to take this exciting journey with us.

Here is a brief explanation of the strategies we explore in each chapter:

Strategy 1: Understand the Culture and Dynamics of Conflict.
Every conflict is significantly influenced by the culture and dynamics in which it takes place. Understanding these elements will help you discover the hidden meaning of your conflicts,

not only for yourself but for your opponent and the organization in which you work. Identifying the culture and dynamics of conflict for individuals and organizations can lead to increased awareness, acceptance, and resolution of the underlying reasons for the dispute.

Strategy 2: Listen Empathetically and Responsively. Listening with an open mind and an open heart to your opponents will encourage them to do the same for you. This will lead you to recognize the real issues in dispute, and thus to the center of your conflict, where all strategies for resolution and transformation converge.

Strategy 3: Search Beneath the Surface for Hidden Meanings. The language we use to describe our disputes, our opponents, and ourselves reveals a set of attitudes and underlying assumptions that can block resolution. Beneath the superficial issues in every conflict lie a set of subterranean fears, desires, interests, emotions, histories, expectations, and intentions that reveal what is actually wrong, and can become a powerful source of resolution and transformation.

Strategy 4: Acknowledge and Reframe Emotions. When intense emotions are brought to the surface, communicated openly and directly in a way that your opponent can hear, and are acknowledged, reframed, and integrated, then invisible barriers are suddenly lifted to problem solving, collaboration, resolution, and transformation.

Strategy 5: Separate What Matters from What Gets in the Way. The road to resolution and transformation lies less in blaming people than skillfully addressing joint problems; less in asserting differences than finding commonalities; less in asserting positions than satisfying interests; less in debating who is right than engaging in dialogue over what both sides care about; less in resurrecting the past than redesigning the future.

Strategy 6: Solve Problems Paradoxically and Creatively. Transformation requires the energy, uncertainty, complexity, and duality of enigma, paradox, riddle, and contradiction, which form an essential part of every conflict. These complex, paradoxical elements can lead to expanded creative problem-solving techniques that can assist you not simply in reaching agreements, but in building diverse, overlapping, simultaneous options into whatever solutions you are able to agree on.

Strategy 7: Learn from Difficult Behaviors. In many workplace conflicts, people are rewarded for engaging in difficult behaviors. These behaviors offer excellent ongoing opportunities for you to learn how to improve your skills in responding to them while increasing your capacity for empathy, patience, and perseverance; to discover what makes their behaviors difficult for you; and to become more grounded and effective in the way you respond.

Strategy 8: Lead and Coach for Transformation. Because conflicts are places where we get stuck, leadership and coaching are useful in helping us find a way out. Leadership competencies in conflict resolution can be learned and developed, and "conflict coaching" can aid us in shifting our attitudes, developing skills, and locating our own unique path to resolution and transformation.

Strategy 9: Explore Resistance and Negotiate Collaboratively. We begin with the idea that "all resistance reflects an unmet need," and can therefore be interpreted as a *request* for improved communications, processes, and relationships; for greater authenticity; for increased involvement in decision making; or for a deeper and more collaborative relationship. Exploring resistance can unlock conflicts, allowing us to collaboratively negotiate solutions and, if other approaches fail, to mediate the issues that seem too difficult to resolve.

Strategy 10: Mediate and Design Systems for Prevention. Chronic conflicts emanate from systems rather than personalities, and can be addressed organizationally through a "conflict resolution systems design" process. Designing conflict resolution systems enables individuals and organizations to prevent or reduce the severity of chronic conflicts, to eliminate them at their source, to orient the organization toward the institutionalization of resolution practices, and dramatically reduce the cost of conflicts.

In your exploration of these strategies in the chapters that follow, we believe you will find that if there is any set principle in conflict resolution, it is that there are no set principles. Success flows from a synergistic combination of curiosity and authenticity, discovery and invention that seek to integrate intellect and emotion, honesty and empathy, reason and intuition, head and heart, and allow each to guide the other.

We hope you will follow the strategies we describe and endeavor to create a workplace or organizational environment in which conflict resolution is seen as an important creative and strategic element in overall improvement, in which collaboration is integrated, celebrated, and continually reinvented—an environment where settlement is not settled for, and resolution opens opportunities for personal and organizational transformation.

We believe that *everyone* can improve their objective and subjective conflict resolution skills and learn better ways of expressing their needs, feelings, and ideas, even in the midst of the most bitter and painful conflicts. Our basic message to you is to strengthen, calibrate, and follow your intuition; to be guided by your heart; to deepen and expand your empathy; and to risk being deeply and compassionately honest about what you have seen and experienced, while making ample room for others to do the same.

We understand that there are times and places where being open and honest may seem more likely to get you into trouble, but for the most part, we hope you will recognize that you have been suffering primarily from being stuck without the requisite skills and techniques to reach genuine resolution and, in the process, have been cheating yourself, your opponent, and your organization out of learning and growth.

Because everyone is different and each person is different from moment to moment, there can be no single tried-and-true response to conflict that will work for everyone, always, and everywhere. There are no simple step-by-step formulas or methods for shifting a paradigm, opening your opponent's heart, or becoming a different person than you were before. All you can do is find your own way by moving into your conflicts, and by combining honesty and empathy, analysis and intuition, reflection and curiosity, precision and kindness, awareness and equanimity, and applying them to the particular conflict and opponent you are facing, then seeing what works and what does not and being courageous enough to alter your approach as you go.

To obtain the resolution or transformation you desire, you will need to learn to move toward, into, and through your disputes. In conflict resolution, the way *out* is *through*. If you are willing to take the risk of being deeply empathetic and honest, we can promise you that your conflict and the strategies you need to resolve it will open up as you go, together with extraordinary opportunities for personal growth, improved morale, and deeper and more satisfying relationships at work.

Finally, we encourage you to learn from your *opponents* and all the people with whom you are in conflict. If you do not, it will be impossible to understand fully what your conflicts are trying to teach you. We know we cannot teach you anything you do not want to learn, and it is difficult to decide to learn from your opponents. Nonetheless, we invite you, in the midst of your most difficult and trying conflicts, to become more open to yourself, your opponents, and your organizations, and commit to a radically different approach to conflict and resolution. We wish you an exciting and successful journey!

STRATEGY 1

UNDERSTAND THE CULTURE AND DYNAMICS OF CONFLICT

Only someone who is ready for everything, who doesn't exclude any experience, even the most incomprehensible, will live the relationship with another person as something alive and will himself sound the depths of his own being. For if we imagine this being of the individual as a larger or smaller room, it is obvious that most people come to know only one corner of their room, one spot near the window, one narrow strip on which they keep walking back and forth. In this way they have a certain security. And yet how much more human is the dangerous insecurity that drives those prisoners in Poe's stories to feel out the shapes of their horrible dungeons and not be strangers to the unspeakable terror of their cells. We, however, are not prisoners.

—Rainer Maria Rilke

How many of us work in organizations where we know only one small corner of what is possible, where we continue walking back and forth along a narrow, limited, controlled strip of existence? How many of us think, feel, and act this way in our conflicts and, in exchange for peace or security, become their prisoners, along with our opponents and organizations?

As we begin this examination of the conflicts in our work lives, let us not be prisoners of their hidden dynamics, or strangers to ourselves and one another. Let us agree to explore the cultural shapes and dynamics of our conflicts, where their hidden meanings suddenly become clear. Let us no longer experience them as dungeons, but as opportunities for learning and improvement, and as journeys that can take us far beyond the seemingly insurmountable differences that somehow keep us imprisoned.

Decoding the Culture of Conflict

What is it that keeps us imprisoned and stuck in conflict? In the first place, it is our *perceptions* of what has happened, including the issues over which we are arguing, the character of our opponent, our own inner nature, the ways we are able to think about and respond to it, the history of our relationship, and the unspoken expectations and assumptions in our workplaces and organizations about the *meaning* of conflict, whose fault it is, and what can or ought to be done about it.

A useful way of thinking about all of these perceptions, expectations, and assumptions is that they form part of, and are influenced and defined by the *culture*, or more specifically, by what we think of as the "culture of conflict" that is present, though largely unspoken and undiscussed, in every workplace and organization.

It may help to think of your own culture of conflict in the following way. Every society, organization, workplace, group, family, and ongoing intimate relationship creates not only occasional conflicts and disagreements, but a complex set of words, ideas, values, behaviors, attitudes, expectations, assumptions, archetypes, customs, and rules that powerfully influence how its members think about and respond to them.

These cultures of conflict are shaped by our previous experiences, particularly in our families of origin. They set the basic parameters and "default settings" for what we consider possible when we are in conflict, and define what we can reasonably expect to happen, both from ourselves and from others. They shape our capacity to ask questions, alter how we see our opponents and ourselves, and tell us what is acceptable and what is not.

Every workplace and organization, school and neighborhood, family and relationship generates spoken and unspoken rules about what people should and should not say and do when they are in conflict. Each of these entities thereby produces a distinct culture that exerts enormous pressure on its members to respond to conflicts and disagreements in ways that reflect the boundaries and traditions of the culture.

Conflict is a kind of social rupture, a potential dissolution of the bonds that keep people together, and it is important that there be rules to make sure this does not happen when disagreements are trivial, or can easily be resolved. At the same time, conflict is a time-honored way for people to get more of what they need or want, and a method of introducing necessary improvements, so it is important that disagreements not completely disappear.

For these reasons, many organizational cultures place a premium on conflict suppression and avoidance. Many highly competitive corporate cultures give rewards for aggressive conflict behaviors; others reward accommodation or compromise, and still others *preach* collaboration but practice avoidance and accommodation. Each of these cultures possesses a subtle set of rules regarding how their members should behave, with whom, over what, and what will happen to them if they don't.

In many workplaces, we find dismissive attitudes that regard conflict resolution as pointless or "touchy-feely"; conflict-averse cultures that reward avoidance and accommodation; aggressive, hyper-competitive cultures that permit bullying and retribution or reprisal for speaking the truth. Others develop bureaucratic rules and regulations regarding conflict that encourage passive-aggressive behaviors, promote hypocritical, self-serving leaders, or tolerate covert systems that generate chronic, morale-crushing, yet completely avoidable conflicts.

As we scan our current organizational and workplace cultures, we search in vain for signs of support for genuine collaboration with our opponents; for cultures that value open, creative dialogue regarding problems; for honest, empathetic, self-critical leadership in addressing and responding to conflicts; and for preventative, persistent, systemic approaches to resolution and learning.

It is rare in most organizational cultures that aggression, avoidance, and accommodation require explanation, whereas collaboration, honesty, openness, and forgiveness seem vaguely unacceptable. Novelist Albert Camus, observing a similar phenomenon during World War II, wrote, "Through a curious transposition peculiar to our times, it is innocence that is called upon to justify itself."

Our colleague, Harvard University Business School professor Rosabeth Moss Kanter, has written a summary of the conflict-generating rules in many organizational cultures that discourage resolution and actively stifle innovation and change:

1. Regard any new idea from below with suspicion—because it's new, and because it's from below.
2. Insist that people who need your approval to act first go through several other levels of management to get their signatures.
3. Ask departments or individuals to challenge and criticize each other's proposals (that saves you the job of deciding; you just pick the survivor).
4. Express your criticisms freely, and withhold your praise (that keeps people on their toes). Let them know that they can be fired at any time.
5. Treat identification of problems as signs of failure, to discourage people from letting you know when some thing in their area isn't working.
6. Control everything carefully. Make sure people count anything that can be counted, frequently.
7. Make decisions to reorganize or change policies in secret, and spring them on people unexpectedly (that also keeps them on their toes).
8. Make sure that requests for information are fully justified, and make sure that it is not given out to managers freely (you don't want data to fall into the wrong hands).
9. Assign to a lower-level manager, in the name of delegation and participation, responsibility for figuring out how to cut back, lay off, move people around, or otherwise implement threatening decisions you made.
10. And above all, never forget that you, the higher-ups, already know everything important about the business.

Conflict Messages in Popular Culture

The seductive, hypnotic power of negative, limited approaches to conflict are enhanced by powerful images in the popular media, to which we are continually subjected. Newspapers are sold with headlines featuring conflict following the classic editorial injunction, "if it bleeds, it leads." Television dramas and news reports alternately accentuate or trivialize it. Sporting events bristle with it and pass it on to their fans. Soap operas play with it. Advertising captures it in images, or creates a phony, superficial world where it cannot even be imagined.

Look carefully at the messages that are broadcast daily through movies, television, newspapers, magazines, radio, and advertising about conflict, and ask yourself: What ideas are being communicated? What behaviors are being reinforced or emulated by paying attention to them? What ideas and actions do others implicitly regard as unworthy of attention or emulation? How often does the hero respond to conflict by mediating, collaboratively negotiating, or resolving it without violence or hostility?

As we experience this continual cultural assault, our threshold of acceptance for violence and aggression is lowered, our capacity for peacemaking is undermined, and we become more and more addicted to the adrenaline rush of combat. Many of the effects of this continuous immersion in conflict are immediate and pervasive. They include a brutalization of the soul, a loss of capacity for empathy with the suffering of others, an overwhelming fear of violence, an anxiety about social acceptance, a numbing capitulation to unacceptable behaviors, a cynicism about human worth, an avoidance of social intimacy, a political paranoia, a retreat into compliant behavior, and a "bread and circuses" atmosphere.

Like addicts, we are alternately being numbed and "shot up" with negative images, not only of conflict but of efforts to resolve it without violence. In common media imagery, if we are to judge by movies and television, pacifism is naive and idealistic, saintly or cowardly, or merely passive and ineffectual; listening and thoughtfulness are regarded as boring or stupid; caution is seen as cowardice; aggression is a sign of passion; and cruelty represents seriousness of character.

These images divert our attention from solving problems that *appear* insurmountable because of the way they are described, or because we are no longer capable of paying attention to them, or we view our opponents as evil-doers who are solely responsible for them.

Increasingly we see ourselves as isolated and alone and cannot imagine banding together to bring about change. More and more we are afraid of public criticism, censure, controversy, or retaliation for violating accepted cultural norms.

In response to this cultural onslaught, many societies, workplaces, and organizations have developed internal ecosystems that promote conflict avoidance, or engage in polite, superficial communications that sweep issues under the rug. In these cultures, people spend an extraordinary amount of time hiding from honest communications, feeling trapped in unresolved disputes, being confused over unclear messages, and unsuccessfully trying to make their needs and feelings heard and understood.

People in these cultures spend little time learning what their conflicts are actually about—what caused them, why people are so upset, why they have such a hard time saying what they really think and feel, or talking directly, openly, and honestly about what matters to them. As a result, they fail to learn from their conflicts, resist change, and cannot see how they might respond more skillfully to their own obstacles and problems, or those experienced by others.

A dramatic example of this self-reinforcing spiral of conflict occurred in an engineering and maintenance division of a Fortune 100 manufacturing company in which we consulted. The engineers saw themselves as a highly skilled, well-educated elite corps. Their mission was to respond to requests from the manufacturing divisions to build equipment that would produce quality products and generate profits. Although they were not a revenue-generating center, they considered themselves to be central to the company's vision, mission, and goals.

Also in the same division was a maintenance crew that consisted of electricians, carpenters, and building managers who saw themselves as craftspeople. They were responsible for repairing the equipment that was built or purchased by the engineers and maintaining the machinery and buildings that housed it. Each group occupied a different status within the division and held the other in disdain. Not only had they developed completely different organizational cultures, languages, and attitudes that disregarded the contributions of others and described them as obstructionist, their mutual hostility began to undermine their ability to successfully complete even routine work projects and sent them into a downward spiral of conflict.

The engineers who introduced new equipment neglected or refused to provide directions, instructions, blueprints, or repair charts to the craftspeople who were required to maintain and repair it. The maintenance staff, in turn, neglected or refused to inform the engineers when they modified the equipment, repaired it, or changed the location of machinery the engineers had installed, leading to frequent and chronic miscommunications, petty disputes, and conflicts.

When the maintenance staff aggressively challenged the engineers to supply the information they needed, the response they received was hostile and dismissive. The engineers saw these requests as unnecessary incursions into their protected, elite, professional domain, whereas the maintenance staff considered the engineer's reactions as stonewalling what they saw as logical and necessary requests.

Maintenance, on the other hand, considered engineering's requests to know when and how the equipment had been modified, became defunct, was moved, or broke down as "none of their damn business." Needless to say, the division's overall organizational culture resulting from these disputes was characterized by "turfism," competition, mutual suspicion, conflict avoidance, small acts of aggression, and bureaucratic bungling, all of which cost the organization a great deal and took months to fix.

To their credit, they did address the problem with facilitated open meetings that began with confessions of disregard and mutual admissions that they had bungled opportunities for collaboration. A joint team of six engineers and craftsmen came up with a set of guidelines for timing and a list of communication ground rules that everyone agreed to follow and revise when necessary. It was not easy, but with effort and commitment, they were able to shift their culture of conflict in a positive direction.

Shifting Conflict Cultures Globally and Locally

Our challenge, like that of the organization described above, is to release ourselves from pointless, unproductive cultural patterns and build organizational cultures that value openness, honesty, dialogue, collaboration, negotiation, conflict resolution, and the ability to learn from our conflicts and our opponents. The difficulty is that we can no longer do so exclusively locally, or in isolation from conflict cultures around the world.

Our local conflict cultures are now directly impacted by international events, including wars, arms races, religious intolerance, environmental disasters, and outbreaks of terrorism, as well as by drug and arms trafficking, climate change, global pandemics, cutbacks in scarce resources, and international financial crises that lead to constricted public budgets, downsizing, layoffs, mergers, unfriendly acquisitions, and strikes.

Moreover, cross-cultural conflicts have become a fact of life in many of our organizations, due not only to the increasing globalization of manufacturing, finances, services, and culture, but to the development of diverse leadership and staff; to the growing interdependence of worldwide customers, markets, vendors, and suppliers; and to the explosive impact of technology on creating instantaneous global cross-cultural communications.

As a result of these developments, globalization is also having an impact on dispute resolution, increasing the frequency and consequences of conflicts in today's corporations, nonprofits, educational institutions, and government agencies. These worldwide ripples can no longer be dismissed as isolated or trivial. In response, we require a new approach to conflict, and a new, invigorated *international* culture of resolution.

Each of us can improve the way we respond to the conflicts that touch us, whether they are local or global in scope. As we do, we gradually begin to shift the cultures of conflict that we have created or tolerated around us—in our homes, families, schools, organizations, communities, and nations. As we achieve a critical mass in favor of conflict resolution, our larger cultures and societies will begin to change in the way they respond to conflict as well.

We think of this as a conflict resolution "butterfly effect," in which every tiny effort at resolution ripples outward to produce a subtle, yet cumulatively positive effect, on a local level in our families and workplaces, and on a global scale in the cultures and attitudes of people toward their conflicts and the resolution process.

For example, it is possible for us to reduce the level of conflict avoidance in our workplace cultures simply by listening empathetically and responsively to our opponents, honestly and nonaggressively communicating our differences, and collaboratively discussing our issues with others in a spirit of trying to find better solutions. In doing so, it is possible to share our cultural traditions, expectations, and assumptions with our opponents, and reach across our cultural differences to find ways we can each communicate more effectively. Here are some small yet powerful ways you can "think globally and act locally," and begin to shift the conflict culture in your workplace, organization, school, community, or family:

- Increase your ability to empathize with your opponents and colleagues, and generously acknowledge their contributions to your learning and improvement.
- Discuss disagreements publicly and don't allow them to be swept under the rug.
- Be self-critical about the role you have played in your conflicts.
- Agree not to engage in caustic insults, accusations, or vitriolic attacks on others.
- Encourage your opponents and colleagues to let go of ancient, unresolved grievances and create common ground with each other.
- Build consensus, particularly over vision, mission, goals, ground rules, and shared values.
- Reach out to communicate across cultural boundaries or borders, and publicly resist the temptation to slip into "us versus them" thinking.
- Publicly identify avoidant, aggressive, and covert or passive-aggressive behaviors, and ask yourself and others whether you *want* to engage in them, or believe they will prove helpful in the long run.
- Encourage your opponents and coworkers to honestly and empathetically communicate their thoughts and feelings about how you and they are interacting, and ask them how they would like to interact with you in the future.
- Publicly invite your opponents and colleagues to engage in dialogue and collaborative negotiation or mediation with you in order to solve your common problems.
- Seek forgiveness and reconciliation within yourself, with your colleagues and your opponents, and let them know how and why you did so.
- Collaboratively identify the elements of your conflict culture that are blocking or supporting resolution and continually improve them.

In these ways, we can begin to change the conflict-averse, avoidant, and aggressive elements in our conflict cultures—and, more important, increase our awareness of the subtle forms of violence and prejudice that are routinely practiced and rationalized around the world, thereby encouraging others, both locally and globally, to be more open, honest, empathetic, committed, and collaborative when they are in conflict.

Altering the Dynamics: Seeing Conflict as an Opportunity

It is difficult in the midst of conflict to deepen our capacity for empathy and understanding with our opponents. For example, we commonly get angry at things that go wrong, and our anger transforms a person who may have made an innocent mistake into a stereotypical demon or villain. We then become upset, get stressed, feel victimized, and believe we are powerless to respond or to change their attitude or behavior.

Similarly, we commonly become defensive in response to anger that is directed at us by others for what we believe is some innocent mistake, causing us to feel upset in response and unable to communicate openly and honestly with people we now view as our opponents, or to listen deeply and carefully to what they mean beneath the angry, negative, judgmental words they are repeating.

On the other hand, when we engage in dialogue with our opponents we resurrect their human side—and become able to express our own as well. By acting with integrity in conflict, we increase our awareness and stimulate self-improvement in others. Uncontrolled anger, defensiveness, fear, and shame defeat these possibilities and leave us feeling weaker. We all feel more powerful when we face our problems, negotiate our differences, and search for resolution; and we all feel weaker when we succumb to negative emotions and refuse to talk with the other person, or even try to resolve our differences.

It is a bitter truth that victories won in anger lead to long-term defeat. Anger causes everyone to feel they lost and leads to additional problems in the future. In conflict, everyone suffers, everyone feels betrayed and unjustly accused, everyone feels hurt and brokenhearted. If there is no resulting dialogue or resolution, both parties carry these unresolved injuries with them into their ongoing relationship, making their next conflict more probable and more serious.

If, on the other hand, both parties are genuinely able to experience their conflicts as opportunities to learn what is not working and how to fix it, they will not be so frightened by their anger. Instead, they will experience it, perhaps, as an indication of frustration and caring, as an opportunity to learn how to be honest without making others mad, or as a chance to experience their own feelings and become more aware of how their anger and other negative emotions work.

Clearly, finding a solution to your conflicts depends on your ability to understand what caused them. This depends, in turn, on your ability to listen to your opponent as you would to a teacher. Doing so will allow you to halt the cycle of escalation and motivate a search for insight and opportunities for improvement. Thus, different—even antagonistic—points of view can help you create a larger, more complex analysis of what may otherwise appear as a simple, narrow problem, and identify richer, more creative, comprehensive, and effective solutions.

Finally, your conflict can lead you to a deeper understanding, not only of your opponent, yourself, your conflict, and your organizational conflict culture, but also of the complex relationships, holistic interactions, and large-scale evolution of these elements at your workplace and within its culture. Increased awareness of the deeper causes and subtle nature of conflicts in general, the intricacies of interpersonal communication and group process, and understanding the reasons why people become angry with each other, can help you develop a more profound understanding of the chronic *systemic* sources of conflict throughout the organization and lead you to more effective methods of resolution.

The Dynamics of Conflict

If it is possible for us to see our conflicts as opportunities, why do we persist in engaging in them as forms of combat? What fuels our negative attitudes in conflict? How do we get trapped in them? Why do we respond to perceived hostility or aggression in such futile, counterproductive, self-defeating ways? Why do we respond with automatic reactions and responses that make us less inclined to listen to our opponents?

The principal driving force in determining the character of our participation in conflict, the nature of our conflict cultures, and our perception of the choices available to us when confronted with aggression, hostility, or opposition, has been a powerful and instinctual, habitual response that is embodied in what is commonly called the "fight-or-flight" reflex.

Let's begin by diagramming the typical neurophysiological responses most of us have to perceived aggression. Assume that the first move in our conflict is made by the other person, whom we will call A, and let's assume that A has engaged in some action that we, B, perceive as aggressive, hostile, or directed against us. To make this clear, let's illustrate the opening move in the conflict, as B sees it, as follows:

$$A \rightarrow B$$

We are not concerned here with what A actually did or intended, or with the subject matter of the dispute, or with whether some third party did something to trigger A's actions. Instead, we are concerned solely with what B *perceives*. From B's perspective, A is behaving hostilely, and if we analyze B's initial instinctual response, B's view of the action is the only one that counts.

On the basis of this diagram, what can we predict about what B will do next? Based on the perceived hostility that is coming from A, what options does B perceive? The next chart illustrates the most common responses B might make to A's perceived aggression. As you scan this chart, think about the responses you make most often when you are in conflict. If you recognize any of B's typical responses in what your opponent is directing toward you, you can assume you have become A in your opponent's eyes.

It is therefore likely that B will respond to A's perceived attack in one of the following ways:

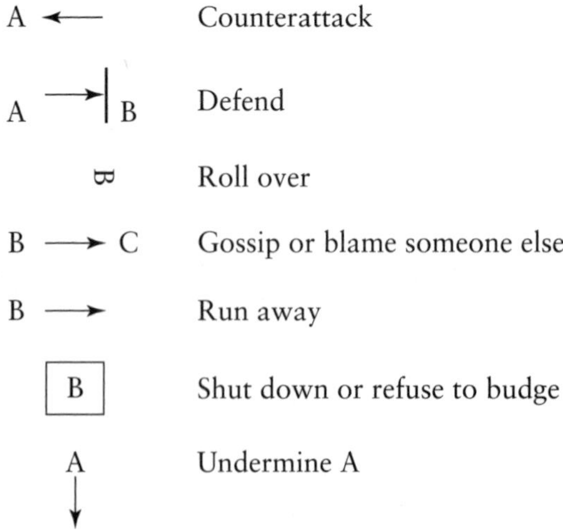

Notice that in each of B's possible responses, A appears more dominant and powerful while B seems weaker and merely responsive to A's cues. Notice also that A "gets something" from every one of B's responses:

- If B counterattacks, A will succeed in getting B's attention and earn support or sympathy from others by no longer appearing to be the one who initiated the dispute.
- If B withdraws, A wins, and can say that B refuses to talk or is never available.
- If B becomes defensive, A can say that B is not listening or is just being defensive.
- If B gossips to C, blames A, or refuses to budge, A can criticize B for gossiping, defensiveness, bad-mouthing, and refusing to accept responsibility for solutions.
- A may even, as a result of B's responses, look like the innocent victim of B's unprovoked attack to an outside observer who did not actually see A attack B first!

In each of these responses, B actually does A a *favor* by entering the conflict, and paradoxically increases A's power by responding in the ways diagrammed. B also loses the moral high ground and aura of leadership by sinking to A's level. Notice, in addition, that to someone who does not know A or is unaware of A's prior aggression, B may not only seem to be the aggressor, but may appear to be "troubled," "crazy," or "a difficult personality" who should be avoided at all costs.

Yet the truth is that A and B are both acting out of a context in which anyone who is an opponent is regarded and treated as an enemy. This warlike approach encourages defensive responses based on ancient instinctual reactions and primitive strategies of fight, flight, or freeze that originate in an area of the brain called the amygdala, which regulates our perceptions and responses to aggression. The function of this area of the brain is demonstrated when the amygdala is disabled by, for example, a stroke, causing fear to disappear.

As a result of the evolution of our brains and increased capacity for higher-level thinking, we have developed a rational prefrontal cortex that advances a set of strategies that are more subtle than simply attacking others, defending oneself, freezing, or running away. These strategies consist, for example, of shifting blame onto others, undermining an opponent's support through covert criticism and hostile forms of humor, disrespectful body language, spreading rumors, and gossiping to C about what A did.

As a result, it is extremely rare that A or B regard their conflict as an opportunity. Neither is likely in their initial responses to a perceived attack to ask their opponent to sit down; listen empathetically and responsively; talk openly and honestly about what happened; or jointly and collaboratively define, explore, and resolve the problem. This is largely because they have each already labeled the other's behavior as an attack and automatically reverted to more primitive responses. If they had labeled the incident as a misunderstanding, a natural response to rejection, a request for honest communication, an effort to identify something that is not working as well as it might, or a barrier that could be overcome through joint problem solving, their responses would be quite different.

The difficulty with all the options outlined so far is that none of them have anything to do with listening. None support either side in understanding or coming to terms with the underlying issues in the dispute. None assist them in finding solutions to problems or contribute to improving the quality of their relationship. Instead, these options encourage them to think of their conflict as a battle, and keep them trapped in ongoing, chronic hostilities.

Once we have defined our opponents as evil, resorting to aggression and warfare becomes automatic. The adjectives we use to describe them, the metaphors we use to communicate and think about the conflict, the ways we analyze our options, and what we feel it is intelligent to do in response become limited to a set of instinctual, counterproductive, mutually reinforcing reactions to our perception that we are facing a hostile, adversarial opponent.

Whether we are A or B, we are likely to remain in impasse until we commit to listening and understanding the other person, critically examine our own assumptions, determine whether either side is being *irrationally* aggressive, and halt our instinctual responses. Only then will we be free to identify the opportunities that are hidden in our conflicts, to focus on finding solutions to common problems, to develop a deeper understanding of the issues, to stop reinforcing the other side's negative behaviors, and to become more skillful in responding to perceived aggression.

From Fight or Flight to Tend and Befriend

So how *do* we overcome our initial fight-or-flight reactions and join someone we fear, dislike, or distrust who seems to be continuously attacking us? How do we respond more positively, consider conflicts as opportunities, and achieve the ends we and our opponent desire? How can we benefit from learning how to disarm our instinctual responses, listen to what our opponent is actually saying, and search together for constructive, collaborative solutions?

The answers, although simple to suggest, are not at all simple to implement—particularly if you are in the grip of an ancient, powerful, and hypnotizing emotion like fear or rage. To make this shift, you need to create a new dynamic, try to understand your opponent, critique yourself, and search for the real content of the dispute and ways of improving your relationship, thereby deepening your understanding of the nature of conflict in general.

Several years ago, researchers discovered that there are in fact *two* principal pathways or responses to aggression: one is "fight or flight" and the other is "tend and befriend." The first is regulated by adrenalin, the second by oxytocin, sometimes referred to as "the bonding chemical." Oxytocin stimulates trust, collaboration, and caring, and is increased by listening, acknowledgments, and concessions, including unilateral ones. The release of oxytocin dramatically alters the way we see and interact with our opponents, which automatically and simultaneously alters our definition of ourselves, and our understanding of the causes, content, and context of our disputes.

By experiencing our conflicts as opportunities, we automatically increase our capacity to listen and resolve our disputes, thereby strengthening our relationships and improving the way we approach conflicts in the future. Listening is therefore the "opportunity of opportunities," because it is through listening that it becomes possible to increase trust and collaboration, gain deeper insights, act with greater self-awareness, prevent conflicts from escalating, and begin to see how we can shift our communications and relational dynamics in a more constructive direction.

If, for example, instead of assuming your opponent is attacking you, you assume they have merely confused you with the problem, you may be able to respond by shifting your opponent's attention by describing the problem as an "it" rather than as a "you." Or if you can hear the other person's attack as a request for assistance, attention, or support, you may be able to say, "How can I help you?" or "How could we work together to solve this problem?" Or if you can hear the attack as a critique of the way you have communicated, or as a request to adopt a more effective way of speaking, you may be able to apologize for not communicating clearly enough, or to say, "Can you give me some feedback so I can communicate with you better next time?"

None of these responses, in the beginning, is likely to be effortless, but each will lead you away from aggression and toward collaboration, thereby revealing opportunities for improved solutions. As illustrated in the following chart, there are a number of practical, realistic ways you can shift your response from one that is based on adrenalin and a perception of aggression to one that is based on oxytocin and a perception of commonality and misunderstanding.

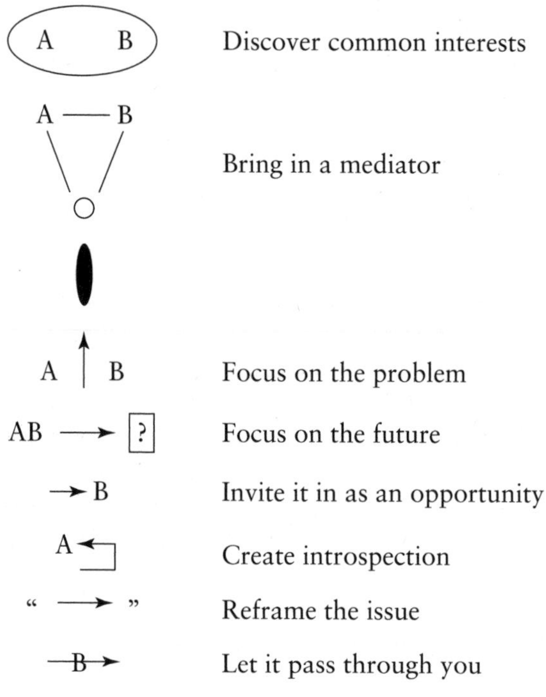

In each of these collaborative responses, the cycle of aggressive or defensive responses is halted for a variety of reasons. B is no longer responding as though A were the aggressor. The focus has shifted from people to problems. A and B are engaging in dialogue over common problems. They are attempting to satisfy each others' interests. They are not arguing about the past but considering what they want to happen in the future. In other words, B is being responsive, empathetic, and collaborative, rather than acting out of a fight-or-flight reaction.

Notice also that in the second chart B *gains* power by engaging in these actions, while at the same time eliminating the reasons that prompted A's original and continued aggression. B's collaborative "tend and befriend" approach rewards A for engaging in dialogue, while not giving A attention or similar rewards for aggressive behavior. This new response by B makes A appear uncooperative if he or she continues to act in an aggressive manner.

Despite the simplicity of these approaches, it may be difficult in practice to convert your initial responses to A from negative to positive. In attempting to do so, it may help you to recognize that A could be behaving aggressively for reasons that have more to do with A's *own* needs than with B's actions. It may also help you to recognize that A could be using aggression more to communicate to B what A is feeling, or how important the issues are to A, and that B's defensive responses are blocking and frustrating this communication. If B can find a way to listen, discover, and satisfy A's legitimate interests while not rewarding A's aggressive behaviors or taking them personally, even by silent acquiescence, in most cases A's aggression will gradually disappear.

If you are B, you may also be able to halt the escalation of the conflict by refusing to accept the role as perpetrator that A has created for you. If you are B, you do not have to be the victim of A's aggression, or accept A's definition of the problem, or allow A's version of your role in the interaction to go unquestioned. The goal is not to give in to aggression, but to sidestep it, not allowing it to determine what you will do in response, and become more skillful and self-confident when confronted with it. In other words, it only takes *one* to stop the tango, and that one could be you.

Creating Learning Organizations

Transforming your response from one of counter-aggression or defensiveness to one of listening and collaboration is not easy, yet it is possible in every conflict. Collaborative responses begin with simple steps that each person can begin to take in the direction of learning and resolution. In this way, a larger strategy is created that focuses on solutions rather than obstacles, thereby dramatically improving communication and relationships throughout the workplace.

Yet it is also possible for families, organizations, and institutions that are experiencing chronic conflicts to become more proactive about preventing and resolving them, and similarly shift their perspectives and orientations in responding to conflict from avoidance, accommodation, or aggression to engagement, collaboration, and learning.

Doing so automatically transforms their conflicts into opportunities, and themselves into learning organizations.

Learning organizations are able to discover the opportunities in conflict, creatively solve their problems, and continuously find ways to improve. They encourage employees to take responsibility for their disputes and routinely initiate open and honest communications that emphasize commonalities while valuing diversity and dissent. According to our colleague, Peter Senge, who brilliantly conceptualized learning organizations in *The Fifth Discipline*, they are able to reduce chronic conflicts by creating

- *A Shared Vision:* They articulate personal visions, communicate, ask for support, use visioning as an ongoing process, blend extrinsic and intrinsic visions, and distinguish positive from negative visions.
- *Mental Models:* They encouraging leaps of abstraction, balance inquiry and advocacy, distinguish espoused theory from theory in use, and recognize and defuse defensive routines.
- *Systems Thinking:* They value interrelationships rather than things and processes, move beyond blame, distinguish detailed complexity from dynamic complexity, focus on areas of high leverage, and avoid symptomatic solutions.

In these ways, learning organizations empower people to analyze their conflict culture, discover what prevents them from learning from their disputes, and develop ways of encouraging resolution and prevention. They generate knowledge-enhancing systems that work to improve processes and relationships so as to increase collaboration and spread best practices throughout the organization.

The complex process of creating learning organizations begins by fostering and supporting individual learning, which is especially powerful in connection with conflict. Because individuals are not completely isolated at work and require support to learn from their conflicts, in order to create learning organizations with positive conflict cultures it is necessary to

- Design, detect, and nourish local learning practices
- Create shared understandings of conflicts as learning opportunities

- Empower people to analyze what in the culture prevents their learning and to change it
- Generate knowledge-enhancing systems
- Regularly assess the impact of each new conflict on desired results, high-achieving processes, and collaborative relationships
- Diffuse appropriate lessons and meditative processes throughout the organization

Every conflict culture, dynamic, and organizational orientation begins with a single action on the part of some individual who is willing to model a new way of responding to divisiveness and disagreement. To shift large-scale personal and organizational attitudes toward conflict, it is necessary that the responses, behaviors, and actions of large numbers of individuals become more conscious, responsible and oriented to learning, resolution, and collaboration. To better understand how this is possible, it may be useful to deepen your understanding of conflict dynamics, and the reasons people respond in the ways they do.

Five Responses to Conflict

Aggression and collaboration are not the only responses you can have to conflict. There are several other ways you might respond, each reflecting a different attitude toward yourself, your opponent, and your conflict. The most common responses to conflict, shown in the list that follows, focus either subjectively on the *people* in dispute or objectively on the *result*, goal, or outcome. These responses are

- Avoidance
- Accommodation
- Aggression
- Compromise
- Collaboration

The following chart, drawn from research by Thomas and Kilman, reveals the relationship between these approaches by differentiating them according to whether the concern for people is stronger or weaker than the concern for results.

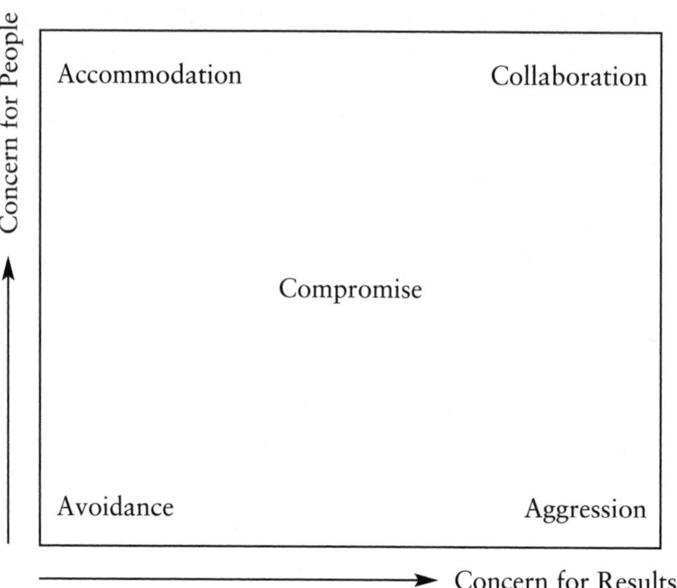

The key to choosing an effective response is deciding what kind of relationship you would most like to have with your opponent, and what results you would most like to achieve. If you are primarily concerned with people as opposed to results, you will be more likely to choose accommodation.

More significantly, however, whenever you accommodate, you *automatically* communicate to other people that you are more concerned about them than you are about results. And when you act aggressively, you communicate the exact opposite—that you care more about results than you do about them. When you are collaborative, you communicate that you care about both, that your relationships with them and what you want to achieve are equally important to you.

To understand the differences between these responses, imagine that you are about to be asked to work late. If you use avoidance, you may decide to hide in your office or duck out the back. If you use accommodation, you may decide to do the work, but feel resentful and perhaps do it poorly or not complete it. If you use aggression, you may decide to refuse to do it and create an argument. If you use compromise, you may agree to do it today if someone else agrees to do it tomorrow. And if you use collaboration, you will decide to do it together.

None of these responses is wrong. In fact, a skillful person is able to employ each response at the right moment, with the right person, to solve the right problem in the right way. Each is simply a choice of how you will respond to conflict. Here are a few of the reasons you might choose one response over another in any given conflict.

Reasons for Avoiding Conflict

- You regard the issue as trivial.
- You have no power over the issue or cannot change the results.
- You believe the damage due to conflict outweighs its benefits.
- You need to cool down, reduce tensions, or regain composure.
- You need time to gather information and cannot make an immediate decision.
- You can leave it to others who are in a position to resolve the conflict more effectively.
- You regard the issue as tangential or symptomatic and prefer to wait to address the real problem.

Reasons for Accommodating to Conflict

- You realize that you were wrong or want to show you can be reasonable.
- You recognize that the issue is more important to others and want to establish good will.
- You are outmatched or losing, and giving in will prevent additional damage.
- You want harmony to be preserved or disruption avoided.
- You see an opportunity to help a subordinate learn from a mistake.

Reasons for Being Aggressive and Engaging in Conflict

- You want to engage in quick, decisive action.
- You have to deal with an emergency.
- You are responsible for enforcing unpopular rules or discipline.
- You see the issues as vital, and you know you are right.
- You need to protect yourself against people who take advantage of collaborative behavior.

Reasons for Compromising Conflict

- Your goals are moderately important but can be satisfied by less than total agreement.
- Your opponents have equal power, and you are strongly committed to mutually exclusive goals.
- You need to achieve a temporary settlement of complex issues.
- You need a quick solution, and the exact content does not matter as much as the speed with which it is reached.
- Your efforts at either competition or collaboration have failed, and you need a backup.

Reasons for Collaborating to Resolve Conflict

- You believe it is possible to reach an integrative solution even though both sides find it hard to compromise.
- Your objective is to learn.
- You believe it is preferable to merge insights that come from different perspectives.
- You need a long-range solution.
- You want to gain commitment and increase motivation and productivity by using consensus decision making.
- You want to empower one or both participants.
- You see it as a way to work through hard feelings and improve morale.
- You want to model cooperative solutions for others.
- You need to help people learn to work closely together.
- You want to end the conflict rather than paper it over.
- Your goals require a team effort.
- You need creative solutions.
- You have tried everything else without success.

(*Source:* Adapted from Thomas-Kilman Instrument.)

Each of us should be able to use all of these responses under the appropriate circumstances. Thus, there will be times when the most effective approach is to walk away or surrender. There will be times when there is no alternative than to fight or be aggressive. Nonetheless, it is clear that responding with collaboration produces the best and most satisfying results, especially when there is an ongoing relationship between them.

Consider, for example, the kind of person you are likely to *become* if you can only respond in one of these five ways. If all you ever do is avoid conflict, after a while you will begin to feel numb and disengaged. If all you ever do is accommodate, after a while you will feel used or like a doormat. If all you ever do is respond with aggression, you will increasingly feel angry, guilty, or incapable of empathy or compassion. If all you ever do is compromise, you will end up feeling dissatisfied and compromised. But if all you ever do is collaborate, you will feel connected and successful.

The difficulty, however, is that of all these responses to conflict, collaboration requires the highest level of skill, the greatest investment in time and energy, and is the *last* approach we learn, Most of us discover the power of avoidance by the time we are two. We learn to accommodate from our parents as children. We learn aggression from our siblings and in school, and to compromise as we grow older. Collaboration is the last skill we learn, but it is increasingly critical in the workplace, because it is the basis for all teamwork, and the method by which conflicts are transformed into opportunities.

The Opportunity of Collaboration

Most people prefer to use the collaborative approach, not because it is quicker or easier or necessarily the right response under the circumstances, but because it

- Is more pleasurable
- Allows people to penetrate deeper into their problems
- Seeks to satisfy interests
- Produces better and more lasting results than the others
- Is more respectful
- Is versatile and satisfying
- Builds better relationships
- Encourages learning

As an illustration, a large communications firm in which we were consulting was attempting to implement a sweeping new structure that had been designed by the CEO with hardly any input from below. As a result, the change process had produced many disgruntled managers, and even the custodians were skeptical! As we probed the sources of covert resistance, we found that the conflicts and disagreements that had been triggered by the change process were being avoided and swept under the rug by the top leadership, who hoped these problems would simply disappear over time.

Instead, they were festering and simmering behind closed doors and fueling a growing resistance to change. We interviewed a cross-section of employees, opened conversations about the real barriers, and drew the underlying conflicts out into the open. As we did so, we were able to see relief and renewed energy bubbling to the surface among staff members who had become frozen in rage, avoidance, and despair.

This renewed energy represented a widespread unspoken desire to collaborate in making the change more effective and successful. Allowing staff input on how the CEO's ideas could work better transformed staff resistance into collaborative problem solving. The transformation was so complete that the leadership council, which included several executives who had resisted the change, volunteered to make their annual bonuses contingent on its success.

In our day-to-day lives, we face an unending array of choices about what to say and do and how to behave when we are in conflict. When we step back from our instinctive responses and the pressures and demands of the moment, and allow a collaborative approach to guide our behaviors, we feel more empowered and proactive, open to experience, and better able to locate the transformational potential that is hidden in our conflict.

The shift from feeling victimized, reactive, overwhelmed, destructive, or passive in our conflicts to feeling powerful, proactive, challenged, constructive, or collaborative is *already* a transformation in the attitude, culture, dynamic, and context through which we are participating in our conflicts, and thus in our ability to select a strategy that supports our deepest intentions and commitments. Consciously choosing a strategy and sticking to it makes us feel less driven by the choices of others, or the emotional whims of the moment, or the dictates of circumstance.

How to Collaborate in Conflict

Once you have decided to use collaboration in your conflicts, the next step is to learn how to respond to your opponents in ways that bring them closer, rather than push them farther away. Instead of papering over your conflicts, giving in to them, sweeping them under the rug, escalating them through rage, or compromising them, you will want to improve your skills in being able to engage in conflict in a collaborative way. The key is to find ways of combining a concern for people with a concern for results.

The following exercise and questions are designed to assist you in reaching out and creating a more collaborative relationship with your opponents. As you review these suggestions, consider a conflict in which you are presently engaged and answer the questions with it in mind. Allow each question to point you toward ways of collaborating and learning from your conflicts.

1. Begin by recognizing and affirming that conflict can be a positive experience, try to clarify where the opportunities for growth and learning lie, and ask yourself whether they indicate a need to change the culture or dynamics, or shift an organizational paradigm.
   - Can you think of any ways your conflict might be experienced positively?
   - How could this conflict become a learning opportunity, or a trigger for growth?
   - What positive changes and options for learning does this conflict suggest?
2. Use empathy to place yourself in other people's shoes and try to see things from their point of view, while at the same time recognizing that there are differences between understanding their behavior and condoning it, between forgiving them and forgiving what they did.
   - Why do you think they acted as they did? What might make you act that way?
   - How do you think they see your actions?
   - How could you learn more about their motivation that could help you understand what they want?
   - How could you respond to them more skillfully as a result?
3. Shift your focus from holding on to power and defending your position to focus on sharing responsibility and satisfying both sides' interests.

- If you let go of the desire to hold on to your power or position in the conflict, what might you learn as a result?
- What changes would you be willing to make to increase collaboration?
- What would happen if your opponent were willing to do the same?
- What are your interests? What are your opponents' interests?
- What interests do you share? How might both sets of interests be satisfied?

4. Focus your efforts beyond settlement and to commit to fully resolving all the underlying issues in your dispute.

   - What would accommodation, or settlement for settlement's sake, leave out of the equation?
   - What are the deeper underlying issues in your dispute?
   - What would it take to resolve them?
   - How can you bring these issues up so they can be resolved?

5. Be deeply honest with yourself and your opponent, and give empathetic and timely feedback.

   - What feedback can you give your opponent that is empathetic and truthful, and at the same time constructive and likely to move the conflict toward resolution?
   - How long has it taken you to give honest feedback? Why has it taken so long? What could you do to respond more quickly?
   - What feedback do you think the other person might give you?
   - Have you requested their feedback? If not, what is stopping you?
   - How might you benefit from your opponent's feedback?
   - What honest feedback can you give yourself?

6. Speak and act with integrity and clarity, without judgment, and with your heart and spirit, rather than only from your head.

   - Have your actions and communications been crystal clear, and have you had the highest integrity?

- If not, why not? What might you do to change or correct it?
- What can you say to the other person that comes straight from your heart and at the same time is clear and nonjudgmental?
- Instead of holding on to judgments and answers, can you ask questions that do not assume the answer?

7. Search for small-scale collaborative alternatives that increase cooperation, create common ground, and focus on shared interests.

    - What are some things you might do together to increase your cooperation and partnership?
    - What interests, values, or concerns do you both share?
    - What could you both do to find or create what you both need and want?

In answering these questions, remember that collaboration, resolution, and transformation are real, practical possibilities that become available whenever we begin to search collaboratively for the opportunities in our conflicts. To become genuinely collaborative and transform your conflicts into opportunities for learning and improvement, empathetic and responsive listening is a critical skill. If you listen in a committed way, even to your opponents, and especially to people you do not trust or like, you will start to discover, and then to create, the magic of resolution.

STRATEGY 2

LISTEN EMPATHETICALLY AND RESPONSIVELY

I want to write about the great and powerful thing that listening is. And how we forget it. And how we don't listen to our children, or those we love. And least of all—which is so important too—to those we do not love. But we should. Because listening is a magnetic and strange thing, a creative force. . . . This is the reason: When we are listened to, it creates us, makes us unfold and expand. Ideas actually begin to grow within us and come to life. . . . Who are the people, for example, to whom you go for advice? Not to the hard, practical ones who can tell you exactly what to do, but to the listeners; that is, the kindest, least censorious, least bossy people you know. It is because by pouring out your problem to them you then know what to do about it yourself. . . . So try listening. Listen to your wife, your children, your friends; to those who love you and those who don't; to those who bore you; to your enemies. It will work a small miracle—and perhaps a great one.

—BRENDA UELAND

We have all participated in countless ineffective, pointless, and destructive communications. We have all felt unheard, misunderstood, and unrecognized, and know firsthand the immense cost and destructive consequences of miscommunication. Yet despite this wealth of experience, the personal and organizational price that is paid every day for poor communication is not fully appreciated, and it is rare that any of us devotes sufficient attention to improving our communication skills.

Many of the conflicts and miscommunications we experience in life result from the assumption that we communicate successfully merely by speaking clearly, and that if we can make other people listen they will immediately understand and agree with us. Yet even when we speak a common language, each of us hears what was said from a somewhat different context or frame of reference and attributes an entirely different meaning to the words that were spoken.

Even ordinary differences in backgrounds, including gender, ethnic and cultural assumptions, unacknowledged biases, slight variations in perception, and unstated needs and desires, can lend words a meaning entirely different from what was intended. This capacity for distortion caused playwright George Bernard Shaw to wryly observe, "The greatest problem with communication is the illusion that it has been accomplished."

Each of us filters what we hear through a largely unconscious, unspoken backdrop of personal histories, ideas, emotions, experiences, cultures, expectations, needs, desires, fears, and values that profoundly shape the way we understand and interpret what is said. These personal frameworks have a powerful impact on our interpretation of the *meaning* of the communications we receive, and on the choices we make as a result. Successful communicators are those who listen for, seek out, and endeavor to understand these historical, cultural, emotional, and contextual frameworks and, as a result, send messages that stand a better chance of being understood.

For example, some people interpret statements of sympathy as expressions of support, whereas others interpret them as signs of weakness. For some people, a request by their boss for a status report is heard as an invitation to communicate, while others experience it as an indication that there is something wrong with their work. For some employees, it is important to have their feelings recognized and validated, whereas for others, talking about negative emotions implies giving in to them.

As a result, effective communication begins with speakers taking responsibility for understanding the language, perspectives, and experiences of their listeners and framing their messages in terms that are likely to make sense within the listeners' framework of experience. Communication, ultimately, is not what *we* say, but what *they* understand.

The unspoken perceptual framework or "language" of the listener may be grounded in a vastly different perspective, history, or point of view, or in a wholly different set of needs, interests, experiences, ideas, and emotions that create a completely different interpretive context for understanding the issues that are being addressed. There may also be fundamental differences in style, etiquette, culture, and values between the speaker and the listener. Or it may be that the communication raises collateral issues that have nothing to do with the speaker but make understanding difficult for the listener. In this way, the problem for each communicator becomes one of learning how to be strategic in communicating so that others can listen to what is really meant by the communication.

Understanding the Listener

There are so many important needs, distractions, life crises, and immediate problems that occupy the attention of everyone who is receiving a communication, it's a wonder we are able to listen at all, especially to our opponents in the midst of conflict. When we are preparing to speak to others about our conflicts, we should consider the most important reasons *why* people have difficulty listening before we initiate our communication.

For example, there are significant differences between men and women in how they listen and interpret communications, as well as differences based on ethnic or racial backgrounds and experiences; ethnic and religious orientation; workplace cultures; birth order in families of origin; economic status; social standing in the organization; position in the hierarchy; personal, emotional, and psychological needs; and hundreds of others. Each of these can influence the ability to hear what another person is saying.

As a result, it is important, before beginning to speak about your issues or concerns, to think for a moment about the person you want to listen. To increase your capacity to influence your listener, try the following exercise. First, select a conflict and a person you want to reach or influence. Make a list of everything you think may be diminishing your listener's receptivity, openness, and responsiveness. Consider the following possible influences and how you might take account of them in what you are about to say:

- Gender patterns
- Race, ethnicity, and national origin
- Sexual orientation
- Impact of disability
- Birth order in family of origin
- Family tensions
- Style of communication in family of origin
- Life tensions and concerns
- Work pressures
- Economic stresses
- Location relative to you in organizational hierarchy
- Social status relative to you
- History of relationship and conflict between you
- Attitude and style of approach to conflict
- List any other elements that you think may influence their receptivity

Once you have completed your assessment of the listening orientation of your opponent, create one for yourself. If you want to have a *dramatic* impact on your conflict communications, share these lists with your opponent. Compare the list you created for them with the one you wrote for yourself, circle the items that differ, and discuss the gaps in your perceptions. Consider asking them to do the same. The next step will be to actively search for clues on how to more effectively reach others by tapping into their contexts, concerns, and frames of reference, attempting to understand their cultural frameworks and styles, learning how to speak their language, and saying what you need to say in ways they are more likely to understand.

The Cost of Poor Communication

We all pay an enormous, uncalculated price for poor communication, not only personally in lost jobs, divorces, unhappiness, and ruptured relationships, but organizationally in failed endeavors, gossip and rumors, inefficiencies, wasted time and resources, lost revenues, poor morale, missed opportunities, grievances, and ultimately, strikes, discharges, and litigation.

For example, three members of the executive staff of a large federal agency told us in interviews about the lack of listening in their workplace and the price they and their organization paid for it. Here is what they said:

- Executive staff meetings are not a place where we have true dialogue or air problems, or where there is an effort to understand what people are saying. We don't have a social contract outlining acceptable codes of behavior, so no one hears anyone else, really—there are too many insensitive remarks, confidences aren't kept, and attendance is spotty. There is more of a sense of power tripping and power alliances versus operating on principle.
- One of our major blocks to success is Harry's role in the organization. When he [the director] does come to meetings, which is rare, he says nothing. He just sits there and doesn't seem to hear what we're saying. You wonder, does he think this is a waste of his time, and things will happen according to a grand plan he is controlling? He rarely speaks supportively or in a problem-solving way.
- There is unevenness of commitment here. No one listens to anyone. I am personally offended by people who fall asleep in meetings or say, "OK, it's time to go now, isn't it?" Harry does this. It seems like a favoritism thing. Some people get favored treatment. People are not behaving decently toward each other.

The cost of their poor communication included widespread distrust of management (especially Harry); high rates of absenteeism, tardiness, and stress-related workers' compensation claims; and an increase in bitter interpersonal conflicts. These mishaps in communication paralyzed the organization and made its performance mediocre. Everyone we interviewed was unhappy, and personal feuds and miscommunications escalated as a result.

We facilitated a two-day retreat with Harry and the entire staff who, to their credit, agreed to participate despite their doubts and distrust. The main goal for the session was to engage in open and honest communication. We agreed on four informal ground rules: everyone would speak with no-holds-barred honesty, each would attempt to listen nondefensively, all communications would be confidential within the group, and there would be no retaliation for anything said during the session.

We surfaced the problems with Harry by asking everyone to identify what was not working in their communications and distributing a summary of what people told us in interviews. We reached consensus on a set of standards for effective communication that everyone agreed to implement, starting immediately. As they did so, we could feel the sense of depression starting to lift.

We next asked them to give themselves and each other feedback, beginning with Harry. We asked him to evaluate his communication style and suggested he then invite each person present to give him honest feedback. We recommended that he not respond defensively, even if he thought the feedback was inaccurate or unfair, and instead try to figure out *what was true about it*. We asked him to thank each person afterward for the gift of honest feedback, and identify what he was willing to do to communicate more successfully. After Harry completed his comments, it would be the next person's turn.

We made sure the feedback was constructive and specific, and asked the group to practice their best communication techniques during the exercise. We interrupted them occasionally to encourage listening and responsiveness, and to assist them in speaking nonjudgmentally and listening nondefensively. At the end, we asked each person to evaluate the exercise. Everyone agreed it had been a great relief to communicate openly and honestly and finally be able to say what they had been thinking in private.

By the next quarter, productivity had increased significantly and morale began to return. One year later, nearly everyone indicated they were happier to be working there, and noted that Harry had changed his behavior so completely that he was warmly acknowledged and given a hearty, unsolicited round of applause at a meeting where the organization's success was celebrated. In a client satisfaction survey conducted eighteen months later, the group received its highest ratings in client appreciation and quality of client services.

Clearing the Decks for Empathetic and Responsive Listening

Obviously, being able to listen and feeling you have been heard are key elements in job satisfaction, conflict resolution, and organizational effectiveness. But what makes someone a good listener? How can people learn to become better listeners? Here is a personal exercise that may help you clarify what is involved and contribute to improving your listening skills.

Recall a leader with whom you have worked, or someone in your life who was an active, empathetic, and responsive listener—perhaps a friend or team leader who made you feel you were valuable and had something worthwhile to share, or a teacher or boss who mentored you or asked hard questions that encouraged you to be more successful. What did these listeners do that made you feel heard?

Effective listening does not actually *start* with listening, rather it begins when the listener clears the decks and focuses his or her *undivided* attention on the person who is about to speak. This means emptying your mind of all the thoughts competing for your attention—including what you are thinking about the person who is speaking or planning what you are going to say in response.

It means surrendering your ideas about what the speaker should or should not do or be, and being fully present and focused on what is said, not just on the surface, but underneath as well. It means bringing all your senses, including your posture, body language, eye contact, emotions, intentions, heart, and mind to focus on the communication. It means working interactively and collaboratively to clarify your questions and anything you did not completely understand.

Most people think of listening as a passive activity in which they sit quietly and take in whatever is said. But the best listening is a highly active, responsive, and interactive experience on the part of the listener that requires energy, openness, awareness, and a readiness to bring initiative and curiosity to the conversation.

There is a crucial difference between hearing, which is physiological, and listening, which is psychological. Similarly, there are differences between listening *at* people and listening *with* them, listening to what we want to hear and listening to find out what is important to the speaker. There is a similar gulf between listening in a role—for example, as a manager or school principal—and listening as a fellow human being.

Listening, like speaking, is a matter of *intention.* Our effectiveness depends on how important we think the information is to us. When we listen, we can do so in a variety of ways. We can listen only to the facts and details of what the speaker is saying, but not to their deeper meaning. We can listen only for openings or holes in our opponent's arguments—picking out what we think is wrong with them or what they are saying so we can use it against them.

We can also distinguish listening passively from listening actively, listening guardedly from listening openly, and listening sympathetically from listening empathetically. We know when someone is listening only for the facts and when they are listening for desires and feelings. We can feel the difference between listening collaboratively and listening as an adversary. We know when they are listening for problems and when they are listening for solutions.

In sum, we can tell when people are just *going through the motions* and when they are actively committed to understanding what we most want to communicate. *Committed* listening is what we do when we believe *our* lives could change as a result of what we are about to hear. It is what happens when we are told a fascinating story, even one that on the surface has nothing to do with us, but on a deeper level is about issues that are important to each of us. Committed listening is a reflection of openness in our hearts and minds, of our willingness to *act* on what we hear, and of our capacity for integrity and constancy in the face of answers we do not like.

Setting the Stage for Listening

To increase your skills and become a more active, empathetic, and committed listener, start by focusing on the physical and emotional environment in which your conflict communication is about to take place. The sketch below illustrates how many managers arrange their offices, which is where they do much of their listening.

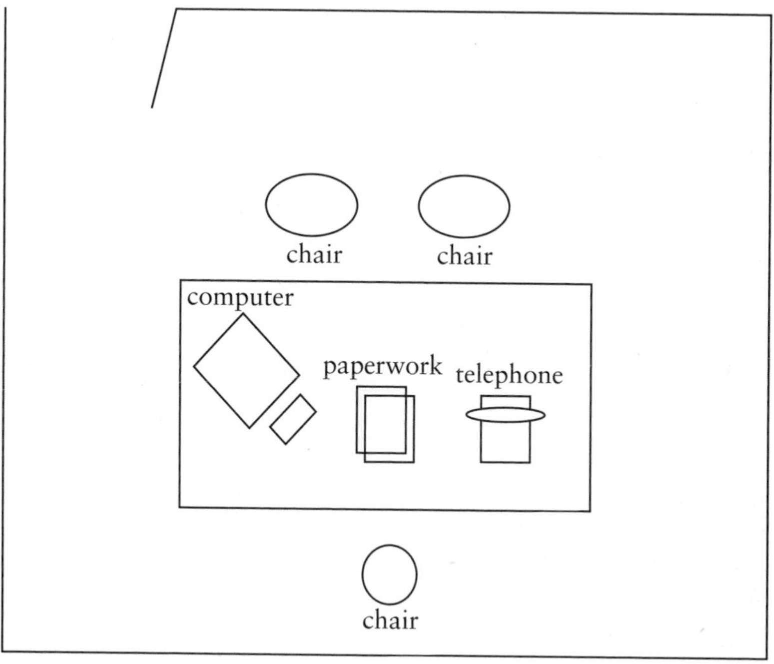

There are several problems with this configuration. First, some conversations should not be held in the manager's office at all because, for many employees, being called into their manager's office implies discipline or a rebuke. Second, in many offices, the manager has a distracting screen saver running on their computer, a telephone, cell phone, or beeper that has not been turned off, and piles of paperwork calling for their attention. Third, the arrangement of table and chairs signifies who is in power and who is not. It suggests that the person sitting behind the desk is an authority, judge, and decision maker, rather than a coach, mediator, or facilitator. Fourth, the desk separates them from each other and obscures much of their body language, which will communicate more about what they are thinking and feeling than their words can ever do.

The next illustration shows two alternative arrangements for the same office that may support more effective communication and feel more satisfying to all parties:

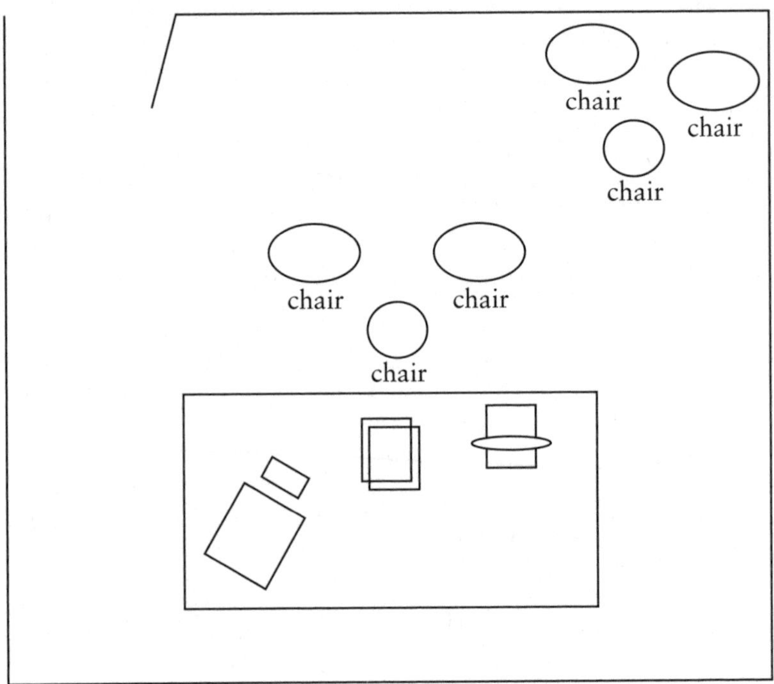

In these arrangements, communication is more likely to take place on an equal footing. Telephones, paperwork, and computers are less likely to get in the way and responsibility for problem solving is more likely to be shared in a team atmosphere. The manager will be seen more as a participant and facilitator, and employees will be able to speak more openly and naturally, allowing listeners to monitor body language for signals of consensus or resistance. Placing the chairs close to one another in a circle at a distance that encourages intimate communication, but far enough apart to respect personal space, conveys two messages: that communication is welcome, and that boundaries will be respected.

You may want to rearrange the environment in your office and try various configurations to see which works best for you. As you rearrange your space, be sure to position your chair so it does not communicate favoritism by being closer to one person than another.

Communication, of course, does not consist primarily of arranging desks and chairs. Yet consciously setting the stage for communication can dramatically improve the mood of a conversation. The atmosphere and ambiance of the setting can also be altered by natural or indirect lighting, plants, art, refreshments, and other "props" that create a friendly, open atmosphere and an environment that suggests welcome, respect, and receptivity.

You may not have enough space or room for these amenities in your office, in which case you may want to move your conflict conversations to a different location, such as an office cafeteria, a nearby restaurant, park, or even your own living room where everyone can listen in a relaxed atmosphere. The object is to try to match the environment with your intentions.

The Elements of Communication

For many years, theorists have suggested that successful communication consists essentially of a combination of the five fundamental elements that are diagrammed in the chart below.

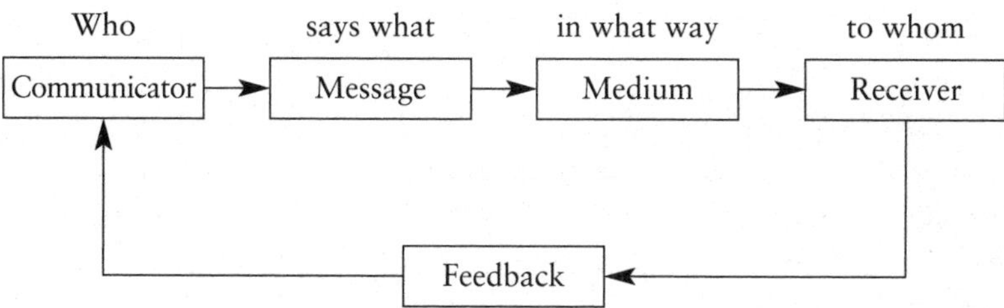

The problem with this taxonomy is that we have all experienced being articulate, expressing our messages clearly and accurately, using a medium that conveys our ideas appropriately, and having a receiver who is awake and listening, yet the communication has failed. Most communications involving employee discipline or termination, divorce, and racial or sexual harassment are examples of how it is possible for someone to be articulate, use an appropriate medium, and have a listener who is awake, yet still be ineffective in their communication and have their meaning distorted.

On the other hand, we may also have had the experience of falling in love, speaking incoherently, using a clumsy, ineffective medium, even communicating in a foreign language to a listener who is half asleep—yet, somehow, our communication is able to get through with no problem. How do we explain these apparent anomalies?

Hidden Frameworks for Communication

Clearly, something else is at work in addition to the elements cited in the diagram. That "something else" is the context, culture, environment, system, history, backdrop, framework, or setting in which the communication is taking place. This includes the largely unspoken real-life pressures and tensions, roles and responsibilities, histories and anticipated futures, needs and desires, thoughts and emotions, assumptions and expectations of the speaker as well as the listener. It includes the messages being communicated by the medium itself, the messages sent by the organizational culture, and the deeper meaning and importance of the communication to each individual.

When we examine these deeper aspects of conflict communications, there are three important hidden frameworks we need to consider. First, there are the words, symbols, metaphors, tone of voice, and body language used in the communication, which often convey its true meaning and significance to the listener. Second, there is the process of communicating, which includes how respectfully, responsively, actively, empathetically, appropriately, and reliably the message is communicated. Third, there is the relationship between the speaker and the listener, which includes their unspoken interests, needs, emotions, and expectations, and the degree to which they have let go of past conflicts, including those from their families of origin.

Each of these hidden frameworks defines our conflict communications more reliably than the literal definitions of the words we use. Yet most of our attention is focused on specific words and their culturally understood definitions—which make up only a small part, and by no means all of our conflict communications. The larger part, to which we pay less attention, consists of the subtle, symbolic significance of the words, gestures, and body language; the process, style, or way we communicate; and the impact our conflicted relationship is having on our willingness to hear what is meant without being said.

Even an innocuous word like "hello" can be interpreted in different ways depending on the context, tone of voice, phrasing, speed, timing, location, personal history, and emotional relationship between speaker and listener. Just a simple sentence can communicate rage, lust, friendship, enmity, admiration, disrespect, happiness, or sadness. For example, consider subtle variations produced by changing the emphasis on different words in the same statement, offered by mathematician and science fiction writer Rudy Rucker:

I'm glad to see you.	(Even if no one else is.)
I'm *glad* to see you.	(What made you think I wouldn't be?)
I'm glad to *see* you.	(Instead of talking to you by phone.)
I'm glad to see *you.*	(But not the schlub you came with.)
I'm glad to *see you.*	(It's wonderful to be with you.)
I'm glad to see you.	(So stop asking me if I am.)
I'm . . . glad-to-see-you.	(Are you glad to see me?)
I'm . . . glad . . . to . . . see . . . you.	(I'm drunk or don't really mean it.)
I'm glad . . . to see you.	(But only as an afterthought.)
I'm glad-to-see *you.*	(Me Tarzan, you Jane.)

As you listen to your opponent, or to your own words, and observe the gestures and emotions that are subtly communicated in every conflict conversation, search for the hidden frameworks that may be giving added and perhaps unintended meaning to your message. Ask yourself, for example:

- What metaphors, body language, and tone of voice am I using?
- What is my communication process and style?
- What is my relationship with the person to whom I am speaking?
- Are there tensions or unresolved conflicts between us, seeping into our communications?
- Do I have unmet, unspoken expectations that are blocking my efforts to convey meaning?

- Is there a perceived difference in our power or status?
- How are these differences altering the meaning of what I am saying?
- What is our history with each other?
- Is there an emotion, tone, or tension in my communication that is not matched by the words I am using?
- What does the listener think will happen as a result of my communication?

How Communication Gets Distorted

There is only one test for the effectiveness of any communication, and that is what the listener understands. If we consider communication from the point of view of the one who is on its receiving end, we can see that there are dozens of opportunities for distortion.

It may help you to think of your communication as a light wave that is bent when it passes through a different medium. Messages in organizations pass through many different layers as they travel from the speaker through a hidden framework of structures, systems, histories, cultures, symbols, processes, expectations, and relationships that suggest different meanings to those receiving them.

Whether we are speaking or listening, we can learn to take account of these ways in which communications get distorted and adjust for their negative impact by noticing what happens as they move along different paths and correcting for it. In organizations, the meaning of a message can be completely altered, for example, by being

- *Refracted* as light is bent by passing through water
- *Diffused* as information becomes less concentrated by passing through many people, or reaches people other than the one for whom it was intended
- *Amplified or diminished* as it expands or contracts as each level and departmental barrier interprets it differently
- *Disrupted* as conflicting messages, needs, and agendas alter or confuse its meaning, or add and subtract meanings that were not intended

- *Diluted* as the message loses meaning or is reinterpreted by each person who passes it on
- *Canceled* as when conflicting messages block it completely

As speakers, we can counter these distortions by being clear and strategic about what we say, how we say it, and why we say it, by designing better organizational pathways, and by tailoring what we say to the ears of a particular listener. We always need to be alert to what is likely to distort our meaning and endeavor to prevent and take account of these distortions.

As listeners, we can become more skillful in trying to understand what the other person *means* to say, by taking account of the ways the communication is being distorted and testing the accuracy of our perceptions by asking questions. As speakers or listeners, we can realize that many of these distortions originate not with the speaker or listener, but with the hierarchical systems, bureaucratic structures, adversarial processes, and conflict-avoidant cultures of many workplace organizations.

How Hierarchy and Bureaucracy Block Communication

Some distortion in communication is inevitable in conflict. Other distortions occur whenever communication occurs inside organizations, based on how they are structured. Consider how communications are distorted by the hierarchical, bureaucratic, and autocratic ways many of our private and public sector organizations operate, and by the impact of power inequalities, job insecurities, racial and gender differences, cultural and ethnic diversity, and similar relational imbalances on conflict communications.

Imagine, for example, a typical hierarchical, bureaucratic organization in the form of a pyramid with vertical levels corresponding to divisions between executives, managers, supervisors, and employees, and with horizontal functions, stovepipes, or silos corresponding to different departments. You may have spent a considerable part of your working life inside such an organization. If not, try to imagine how any communication inside this type of organizational structure is likely to be distorted, as illustrated in the following chart.

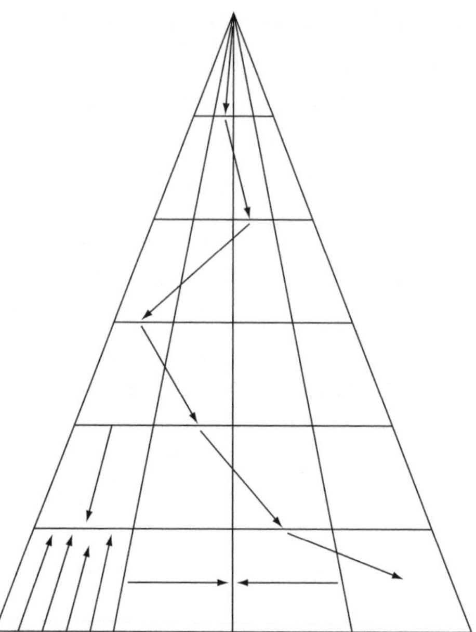

We can predict that any communication that takes place inside a hierarchical structure like this one will be distorted. Any communication that is intended to move from the top to the bottom will be twisted, diluted, and reinterpreted as it passes through each managerial level. Any communication intended to move from the bottom to the top will be simplified and compressed because there are too many communications trying to get to the top.

Moreover, if the communication is critical of some manager or higher-up in the organization who needs to pass it on, it may never get through. On the other hand, "squeaky wheel" communications, those that support upper management or tell them what they want to hear, or messages that are emotionally compelling or that convey a significant threat to the organization, such as accusations of sexual harassment, or communications from attorneys will predictably be favored.

In the process, each level will add its own special spin to the communication, resulting in some messages getting magnified in importance while others get minimized, altered, or nullified. Each department, as it battles with others for budget, staff, and scarce resources, may try to cancel, distort, suppress, or contradict information that favors competing departments, while advancing information that favors itself.

More subtly, competition within the organization, especially as people seek to move up the hierarchy, will encourage them to see each other as adversaries rather than as members of the same team. Because their relationships are systemically and structurally adversarial, communication between competitors is likely to be superficial, aggressive, defensive, blaming, shaming, responsibility-averse, conflict-avoidant, insular, self-promoting, and problematic.

An incident occurred in the midst of a major corporate change initiative that brought these distortions to light. We were asked for advice by an organization that was converting to self-managing teams and flattening its hierarchy. During the change process, the chief financial officer (CFO) decided to meet with the people who reported directly to him to let them know about a predicted shortfall in revenue. He assumed, because of the team initiative, that these managers would discuss the problem with their teams, brainstorm solutions, and let him know what they recommended to solve the problem quickly.

The managers, on the other hand, assumed that because the team initiative was not yet final, the CFO would decide what to do and tell them, or ask them to brainstorm solutions at his meeting with them. As a result, no one dealt with the problem, all efforts to solve it ground to a halt, and each group blamed the other.

The context of their communication was that there was a conflict between two sets of expectations. The first, appropriate to a hierarchy, was that the CFO would make decisions and tell everyone what to do. The second, appropriate to self-managing teams, was that they would work together to define the problem, identify solutions, and communicate what they decided. Either the CFO should have been more explicit in his request that the teams take the ball and run with it, or the teams should have sought clarification and taken the initiative in trying to solve the problem.

Contradictory messages and interpretations proliferate in hierarchical structures, causing them to simplify their messages by translating them into corporate-speak or bureaucratic language to the point that all the subtlety and complexity gets removed from them in an effort to avoid potential misunderstandings. As a result, official organizational messages tend to be formal, obvious, impersonal, and meaningless. A lot of time and energy is then spent by listeners trying to fill in the gaps using informal communications, such as gossip and rumors, which are highly volatile, damaging, and inaccurate.

Hierarchical structures usually place a higher value on uniformity than on diversity in communications, and on standing behind messages that are handed down from the top regardless of their accuracy—rather than raising questions or admitting that they are mistaken. For these reasons, hierarchical communications tend not only to limit creativity and individuality, but to increase suspicion and distrust, causing profound distortions in organizational communications, structures that separate speakers and listeners, perceptions of incongruence and lack of integrity, distrust of official communications, and disregard of communications from the opposite end of the hierarchy.

Phrases for Miscommunication

Many miscommunications in conflict are already latent in the words and phrases we commonly use at work. As speakers, our communications are more effective when we take time to reflect on the precise message we want to communicate, strategically improve our communications, and eliminate words and phrases that are likely to trigger misunderstandings and conflicts.

As a simple illustration, have you used the words "always" or "never" to describe someone else's behavior? If so, you might want to consider substituting a phrase that conveys the same meaning without encouraging the other person to respond with "No, I don't" or "Yes, I do," triggering endless, pointless arguments that distract their attention from your intended meaning.

Instead of saying "You never listen to me," try saying "This is important to me and I would appreciate it if you would really listen while I tell you why." Instead of saying "always," try saying "You do X too often for me," "Could you please do X less often," or "It bothers me when you do X because . . ." And in place of "never," try saying "You don't do X often enough for me," "Please do X more often," or "I really like it when you do X."

The likely reason you said "always" or "never" is that you are getting frustrated because you've asked many times and they haven't responded, leading you to wonder if they really care about you and what you want, so you intentionally exaggerate in order to signal them that you are getting upset. Instead, try asking them if your interpretation is accurate, why or why not, and what you can do to increase the chances of your getting what you want; then prepare to listen.

Try to recall the words you used in a recent conflict or miscommunication, or the words someone else used in a conflicted conversation. Was your communication successful, or did misunderstanding, disagreement, and conflict occur? What could either of you have said differently?

Here are some examples of words and phrases that often lead to miscommunication, misunderstanding, and conflict. As you review each phrase below, note whether you or your opponent have used it, or whether you have heard someone else in the workplace use it, and what you will do to remind yourself to avoid using it in the future.

WORKSHEET

Ordering: "You must . . ." "You have to . . ." "You will . . ."

____

Threatening: "If you don't . . ." "You'd better or else . . ." "You'll pay a big price . . ."

____

Preaching: "It's only right that you should . . ." "You ought to . . ." "It's your duty . . ."

____

Interfering: "What you should do is . . ." "Here's how it should go . . ." "It would be best if you . . ."

____

Judging: "You are argumentative (lazy, stubborn, dictatorial . . .)." "I know all about your problems." "You'll never change."

____

Blaming: "It's your fault." "If you had only . . ."

____

Accusing: "You lied to me." "You started this mess." "You won't listen."

____

Categorizing: "You always . . ." "Every time this happens you do the same thing . . ." "You never . . ."

____

Excusing: "It's not so bad." "It isn't your problem." "You'll feel better."

____

Personalizing: "You are mean." "This is your personality." "You are the problem here."

____

(*continued*)

Assuming: "If you really respected me, you would . . ." "I know exactly why this happened."

Diagnosing: "You're just trying to get attention." "Your personal history is what caused this to happen." "What you need is . . ."

Prying: "When?" "How?" "What?" "Where?" "Who?" "What are you hiding?"

Labeling: "You're being unrealistic (emotional, angry, hysterical . . .)." "This is typical of you . . ."

Manipulating: "Don't you think you should . . ." "To really help, you should . . ."

Denying: "You did not . . ." "I am completely blameless . . ."

Double binding: "I want you to do it my way, but do it however you want."

Distracting: "That's nothing, listen to what happened to me . . ."

Creating a Commitment to Communicate

To be a more effective communicator in conflict, it is helpful to clarify your commitment to open and honest communication. Being a *committed* communicator means taking responsibility for observing and managing the context of your communications, improving your skills with each person you meet, and eliminating negative and ineffective communication behaviors. It means proactively seeking feedback and not waiting for others to volunteer it. It means asking coworkers, family, friends, and colleagues to support you in making good on your commitments, and calling you on them when you do not.

For example, we worked with a small operations unit in a large corporation that revealed how even minor miscommunications and unclear commitment can lead to serious misunderstandings. Mike, the manager, was described in interviews with the people who reported to him as follows:

- Mike's style is too much micromanaging and detail oriented. We get paralyzed if he isn't available, and he is not committed to helping us.
- Mike's style is talking and not listening. He doesn't follow through.
- Mike is unwilling to delegate to his managers—he says he does but doesn't really mean it.
- Mike needs to be less negative, political, and confrontational.

Mike's aggressive, personalizing, controlling, disrespectful behavior, and his lack of committed listening were getting in the way of his ability to lead. As a result, a number of conflicts arose that made him look ineffective and uncollaborative. We gave Mike some strong, empathetic, and honest feedback about his staff's feelings and persuaded him to work on improving his effectiveness as a communicator by practicing committed listening.

We asked the people who reported to Mike to anonymously identify specific actions he could take to improve his communication style and create greater trust in their relationship. They gave him some painful, risky feedback. We prepared a written document summarizing their feedback and, with their permission, gave a copy to each member of the team. Mike was able to take their comments not as personal accusations from his enemies, but as objective information from his friends that would make him a better leader.

Before our intervention, his direct reports were unwilling or unable to give Mike honest feedback out of fear that he would retaliate against them. Yet, by their silence they condemned him to continue making the same mistakes, and themselves to continue suffering from and misunderstanding his intentions. By ignoring the problem, everyone paid a stiff price, and it wasn't until their growing demoralization and inability to resolve their conflicts demanded their attention that they finally confronted the obvious.

As a result of their honesty and our coaching, Mike was able to dramatically improve his communication skills. He started the next meeting by thanking everyone publicly for their feedback. He met one-on-one with every member of his staff to gather more information about how he could improve. He took all their suggestions seriously, and though he did not do everything everyone asked and experienced several failures, he demonstrated genuine commitment to learning from his mistakes and changing his behavior. The group responded by giving him the support he needed to improve, and acknowledged him when he did.

Only by reality testing your commitment and requesting feedback from those who do not understand what you are trying to communicate will you be able to learn whether you are making good on your commitment and effectively reaching them. If your listeners do not think you are committed, it is *not* real to them and you are probably kidding yourself.

Making a clear commitment to yourself and an open declaration to others is the first *active* step in this process. The second step is learning the skills needed to make good on your commitments and actually implementing them. The third step is inviting feedback, making corrections, and generously acknowledging others for contributing to your growth and learning.

Fifteen Steps for Effective Communication

Effective communication includes not only how we listen, but how we speak. Even in extremely hostile confrontations, if you are the speaker, you can defuse misunderstanding through a variety of empathetic and responsive speaking techniques.

The difference between a communication that is recognized by your listeners as authentic and believable, and one that is experienced as disingenuous and untrustworthy, will not be based principally on the words you use or their dictionary definitions, but on the *congruity* of your communications, subtle indications of your intent, and the integrity of your commitments, as demonstrated by what you do afterward.

If these elements in your communication are weak or inappropriate, your questions—no matter how polite—will strike your listeners as prying, your statements as self-righteous, your assertions as accusations, your declarations as egotistical and autocratic, your requests as manipulations, your agreements as insincere, and your commitments as inauthentic. Here are fifteen methods you can use to encourage others to recognize your true meaning.

STEP ONE: LET GO OF YOUR OWN IDEAS, ROLE, AND AGENDA AND TRY TO UNDERSTAND WHAT THE OTHER PERSON IS SAYING. The first step in communication is not speaking. It is not even listening.

It is preparing to listen by emptying yourself of your own preconceived ideas, dropping predefined roles, and letting go of the agendas, assumptions, judgments, and expectations that can twist what you hear into something other than what they meant. The greatest enemy of learning is not ignorance, but what you *are sure* you already know. The greatest challenge in listening is letting go of what you are certain of, realizing that your version of the truth could be preventing you from hearing or understanding theirs, and allowing their experience to lead you to a higher, more integrated, and composite truth.

STEP TWO: BECOME CURIOUS ABOUT WHAT MAKES THEM TICK. Try to become genuinely curious about what is motivating them. Consider, "What do I really know about who they are when they are not in conflict with me? How could I find out more?" Ask yourself, "What is going on in my mind when they are communicating with me?" "Am I open to learning and poised to understand what they are saying, or am I thinking about what I am going to say in response?" "Am I listening as a curious human being, or as a manager or employee or teacher with an agenda?" "Which one would I rather have listen to me?"

STEP THREE: BEFORE YOU SPEAK, DRAW OUT THE OTHER PERSON'S IDEAS. Start by asking open-ended questions so your ideas can be targeted to your *specific* listener. This does not mean watering down what you want to communicate, but recognizing there are a multitude of ways you can say what you mean so the other person will feel invited into the conversation and personally engaged. Ask detailed, respectful questions that do not presuppose an answer and curiously explore their beliefs and ideas.

STEP FOUR: SEARCH BEHIND THE WORDS FOR THE OTHER PERSON'S MEANING, ESPECIALLY IF HE OR SHE DISAGREES WITH YOU. After you empty yourself, let go of your judgments and genuinely listen to the words used by the other person, trying to sense the deeper unspoken issues and hearing the assumptions, expectations, and hidden meanings that lie beneath what is said. Ask yourself, "What does my opponent really want?" "What are his or her real best intentions?" "What is going on beneath the surface?" "Am I aware of and considering the subtleties that are hidden in the words being spoken?" "Am I listening to what is intended and not just to the words that are being used?"

STEP FIVE: DISCOVER AND MANAGE YOUR LISTENER'S UNSPOKEN EXPECTATIONS. Make sure you do not base your comments on false expectations regarding what the other person wants or is willing to do. Do not encourage your listener to have false expectations of you. Ask, "What are the unspoken expectations that might lead them to speak or act this way?" "What role do they want me to play?" "How can I correct their false expectations?"

STEP SIX: RESPOND RESPECTFULLY AND NONDEFENSIVELY, ACKNOWLEDGING AND ADDRESSING THE OTHER PERSON'S CONCERNS FIRST. Address the speaker's point of view first, rather than immediately countering with your own and ignoring what was just said. When people feel they have not been heard, they repeat their comments over and over and become frustrated, strident, and angry. Try saying, "Thank you for that information. I really appreciate your willingness to tell me what you saw and heard, and how you experienced it." When you respond seriously to what other people say, they feel heard and can relax and listen better to you. Put yourself in their shoes and walk a while inside their perceptions before you disagree. Speak to them in ways that could make a difference, rather than simply discounting their ideas and replacing them with your own.

STEP SEVEN: CHOOSE AN APPROPRIATE FORM OF COMMUNICATING. Decide what you want to communicate and choose the form of communication that best supports your intention. If you want to make a declaration, make an "I" statement rather than a "you" statement, which may be heard as an accusation. Make sure your questions are genuine and not disguised statements. Let them know you genuinely want to know what they think and feel. Be clear when you make a promise that you mean it and will follow through with actions.

STEP EIGHT: SPEAK RESPECTFULLY, EMPATHETICALLY, AND RESPONSIVELY. Make sure you speak respectfully to your opponents, especially if you disagree strongly with them or disapprove of their behavior. Make sure you are responsive to the issues they have with you, and adopt the Golden Rule by communicating to them as you would want them to communicate to you. Ask yourself, "What would make me speak or act like that?" and "What would I want someone else to do in response if I did?"

STEP NINE: DEMONSTRATE THAT YOU HEARD THE OTHER PERSON'S DEEPER NEEDS AND FEELINGS. Put the listener at ease. Speak informally in a way that relaxes your listener and encourages trust in what you have to say. Make positive references when you speak to their issues and feelings, especially those that demonstrate you were paying attention to what they've been telling you, and summarize their remarks without watering them down and even making them stronger. Say, "Here is what I hear you are most concerned about . . ."

STEP TEN: ANTICIPATE OBJECTIONS AND ADDRESS THEM *BEFORE* THEY ARE RAISED. Try to anticipate what the other person is likely to say in response. Address those issues *in advance* as a way of demonstrating that you understand your listener's concerns. Say, "Here is what I understand your main objections are . . ." "Is that right?" "Do you have any to add?" "Here is what I propose to do to respond to them . . ."

STEP ELEVEN: CLARIFY AND EMPHASIZE YOUR AGREEMENTS. Do not lose sight of what you actually agree on. Start by thanking the other person for agreeing to discuss their issues openly with you. Emphasize even minor points of agreement. There will always be something you can agree on, even if it is only your agreement to talk directly with each other rather than ignore the problem or take it to someone higher up. Say, "Here are the areas where I think we are in agreement . . ." "Are these right?" "Great! We've made a lot of progress."

STEP TWELVE: ACKNOWLEDGE DIFFERENCES AND RESTATE ISSUES POSITIVELY. Acknowledge your differences openly and state them neutrally, then summarize the main issues positively so they can be resolved. Afterward, test for understanding and agreement or disagreement with your remarks and respond proactively to the other person's concerns. Say, "Here are the issues I think we still disagree over and have to work out . . ." "Do you agree?" "Which one should we tackle next?"

STEP THIRTEEN: STATE YOUR INTERESTS INSTEAD OF YOUR POSITIONS. Rather than repeat *what* you want, explain in a personal way the reasons *why* you want it. Address problems that can be solved rather than trying to assign blame or citing conditions that are beyond your or their control and be open to creative solutions. Ask the other person, "Why is that so important to you?" "Why do you feel so strongly about that?" "What solutions would you suggest that you think would work for both of us?" "How might we combine our interests?"

STEP FOURTEEN: ASK FOR FEEDBACK. Asking for feedback on how you communicated and might communicate better is a powerful way of demonstrating positive intentions. At the end of your comments, turn the conversation over to the listener and ask them to respond to what you said. Try to formulate a question that, if answered correctly, could result in your actually changing your mind. Ask, "Could you give me some feedback on how I am communicating with you?" "If there is one thing I could do to communicate better with you, what would that be?" "Would you be willing to receive some feedback now on how you can communicate better with me?"

STEP FIFTEEN: COMPLIMENT THE OTHER PERSON FOR LISTENING. Offer unconditional positive reinforcement for listening without adding "but..." and indicate your willingness to listen with an open mind in return. Say, "Thank you for listening." "I feel heard and want to thank you for really listening to me." "Thanks for meeting with me today; I appreciate your willingness to be here and listen."

Effective Communication for Listeners

It is rare for us to sit down with our opponents and engage in open, honest, problem-solving dialogue and actually listen to each other and learn from our problems. Instead, we spend most of our time trying unsuccessfully to win, defending ourselves, asking our opponents to understand our point of view without caring about understanding theirs, wanting not to lose or suffer or look bad, and trying to make the problem go away. As a result, we spend sleepless nights obsessing over emotional slights, focus on superficial issues, and plan responses to our opponents' positions without being curious about their interests and deeper motivations.

If this is how we behave, we are likely to experience little more than anger, fear, and shame from feeling attacked, loneliness and sadness from not being listened to, sadistic pleasure and guilt from attacking others, pain and grief from lost relationships, and occasionally, pyrrhic victories from authoring our opponent's defeat.

As a result of these adversarial responses, we may fail to realize that, like all self-fulfilling prophecies, hostile attitudes generate hostile realities. When we believe our opponents are "out to get us," we behave toward them with reciprocal hostility and defensiveness. Seeing our hostility and defensiveness, they naturally respond in kind, proving to us that we were right in the first place. As a result, many people come to feel, as critic and writer Gore Vidal quipped, "It is not enough that I succeed—others must fail."

When we do not listen to our opponents or recognize the legitimacy of their needs and interests, we become incapable of participating in honest, empathetic dialogue and unable to communicate effectively or solve the problem. As a result, we are left with few alternatives other than to surrender, engage in aggressive opposition, or paper over our disputes with temporary, inadequate, superficial settlements.

On the other hand, as Mahatma Gandhi, Mikhail Gorbachev, Martin Luther King Jr., Nelson Mandela, and countless others have amply demonstrated, even an entrenched military opposition will find it difficult to continue acting aggressively when a leader with sufficient courage refuses either to surrender or to become its enemy.

Listening is the first step in transforming our opponents into collaborative problem solvers. Empathetic and responsive listening automatically arises when we genuinely care about what our opponent is trying to tell us, and actively reach out with questions, tone of voice, and body language. It arises when we participate in open, honest, responsive dialogues that move back and forth, and both sides are authentic in their responses. It occurs when we search for creative solutions or work together to come up with fresh ideas and approaches to solving problems. It happens when we listen as *we* would want to be listened to if we were speaking.

Committed listening arises when we listen as though *our* lives depend on understanding what our opponent is saying, when we are no longer even aware of our separate presence as listeners, and completely merge with the speaker and the story. When we listen in this way, with our hearts as well as our minds, we may even feel love and affection for the one who is speaking.

Thus, there are many ways you can listen to your opponent that range from going through the motions to listening with deep commitment and an open heart. As your listening moves deeper and further along this continuum, you will develop improved skills and discover increasing opportunities for problem solving, resolution, and transformation.

For example, we coached a client who made considerable progress along this continuum. Tim was a well-meaning, much-loved leader in city government who became isolated as a result of his communication problems. His staff respected and valued him, but felt blocked in their communications with him, which they described as follows:

- The volume of work is such, and the number of crises and emergencies is so great that even if he were organized, Tim would be pulled off constantly. Calls and messages interrupt Tim's meetings all the time. His availability to hear what we have to say is missing. It's hard to get his time and attention to focus on issues.
- Tim is marvelous, smart and a good people person, but he is disorganized and lacks follow-up. He never has time to hear our problems.
- Tim is disorganized and there often is no follow-up because his job is so overwhelming and challenging that no one can do it. Tim loses the points we are trying to make as we give them to him. He doesn't seem to hear us anymore.

We encouraged Tim to use the phrases for empathetic and responsive listening that follow in his conversations with the employees who reported to him. His consistent practice using these phrases and strengthening the *attitudes* that lay behind them over several months paid off in better relationships with his staff. Tim found it was easy to think of effective ways of responding, but more difficult to consistently use them in practice. In your next encounter, try to apply them and notice what happens as a result.

Techniques for Active, Empathetic, and Responsive Listening

Using the following techniques can help you speak and listen more effectively and encourage others to listen when it's your turn to speak. Remember that the point is not to *substitute* these techniques for positive intentions, but more fully express your intentions by making a real connection with another person.

ENCOURAGING. Making encouraging comments and asking questions that invite others to share their feelings, perceptions, and ideas can quickly transform negative into positive interactions. Comments such as "Please tell me more," "I'm interested in what you are saying/thinking/feeling," "I would like to know your reactions," or "I hear what you are saying" are inviting statements. You can even say, "Tell me more about why you disagree with me," which will elicit more conversation and dialogue. What statements could you make to your opponent in a conflict you are now experiencing that would be encouraging?

CLARIFYING. As the discussion unfolds, ask questions that clarify the points being made by the speaker. Send a signal that you are interested in the speaker and the content of what is being said. Clarifying questions de-escalate emotions by focusing the speaker on facts rather than feelings. Be careful not to create the impression that you are trying to interrogate or pry. Your tone of voice and intention will make the difference. Questions like "When did this happen?" "Who else was involved?" or "What did it mean to you?" elicit detail and precise meaning. What are some clarifying questions you might ask?

ACKNOWLEDGING. You can encourage greater openness by recognizing, naming, and acknowledging feelings, emotions, and intentions. Comments like "I can see you are pretty upset about that. Can you tell me why?" or "Thanks, I can see now why you might feel/think that way" give permission for deeper communication. Be careful not to assume you know what the other person is feeling. You can also use acknowledgments to give people permission to say what they are actually feeling. Avoid popular catchphrases such as "It sounds like you are very angry right now" because they can be taken as an attempt to manipulate the speaker, and betray a lack of empathy rather than a presence of heart. What acknowledging statements might you make when a coworker or friend gets upset?

NORMALIZING. As feelings are expressed and opinions offered, you may want to communicate to the speaker that it is natural or normal to have those feelings. Statements like "I think I might have felt/thought the way you do if that had happened to me" allow the person to feel accepted while expressing difficult emotions or critical thoughts. These statements encourage the speaker to go deeper in the conversation with you. Can you think of a way of normalizing the feelings of someone with whom you are in conflict?

EMPATHIZING. Put yourself in other people's shoes to better understand their perceptions and feelings. Look inward and find a time when you had a similar experience, reaction, or feeling. You might say, "I think I can understand why you feel so strongly about this subject because I experienced something similar in my own life." Or, "I can appreciate why you might feel that way." Or just, "I understand." Do not say, "I know exactly how you feel." You don't. What are some empathizing comments you might make?

SOLICITING. Ask questions to solicit advice and identify potentially acceptable solutions. You might say, "I would like your advice/help on how we might resolve this." "What do you think we should do?" "Tell me more about what you want." "What would you like to see happen?" "Why do you think that would work?" What questions could you ask to solicit advice about a disagreement or conflict you are having?

MIRRORING. Mirroring reflects back the emotions, affect, demeanor, body language, tone of voice, metaphors, and even breathing patterns used by the speaker to encourage the feeling that you are a companion in whatever he or she is thinking and feeling, rather than a dispassionate observer who does not really care or understand. If the speaker takes a defensive posture, you can try taking one yourself, then move to a more open one. In doing so, don't make it appear you are mimicking or being disrespectful. How might you mirror someone you have not been able to reach and let them feel you are with them?

AGREEING. If you disagree with a speaker about a topic, it doesn't mean you have to disagree about everything. It is useful in the midst of your disagreements to point out the issues on which you are in agreement. You might say, "What I like about what you just said is . . ." "I really agree with you about that." "What I think we disagree about is . . ." What might you say to someone with whom you disagree to let the person know you share areas of agreement?

SUPPLEMENTING. Instead of "yes, but . . ." say "yes, and . . ." In this way, rather than relating to others as adversaries, you can convert them into allies. You might say, "Let me build on that and see if we are on the same track," "Let me support what you are saying with another point," "Not only that, but . . ." What could you say to add to what your opponent said or to supplement the other person's points and clarify your disagreements?

INVITING ELABORATION. Asking open-ended questions that do not have a fixed answer lets the speaker know you respect his or her point of view. You can ask wide-open questions, such as "Why?" "What would you like to see happen?" "Why is that important to you?" Or more directed questions, such as "I'd like to ask a question about that," "How would you . . . ?" "Help me understand why you . . ." What do you really want to know from or about the person with whom you are in conflict? What might you ask that could get you that information?

REFRAMING. Reframing or rephrasing is preserving the basic content and message in a communication while altering its expression so it can be heard nondefensively and encourage dialogue. For example, you can reframe by turning "you" statements into "I" statements or by identifying the reasons for your disagreement. You can turn the statement "You are incompetent!" into "Why did this happen?" "What did I say that created that expectation?" "What did you think you were supposed to do?" One format for reframing is, "I feel . . . when you . . . because . . ." How might you reframe a statement in your conflict to suggest a solution?

RESPONDING. Listening respectfully means responding authentically to what is said and not using listening techniques to manipulate the speaker. The speaker is entitled to a response that comes to grips with what was said. You might say, "If I understand you correctly, you see the problem this way . . . Here's how I see it." "Would you like to know how I experienced what happened?" Try to respond without being defensive or angry yet still make your point clear. If your purpose is to learn from your conflict, you will not do so either by backing away from disagreement or getting drawn into angry, defensive responses. What could you say to someone with whom you disagree that would allow you to achieve both these goals?

SUMMARIZING. If you want the other person to feel heard, summarize what was said in your own words. You might say, "Let me see if I understand what you just said—[summarize]. Is that right?" This feedback will help the speaker feel heard and provide an opportunity to confirm, correct, or improve your understanding. It discourages them from repeating what they just said because they think you didn't really get it. It demonstrates your interest in what was said and your desire to grasp their essential meaning. It is useful to summarize at the end of a conversation to see if you have the same perception of what was said. In doing so, you risk making a mistake, but it is better to be mistaken and get clarification than to continue based on false assumptions. How might you summarize the point of view of someone with whom you are in conflict, with whom you totally disagree?

VALIDATING. Recognize the speaker's contributions and thank the person for communicating with you. Validate specific points the speaker made that you found useful. Consider saying "I appreciate your willingness to raise these issues with me." "I learned a great deal from what you said, specifically . . ." "I know it took a lot for you to be as open as you were, and I want to acknowledge you for taking that risk." "I appreciate your willingness to talk to me about this." "I didn't know you felt that way before." What comments might you make to validate your opponent in a way that is authentic and communicates your genuine interest and respect?

Obviously, you don't always have to do everything listed above in order to communicate effectively. We rarely remember to use all these phrases and techniques in the heat of battle. We hope, however, that you will commit to improving your listening skills by becoming more conscious and aware of how you are communicating, identifying what got you into trouble or triggered a defensive response in the listener that you did not intend, and being open to honest feedback.

None of these methods will guarantee successful communication and each can be used by an uncommitted listener to give an *appearance* of listening while holding firmly to a private agenda. All the words and techniques can be right, but if the listener *really* does not care about the speaker and the message being delivered, their inauthenticity will be clear nonetheless.

In other words, you can have every one of these techniques down perfectly, but if your heart is not in it, your opponent will know. Conversely, you can never use a single one of these techniques, but if your heart is genuinely in it and you are *actually* interested in the other person and what they think, they will know that as well.

We each face four challenges in listening: first, being as deeply honest, empathetic, and responsive as we can possibly be; second, being sincerely curious about our opponent; third, listening with our hearts for other people's unspoken needs, interests, desires, and intentions; and fourth, continuing our search for the best ways of clarifying our communications, improving our relationships, and manifesting our integrity and authenticity.

Listening with the Heart

The most important organ in listening is neither the ear nor the mind, but the heart, and it is within your heart that you will discover the true meaning of any communication you want to make or receive. When you listen with your heart, you become one with the speaker and discover their truth inside you.

Heart-based listening, for this reason, is much deeper than merely empathetic or responsive listening. It requires you to focus your awareness not on the words being used, but imagining what the speaker may be thinking or feeling and not expressing directly through words. It means asking yourself what it might feel like to walk in your opponent's shoes, and what would cause you to make that statement and communicate or behave as she did.

When you listen within a role—the way, for example, that managers typically listen to employees, teachers listen to students, service representatives listen to complaining customers, and government clerks listen to members of the public—you are likely to listen primarily to the *facts,* so you can decide what to *do* in response. But in addition to facts, you can also listen for subtle information about the human being who is speaking to you, what she is feeling, how she perceive the world, and what is really important to her.

To do so, you will need to go inside yourself, expand your heart space, and try to hear the other person's deepest emotions, intentions, biases, and confusions—in addition to the facts. Try to hear

- Emotions and feelings
- Wishes and desires
- Interests and positions
- Dreams and visions
- Intentions
- Humiliations
- Denials and defensiveness
- Openings to dialogue
- Similarities
- Cries for help
- Desire for forgiveness
- Distortions of perception
- Prejudices
- Family patterns
- Role confusions
- Stereotypes
- Self-esteem
- Resistance
- Apologies
- Differences in style
- Admissions of guilt
- Requests for acknowledgment

Each of these is present as possibilities in *all* our conversations. So the next time you listen to a colleague or family member, or to your opponent in a conflict, try to hear these deeper elements in what they are saying. See if you can hear them more accurately by listening with an open heart, and with empathy and intuition. Try to imagine what would cause you to make similar statements and act in similar ways. As the ancient Chinese sage, Lao Tzu, advised many centuries ago, "Take time to listen to what is said without words, to obey the law too subtle to be written, to worship the unnameable and to embrace the unformed."

STRATEGY 3

SEARCH BENEATH THE SURFACE FOR HIDDEN MEANINGS

An autobiography is the truest of all books, for while it inevitably consists mainly of extinctions of the truth, shirkings of the truth, partial revealments of the truth, with hardly an instance of plain straight truth, the remorseless truth is there, between the lines.

— Mark Twain

Resolving conflict is like trying to alter the shape of an iceberg, most of which lies beneath the surface and cannot be seen; or unearthing an archeological treasure and painstakingly brushing away the surface rock to reveal deeper layers that have lain hidden beneath centuries of dust and mud; or reading an autobiography, as Mark Twain suggests, where the truth lies not primarily in, but *between* the lines, hidden well below the surface of what is said.

We rarely take time to search out or excavate these deeper truths in our conflicts, partly because our attention is focused instead on the mistakes and misdeeds of our opponent, or on our own victimization and emotional upheaval. Yet the center and core of all our conflicts, what they actually *mean* to us, is far more profound and important than the relatively superficial issues we are passionately arguing and debating over. In conflict resolution, the deeper you look, the more there is to discover.

There is a vast difference in any conflict not only between what appears on the surface and what lies hidden beneath, but also between what we say in public and what we think or feel in private, between the issues we address and those we avoid and conceal. And it is these deeper, more mysterious, hidden issues that have the power to unlock our conflicts and catalyze our transformations.

When we search below the surface to discover the true source and organizing center of our conflicts, when we genuinely understand how and why they happened, and when we are finally able to listen to our opponents empathetically and responsively and see them as human beings, our conflicts begin to open like flowers, revealing their hidden truths and showing us how to break free of their grip.

Few of us take time before responding to an accusation or criticism to understand the emotions and experiences that may have fueled it, or to search beneath the surface for what our opponent says to find out what they actually mean. More often, we launch an immediate defense or counterattack that, by its aggression, force and personalization, makes it difficult to understand how and why the dispute happened and what we might do to resolve it.

For example, consider an employee who becomes highly irritated when his manager blames him for making a trivial mistake. His irritation is a strong indication that he is concerned about something far more consequential, such as the distrust or disrespect that was communicated by the way the manager spoke about the mistake, or the fact that other team members overheard the manager say it, or the fact that there are so many misunderstandings between them that he is afraid he will be fired.

The employee may actually be responsible for the error, yet is responding defensively because he feels the manager is being hypercritical and disrespectful, or is micromanaging, or has asked him to do something he feels is demeaning, or did not ask for his version of what happened before blaming him for the problem, or he feels the manager is "out to get him."

On the other hand, the manager may actually be responsible for the error, yet feels the employee is being dishonest or disrespectful, or is denying all responsibility for what happened; the manager may also feel humiliated because the employee made a public display of not listening, or she may be uncertain how else to establish her authority, or is too embarrassed to admit having made a mistake.

Or they could *both* be responsible for the problem, yet remind each other of difficult family members, or trigger memories of similar unresolved disputes in the past, or act in ways that make each other angry or uncomfortable, or have very different styles and assume theirs is the only right way to solve the problem, or are engaged in a power contest, or just do not know how to communicate with each other.

Regardless of which of these versions is true, if they become involved in an argument over a relatively trivial or superficial issue they will miss the opportunity to engage in open, honest conversation, solve the problem, and improve their communication process and relationship. Their argument probably seems silly even to them because they know the issues they are arguing over are petty, superficial, and pointless compared to what is *really* bothering them that neither of them is talking about. Why does this happen?

What is *actually* at stake in conflicts at work is not a simple communication failure, or a few dirty coffee cups in the common room, or who gets the best office or parking space. Rather, it is important unspoken issues, such as whether they are going to be fired and lose their livelihood, whether they are being treated fairly and respectfully, whether they feel humiliated and can be honest about what they think, whether they can trust and respect their opponent, whether they are feeling defensive or acting aggressively, and whether it is possible to have an open, honest, empathetic, and collaborative relationship with each other.

The Iceberg of Conflict

One way of understanding the hidden layers and complexities that lie beneath the surface of our conflicts is by using the metaphor of the iceberg, depicted in the following figure.

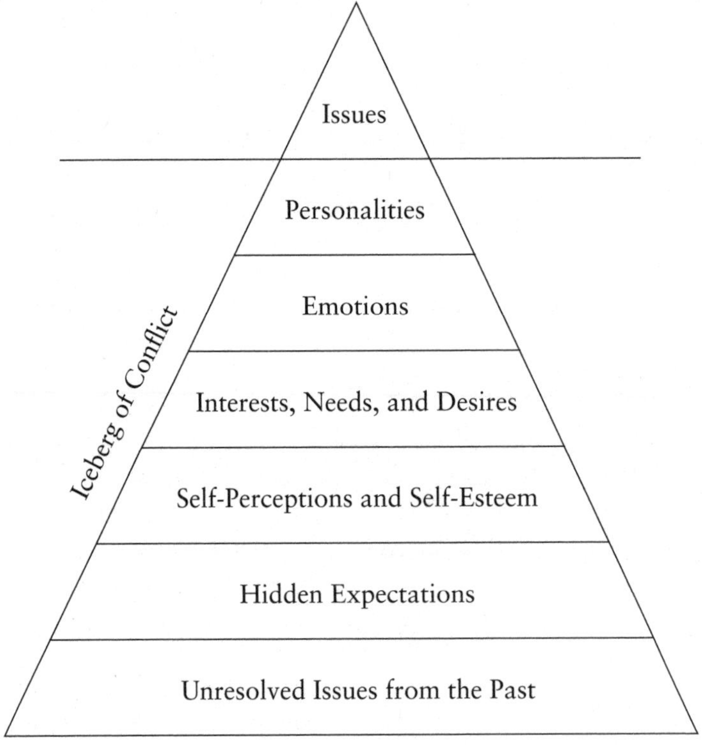

Each successive layer of the iceberg of conflict reveals something that does not appear on the surface, yet adds weight, significance, and hidden meaning to the language, metaphors, and arguments used in conflict. Underneath the iceberg, there is an "awareness of interconnection," meaning that we all have the capacity, if we go deep enough and do not become stuck on the surface, to experience genuine empathy and awareness of our interconnectedness—including even those who are yelling, insulting, or upsetting us. We are all connected as members of the same human family, and we cannot close ourselves off to others without at the same time losing touch with some part of ourselves that we can no longer recognize.

In a university dispute we were asked to mediate, a faculty member stated she had been sexually harassed by her department chair. Both were highly respected and valued for making significant contributions to the academic program. Consequently, everyone was perplexed by Isabel's repeated insistence that Miguel was stalking her, spying on her, and harassing her.

In the mediation, we met separately with Isabel to learn more about her experiences. She told us she was not accusing Miguel of any of the usual sexual harassment behaviors that involve touching, offensive language, or suggestive displays, but merely watching her, standing outside the door of her classroom, and making her feel uncomfortable in faculty meetings. She found she could not get anyone at the university to address her concerns unless she framed her complaint as one of sexual harassment.

When we met with Miguel, he was not only perplexed by her accusation, but extremely upset and angry. He explained that he did sometimes stand outside the door to her classroom because his office was right across the hall and he would meet students at the door when they came to see him. He felt he had not treated Isabel differently from other faculty members, though he acknowledged that he had not scheduled her classes for the times she had requested and he knew she was unhappy about his decision.

As the seriousness of Isabel's allegations and the intensity of their emotions did not match the facts, we realized we were seeing only the tip of the iceberg, and decided our only recourse was to probe beneath the surface to uncover the hidden layers of their conflict. To pursue this strategy, Isabel and Miguel agreed to meet with us in a joint session to discuss the problem and search for solutions.

At the mediation, we discovered they had been colleagues in the early days of the department when there were few other faculty members around. They had worked closely and their friendship had been important to them. As the department grew, the faculty was asked to give each other peer evaluations. Miguel was concerned about Isabel's habit of missing classes, arriving late, and not submitting student grades in time to meet university deadlines. He invited Isabel to lunch to discuss his concerns before putting them on paper in an "official" peer evaluation. True to form, she failed to show up, leaving him fuming and waiting at a restaurant for several hours. In response, he submitted his evaluation without discussing it or informing her beforehand and, as a result, it took her two extra years to make tenure.

Isabel, on the other hand, said she had always admired Miguel and looked to him for support, protection, and friendship. When she found out he had "betrayed" her in his evaluation, she distanced herself and vowed to never trust him again. Five years later, when he became department chair, her distrust escalated, and when he did not give her the class schedule she requested, the feelings of betrayal and abandonment that she had never expressed resurfaced.

As a result of uncovering and sharing these deeper elements in the iceberg of their conflict, Isabel and Miguel were able to acknowledge the pain they had caused each other and apologize for not having been better communicators.

We suggested that they set a new date, have the lunch they missed, and come up with a plan for working together more effectively. They did so and presented a joint proposal at the next mediation that they decided to take to the next faculty meeting. At the meeting, Isabel publicly withdrew her sexual harassment allegation and apologized for making it, Miguel agreed to rotate class schedule assignments, and both indicated an intention to create a more collegial and trusting relationship. Although their friendship never fully returned, their collegiality continued, and their conflicts became more manageable.

A still deeper element in the iceberg was revealed a year later, after Isabel had completed psychotherapy. She called to tell us that in therapy she had recalled that she had experienced sexual abuse by a third-grade teacher who also happened to be named Miguel. As a result of discovering this deeper layer, she became less obsessed with Miguel's comings and goings and his treatment of her. She let the past go and returned to the present.

Applying Your Knowledge of the Iceberg

The past is powerfully present in all our conflicts and communications, yet we are hardly objective historians in describing our own conflicts. We often do not know in the beginning even what we are angry about, which may originate in some incident that happened years ago. We may become angry with someone when in reality we are frightened or in pain or trying to protect ourselves. We may be using the conflict to divert attention from some shameful incident in our past, or to heal our wounds by inflicting them on others.

These emotional experiences can blind us, making it difficult to know or say what is in our hearts or subconscious minds, and to address what lies beneath the surface of our dispute. Instead, we operate semiconsciously, reacting to unseen forces that are detectable only because our reactions are completely out of proportion to the actions that seem to have triggered them. In our confusion, we can easily get hypnotized, and attach importance to superficial issues.

The best option is then to listen to our own inner truth and be willing to reveal these deeper issues to our opponent. By revealing ourselves, we invite similar behaviors in return and may thereby break the conflict system. Even then, we may not succeed. Each of us is so deeply defended that the information we need to resolve the conflict may be unknown or unavailable to us, and we cannot describe what we do not know.

We may hide this information even from ourselves, because it is connected to some highly charged issue or unresolved conflict from the past that we do not want to face. We may think we are in touch with what is going on, yet be completely off track. The only way we can know for sure is by breaking our hypnosis, getting beneath the surface, and opening a deeper conversation with our opponent.

To understand the deeper layers of your iceberg and perhaps an awareness of deeper interconnection, consider a conflict in which you are now engaged and identify what is happening at each level of the iceberg. As you probe deeper, notice whether your definition of the conflict evolves. You may want to identify additional layers to the ones we have cited. Notice any emotions that emerge. Try answering the following questions, first for yourself, and then for your opponent:

- *Issues:* What issues are on the surface in your conflict? What issues lie beneath the surface that neither of you are discussing?
- *Personalities:* Are differences between your personalities contributing to misunderstandings and tensions? If so, what are they and how are they operating?
- *Emotions:* What emotions are having an impact on your reactions? How are they doing so? Are you communicating your emotions responsibly, or are you distorting or suppressing them? What emotions is your opponent experiencing?
- *Interests, needs, desires:* How are you proposing to solve the conflict? Why is that your proposal? What deeper concerns are behind it? What do you really want? Why do you want it? What needs or desires, if satisfied, would allow you to feel good? Why is that important to you? What does getting what you want have to do with the way you are communicating?

- *Self-perceptions and self-esteem:* How do you feel about yourself and your behavior when you are engaged in conflict? What do you see as your strengths and weaknesses? Is any part of the conflict connected to your sense of self-esteem? If you were completely self-confident, would your opponent's behavior bother you as much?
- *Hidden expectations:* What are your primary expectations of your opponent? What do you expect of yourself? Are your expectations realistic? Have you clearly, openly, and honestly communicated your expectations to your opponent? What would happen if you did? How might you release yourself from unrealistic expectations?
- *Unresolved issues from the past:* Does this conflict remind you of anything from your past? Do you have any unresolved or unfinished issues from the past that are keeping you locked in conflict? Why? What would it take for you to let them go?

Notice whether your understanding of the conflict changed as you considered different levels and how your feelings about the conflict, yourself, and your opponent might evolve further if you continue to probe more deeply. Ask yourself, "How many of my answers to these questions have I shared with my opponent?" If there are any that you haven't shared, why have you chosen not to share them? Is there any way you might share them? Is there anyone who could help you communicate more openly? Picture a conversation, however difficult, in which you decide to share your deeper thoughts and insights with your opponent. Practice both parts of the conversation in your own mind or with a colleague or write them down. Notice any shifts in your feelings as you envision each part of the conversation and imagine how the other person might respond. After rehearsing, try it in reality, and see how close the actual conversation comes to what you imagined.

Steps to Get Below the Surface

Most people in conflict never meet with their opponent or have an open, honest conversation—even regarding the superficial issues in their dispute, let alone the deeper issues that are that are keeping them at impasse. When we ask people why they have not communicated important information about the deeper levels of their conflict to their opponents, they often say it is because their opponent is unwilling to listen, would not be interested in the information, or is not trustworthy.

We then ask how can you know your opponent won't listen or is uninterested or untrustworthy if you're unwilling to speak? Are you withholding important information about the conflict, possibly because of your own fear of becoming vulnerable in the presence of someone you don't trust?

Often, we protect ourselves and keep conflict conversations superficial because we lack the language or skills we need to succeed, or we fear becoming vulnerable in our opponent's presence, or we know in our hearts that what we would reveal could change everything, including how we define ourselves, our opponent, and the issues.

Yet at a much deeper level, this level of honesty and openness is *exactly* what we most want and need. Instead, we cover our fear and vulnerability with rationalizations of disinterest or lack of trust, and in the end, deprive *ourselves* of the opportunity to engage in authentic, honest communications with someone who is probably as afraid of being vulnerable as we are. How will they ever learn to listen or become interested or trustworthy if we don't provide them with real information and help them understand who we are and why we are upset?

Getting to the real issues has to start with someone, and it might as well be you because you are the only one whose actions you can control. When you take this risk, other people usually start to listen, become interested, and begin to behave in a more trustworthy way. If they don't, at least you will feel better and more self-confident because you will know you acted with integrity and courage.

How do we break the web of silence and collusion in conflict to discover what is lying beneath the surface when people are behaving aggressively, experiencing intense negative emotions, and unwilling to risk honestly discussing what is happening to themselves and others? Here are some actions you can take to look beneath the surface of your conflicts:

- Start by focusing on yourself and understanding more about the content at each level in your iceberg of conflict
- Use curiosity, open-ended questions, empathy, and responsive listening techniques to probe beneath the surface
- Take a risk and bring a deep level of emotional honesty and vulnerability to what you see, hear, and observe, recognizing that the more honest and vulnerable you are with yourself, the deeper you can go with others
- Be willing to accept whatever you find beneath the surface without shame, anger, or judgment

As you gain more perspective on your own subterranean issues, and those of your opponent and organization, you will become more confident and skillful in taking the next step: which is to ask questions *directly* to your opponent and together address the issues that lie below the surface of the conflict. A simple way of doing this is to become curious and ask naive, honest, even silly questions—the kind that three-year-olds ask. These are often the most powerful questions, and posing them can dramatically alter your conflict.

We suggest that you not censor yourself, but let your questions flow, with only one caution: a probing, attacking, judgmental, or prying style of questioning will not communicate curiosity but reveals a closed mind, which will become counterproductive. Instead, try this approach:

- Begin by asking the other person for permission to ask questions
- Adopt a gentle, respectful, empathetic attitude, no matter what they say
- Ask the kind of questions you would like to be asked by your opponent
- Listen actively and nonjudgmentally to their answers
- Invite your opponent to join you in exploring deeper underlying issues
- Welcome the resulting insights
- Thank your opponent for her responses
- Take her remarks seriously and work to change your behavior

Here are some specific questions you can ask that will deepen the dialogue and turn your opponent's attention toward solutions:

- "What do you think I did or failed to do that contributed to our conflict?"
- "Can you give me a specific example?"
- "How did you feel when I did that?"
- "Can you tell me more what bothered you about what I did?"
- "What do you think *you* did or failed to do that contributed to the conflict?"
- "Would you like to know how that made me feel?"
- "What did you mean when you said . . . ?"

- "How does what I said or did create a problem for you?"
- "What is the worst part of what happened for you?"
- "Why don't you tell me about your experience and I'll listen to you, then I'll tell you about mine."
- "I hope you can hear what I'm saying without getting upset or angry or confused. Will you let me know if what I say starts to bother you so I can communicate with you better?"
- "If you had it all to do over again, what would you do differently?" "Why?"
- "Would you be willing to start over again right now and do it differently?"
- "What is most important to you in solving this problem?"
- "What would you suggest I do to solve my part of the problem?"
- "Would you like to know what I think you can do to solve your part?"
- "Can you think of any solutions that might be acceptable to both of us?"
- "What would it take for you to let go of this conflict and feel the issues have been completely resolved?"
- "How would you like me to communicate with you in the future if we have any more problems?"
- "What should I say specifically if I experience a problem to avoid future miscommunications?"
- "Would you be interested in hearing how I would like you to communicate with me in the future?"
- "What kind of relationship would you *like* to have with me?" "Why?"
- "How would you like this conversation to end?" "Why?"
- "What can we both do to make our next conversation go more smoothly?"

Notice that each of these questions allows you and your opponent to become more honest and authentic with each other, to search beneath the surface of your conflict for its deeper meanings, to share responsibility for having caused it, and to move toward joint responsibility for resolving it.

Sally was vice president in charge of quality, and Ted was vice president in charge of operations at a large high-tech company. They were embroiled in a bitter conflict that was threatening to cause the company to lose customers. In interviews, they blamed each other for starting the conflict, as did the employees who worked for each of them. Both groups identified the other group as the source of the problem, causing communication between them to freeze and the entire organization to become polarized.

Sally felt she was undervalued, both by Ted and by the president. She thought she had little or no voice in executive decisions and was constantly stuck with the responsibility of covering up Ted's bad operational decisions. Ted felt he was losing the president's favor, was not respected or trusted by Sally, and that his only recourse was to resist or sabotage Sally, who was his main competitor for the president's attention. They were both convinced they were completely right and the other one was completely wrong.

We began our intervention by asking them about their family backgrounds. Sally said she was the youngest girl in a family with three older brothers; Ted was the oldest boy in a family with three younger sisters. We asked them to describe what it was like growing up in their families, and they suddenly realized they were reenacting childhood sibling rivalries and competing for the attention of their parents.

We told them that the president had told us he thought they were behaving like children and was considering firing both of them. We also told them we asked the president whether he felt he had been playing favorites, and he admitted that he had been rewarding Sally and Ted for their hyperaggressive, competitive behaviors, but would stop doing so in the future.

As a result, Sally and Ted agreed to stop personalizing each other's behavior and act like members of the same organizational family. They agreed to meet once a week, discuss what they could have done better during the previous week, and plan for the week ahead. Once they began discussing their ongoing issues, the conflicts subsided, they rapidly reached a number of side agreements on how they could support each other, and went together to thank the president for no longer playing favorites.

The president agreed to include Sally on the executive decision-making team and reassured Ted of the vital role he was playing in the organization. He told them he was thrilled that they were now getting along and was impressed that they were taking the initiative to resolve their conflict. Though Sally and Ted continued to have disagreements, they treated each other as allies and colleagues, let their teams know the war was over, and were able to see their conflict as an opportunity for creative collaboration.

The Language of Conflict

The words we use to describe our conflicts reflect the hidden assumptions we have about ourselves, our opponents, and the emotional meaning of our conflicts. These words shape our attitudes, expectations, and experiences, and form our interactions, processes, and relationships. The language we use when we are in conflict reveals a great deal about our secret biases, assumptions, fears, and what we are *capable* of imagining as solutions.

Rather than being static, language evolves dynamically, has an impact on and is impacted by the culture that produces and uses it. National languages divide into thousands of "sublanguages" that include, as Russian language theorist Mikail Bakhtin has written,

> social dialects, characteristic group vernacular, professional jargons, generic languages, languages of generations and age groups, tendentious languages, languages of the authorities, of various circles and of passing fashions, languages that serve the specific socio-political purposes of the day, even of the hour (each day has its own slogan, its own vocabulary, its own emphases).

Each workplace, department, level, and function creates its own language, and each team, group, clique, and relationship does so as well. Similarly, everyone in conflict creates a unique and shared language to describe their experiences, revealing through their choice of words what the conflict means to them, how they see themselves and their opponents, what possibilities they can imagine for resolution, and how they intend to pursue them.

In other words, each of us has a choice about how we describe the conflicts in our lives. We can describe them as experiences that imprison us, as battles, as opportunities for learning and improvement, or as fascinating journeys. Our choices shape the way the conflict is likely to unfold. More important, by changing the language we use to describe our conflict, we automatically change what might happen, and imagine new possibilities in response.

Consider a conflict in which you are currently engaged. Take a moment to write down, without censoring your response, all the words that describe the conflict, your opponent, yourself, and how you feel about resolving it. After doing so, take a look at the words you used and ask yourself what they suggest, how they differ, and what they have in common.

Each language choice reveals as much about yourself as about the conflict and your opponent. If, for example, you describe your opponent as "arrogant," stop for a moment and see if you can think of a positive word you could use instead of the word arrogant. If you wanted to describe your opponent favorably, you might say he is "self-confident" or "determined." By choosing the word arrogant over the word self-confident, you suggest your *own* lack of self-confidence, making you a perfect match for your opponent's arrogance. Here are some questions revealing why:

- If you were completely convinced and unambiguous in your self-confidence, why would someone else's arrogance upset you, as opposed to making you happy that they are self-confident?
- Could your anger be misdirected and actually be anger at yourself, or an overreaction or overcompensation for your own lack of self-confidence?
- Was there anyone in your family of origin who you would describe as arrogant?
- How did you learn to respond to them?
- Was that response successful?
- Are you regarding this type of behavior as arrogant because it reminds you of earlier, similar behavior you experienced in your family?
- Is it possible that your opponents' arrogance reflects *his* lack of self-confidence?
- What would make you *act* like that? Why?
- What other words might you use to describe how you feel?

You can go still deeper and identify the subtleties and nuances of each word. For example, the word arrogant suggests an assumption on your part that the other person does not care what you think, and does not respect your experience or views. If that is the case, it might be possible to say to him or her instead:

> "Let me see if I can summarize what I hear you saying—then I would like to ask if you can summarize what you hear me saying, so we can see if we understand each other."

"I understand that is how you feel/what you think. Would you like to know how I feel/what I think?"

"What kind of communication/relationship would you like us to have? Why?"

"Would you tell me one thing I can do right now to improve our communication? Then I would like to tell you one thing you can do—would that be acceptable to you?"

"It would really help me listen to you, and perhaps do what you are asking, if you could speak to me in a more respectful tone of voice. What can I do to make that possible?"

"Can I tell you what I am feeling right now in this conversation and how we both might make it more successful?"

"Here is what I am doing that is not helpful. I am feeling put off because I sense you don't care what I think and I am getting defensive. Here's one thing I'm willing to do differently. . ."

Thus, every insult hurled at you by your opponent, and every insult you toss back in return, can be traced backwards like a thread into the subconscious of the person using it. The insults your opponent uses to describe you reveal not only what upsets her, but why, and what you could do to create a different response.

If you listen closely, you will discover that beneath each insult and accusation lies a *confession,* and beneath the confession lies a *request.* For example, if your opponent calls you a "bully," you can hear it as a confession that your opponent feels intimidated and is frightened when you raise your voice. More deeply, you can hear it as a request that you treat him more respectfully, and speak softly or less judgmentally in the future.

No matter what insult a person uses, there is a positive way of saying the same thing. Every decision to use a negative word or phrase in place of a positive or neutral one indicates a sensitivity or weakness on the part of the speaker that can be used by the listener to gain deeper understanding of the speaker's motivation. This information can enable the listener to transform the insult into a request, for example, by saying "Can we both agree not to use insults? It's getting in the way of my hearing what you want." "Would you be willing to lower your tone of voice?" "Is the reason you are yelling because you want me to know how strongly you feel about this, or because you feel I haven't been listening to you?" "What can I do to change that?" In this way, even insults and accusations can be turned upside down and transformed into sources of learning, improved relationships, skill building, resolution, and transformation.

The same point can be made regarding the language we use to describe conflict. In conflict resolution workshops, we often ask, "What is one word or phrase that expresses what you do or feel when you are in conflict?" Initial responses usually include words like anger, frustration, silence, shame, fear, stress, avoidance, and repression, nearly all of which are negative. We then ask if there are any *positive* words that describe conflict, and people call out words like change, intimacy, learning, growth, opportunity, communication, resolution, forgiveness, listening, trust, and completion.

These positive words represent what we most want, what is possible, and what is at stake in our conflicts, while the negative words represent how we feel, how we are reacting, and what we are doing to each other. But if we use negative ideas to achieve positive ends, we quickly discover that it is impossible to "get there from here," that anger does not translate into trust any more than shame builds self-confidence.

Try this yourself. Without self-censoring, list the first words, both negative and positive, that come to mind regarding a conflict and see what feelings and ideas emerge. Then ask yourself what led you to use negative words, how you might implement positive ones, and how you might resolve your conflicts by turning the negatives into positives. For example, if you felt frightened by your opponent, consider what it would take to overcome your fear, talk calmly about the problem, and let it go.

You may find that the positive words reflect a deep understanding that working through your conflict could dramatically improve your relationships and communications, whereas the negative ones reflect a profound frustration at your inability to do so, and using them is keeping you locked in conflict and cycles of distrust. You can then decide to get to the bottom of the reasons you came up with the negative words in the first place. Doing so will automatically start to turn negative words into positive ones at their source deep inside you.

Metaphors and the Meaning of Conflict

The language of conflict is highly charged, and filled with allusions, metaphors, and emotional symbols. The reasons we cite for conflict are based on facts and logic, yet our experiences are largely emotional. But instead of participating in direct emotional communications with people we do not trust who are attacking us, we show our feelings *indirectly* by the language we use to describe the facts and reinforce our logic.

Poets, novelists, and lyricists have invented a rich cultural language that allows us to express the complex and convoluted emotional truths in conflict. Listen to your own words when you are in an argument. What metaphors, symbols, and allusions do you use to make your feelings known? What words do you wrap around your emotions to express or disguise them?

Here are three common conflict metaphors and supporting popular phrases that expose our underlying beliefs about the nature and meaning of conflict. These metaphors, drawn from real workplace cultures, translate into phrases with meanings that may or may not be intended. Yet scrutinizing the language we use in conflict lets us discover how simple words and phrases shape what we think and feel, and how we respond. Listen to the symbolism and hidden meanings in the following phrases.

Conflict as War

Following are some common workplace phrases based on this metaphor:

"Your position is indefensible."

"We shot down that idea."

"We've got a battle on our hands."

"He dropped a bomb on me."

"Line up the troops and man the barricades."

"I won."

Using warlike metaphors in conflict reveals an underlying belief that the other person is out to get us, that we have no choice but to fight back using the same tactics, and that nothing can be done to resolve the dispute short of total victory. Yet the other person may only be acting in self-defense, perhaps as a result of hearing our aggressive metaphors and combative language, and may respond favorably to a different set of phrases or tactics and be more willing to negotiate a compromise or interest-based solution.

What is worse, victory often turns into defeat, and defeat is transformed into victory. For example, crushing the other side reduces the winner's capacity for compassion, collaboration, forgiveness, and reconciliation, and increases sympathy for the loser. Also, winners tend to repeat their "winning behaviors" in other circumstances, while losers learn, get creative, and try something new.

Unfortunately, aggressive, hostile, warlike attitudes and a willingness to do battle against our opponents are richly rewarded in many highly competitive organizational cultures. Yet warlike attitudes toward external opponents can easily be turned inward to generate fiercely competitive attitudes toward colleagues *within* the organization, reducing collaboration and increasing distrust among coworkers. Reassessing our language, checking the assumptions hidden in combative metaphors, and using more collaborative terminology can motivate us to use new metaphors that encourage teamwork.

The use of warlike metaphors reveals an underlying assumption that our opponents are evil, allowing us to justify in advance the evil we intend to do in return. Demonizing them disarms our compassion and gives us permission to harm them as we feel they have harmed us. There are a number of reasons why we make our opponents seem like enemy warriors:

- It is possible that we unknowingly caused them harm.
- Someone else may have hurt them in a similar way.
- They may have decided to pass their pain onto us rather than experience it themselves.
- They may feel that a preemptive strike will protect them from future harm we might cause them.
- They may be frightened of losing their jobs and are trying to create a diversion by pointing at our response and minimizing the importance of their behavior.

By attempting to explain their motivation, we do not excuse their behavior. Rather, we question the underlying assumption that lets us think we can demonize them without simultaneously victimizing ourselves, or injure them without hurting ourselves and limiting the effectiveness of the organization. Demonizing others only makes us more brutal, insensitive, and uncaring, inviting similar action in response. It is not necessary that we label the person who hurt us as "evil" in order to communicate our displeasure and refusal to tolerate what they did.

The good news is that while warfare and hatred can be internalized through metaphors, so can love and forgiveness. To see how, contrast the military approach to a different metaphor that sees conflict as an opportunity for learning, transformation, improved relationships, better solutions, and personal and organizational change.

Conflict as Opportunity

Following are some common workplace phrases based on this metaphor:

"This issue presents us with a real challenge."

"What would you like to see happen instead?"

"We now have a chance to make things better."

"You have a good point. What could we do together to address it?"

"Your feedback has helped me see some ways I could improve, by communicating more respectfully. Is that right?"

"What are some creative possibilities we can think of for solving this problem?"

This shift in language reflects a profound transformation. Metaphors that describe conflicts as opportunities signal a transition from assuming our opponents are evil to assuming they are allies in helping solve our problems. They move us from assuming negative outcomes to anticipating positive ones, and open possibilities for learning, creative options, and better relationships.

By adopting metaphors of opportunity, you reveal possibilities for learning and improvement, deeper personal intimacy, improved appreciation of your opponent, better and more lasting solutions, clearer communications, and more trusting relationships. You initiate an open-ended exploration of common problems and a broader range of outcomes that will improve your communication and move you past ideas of victory and defeat. Most important, you become the shaper of your own experiences, in charge of where, when, and how they happen.

These hidden opportunities are not easily revealed. For example, a small but highly successful corporation was being torn apart by a conflict between its two top officers who were battling over who would get the best office, the plushest furniture, the largest head count, and the biggest expense account.

After listening to each of them complain about the other in exaggerated and negative ways, we helped them shift from metaphors of war to those of opportunity by asking them if they would be willing to transfer their competition to something that really *mattered* in the organization, such as who could create the greatest customer satisfaction, who could inspire their teams to produce the best results, or who could reduce costs and streamline operations the most. They laughed, admitted they had been acting like children, saw the opportunities for synergy that were hidden in their differences, and agreed to use their conflict and competition to help drive organizational improvement.

In your conflicts, instead of talking about battling your opponent and exhausting yourself and others in the process, consider whether it would not be more interesting and enjoyable to talk about why your conflict happened and what you can both do to resolve it in better and faster ways, and move it to a higher level of resolution. In this way, you may be able to locate opportunities hidden in your conflict.

Shifting your language to metaphors of opportunity will allow you to take responsibility for what you contributed to the conflict. The more you acknowledge your own contribution, the greater the possibility not only for resolution and innovation, but personal growth and organizational improvement. Your willingness to examine the assumptions that underlie your approach to conflict will also bring you face to face with your own inner nature. The more you can find your authentic conflict voice, the easier it will be to recognize and elicit the authentic voices of others.

Metaphors of war focus our attention on the past, on destroying or undermining our opponent, and on insisting we are right. Metaphors of opportunity, on the other hand, focus our attention on the future, on satisfying both our interests, and on the ways we might learn from the conflict, resolve it, and use it to drive change.

Another metaphor is to think of conflict as a journey that takes place in the present, rather than focusing on the past or the future. The emphasis is then on the *relationship* between you and your opponent, rather than on what you are each doing, saying, thinking, or feeling; and on the *process* of discussing, negotiating, and resolving the dispute, rather than on the difficulty of reaching resolution. When we think of conflict as a journey, we become less concerned with the goal or destination, and more focused on the trip and the adventure. We can then relax and enjoy the ride.

Conflict as Journey

Following are some common workplace phrases based on this metaphor:

"Your ideas point us in a great new direction."

"Here is what I really enjoy about working with you . . ."

"We're off to a good start."

"Where do you want to go with that?"

"Is this process/conversation working for you?"

"We're on the road to a solution."

"I think we've arrived at an agreement!"

By regarding your conflict as a journey, process, or voyage that takes you to a new location, you transcend the idea that you are trapped by it. This metaphor allows you to recognize that the journey is itself worthwhile. In doing so, you increase your ability to move *with* rather than against your opponent, and see that what is new and unknown is interesting, rather than frightening. You may even learn to anticipate with pleasure your next chance to travel the path of conflict in search of growth, innovation, and discovery.

Experiencing your conflicts as journeys will encourage you to explore your relationship with your opponent, discover your "hot buttons" and the reasons you allow them to be pushed, and take pleasure in finding better solutions in partnership with your opponent. Journeys create expectations and anticipations of change, learning, self-improvement, expanded awareness, and even forgiveness. They offer release from the stress of feeling trapped, and from making enemies of people you have not stopped and taken the time to get to know or understand.

A Los Angeles school principal transformed his school by shifting his attitude toward conflict and seeing it as a journey. His school was rundown and needed a facelift. Several teachers told him he should get the district to paint over a faded, peeling mural that had been at the school for many years. He agreed and had the wall painted, but after it was done several teachers and staff protested, telling him they had liked the mural, which respected their ethnic diversity.

Instead of becoming defensive and counterattacking or triggering a battle between rival factions, he implemented an alternative strategy. He met with the entire faculty and staff and asked them to join him in a journey of discovery to see what they could learn from this experience. He invited everyone to express their arguments and defenses and examine their mutual responsibility for misunderstanding and conflict. He began by admitting his own errors, something he would not have done if he were thinking of his conflict as a war.

His approach led to a consensus decision-making process that resulted in an improved educational program that highlighted student diversity, an agreement to replace the mural with a new one designed to display the increased diversity of the school, and a plan that was executed by the entire school community, creating a renewed sense of partnership, respect, and trust.

Your conflict can become an *external* journey in search of a wise opponent, or an *internal* journey in search for an authentic self. Your ability to hear your inner voice will be reflected externally in your ability to listen to others, just as your ability to accept yourself will be reflected in your capacity to experience empathy with others. Each is a journey toward wisdom and more honest, empathetic, and balanced relationships.

There are many other metaphors you might apply to your conflicts. Try to find them in the words you or your opponent use, during angry shouting matches and heated arguments, and in the midst of insults, accusations, and emotional conversations. As you investigate these hidden messages, think about whether you can use the information in metaphors to create better solutions. As you become more skillful, you can intentionally reframe the metaphors your opponent is using and substitute positive metaphors of openness, freedom, and optimism for negative metaphors of entrapment, enslavement, and pessimism.

How Empathy and Honesty Lead to Transformation

One reason for conflict is our inability to empathize with our opponent and imagine what it might be like to be on the receiving end of our communications and behaviors. For this reason, cultivating a capacity for empathy is one of the most powerful methods for resolving disputes. With empathy, we can access the deepest layers of the iceberg, develop an "awareness of interconnection," and realize we share a common set of emotions, interests, issues, and perceptions with our opponents, even when we differ in languages, cultures, beliefs, and personalities.

One way of seeking resolution is to use role play to understand how our opponent might feel, ask a question to find out if we are accurate, and imagine how to build a bridge between us. Most of us have engaged in role plays at some point during our work lives. Empathy is a part of all role-playing and acting experiences, in which vividly imagining someone else's life lets us understand what it might feel like to live it ourselves. When we are acting, we know we are pretending, yet the emotions we feel ring true nonetheless.

Empathy is a skill we can practice and improve in every interaction. In conflict, empathy encourages us to give up the negative characterizations and judgments we have formed about our opponents. Judgments are simply defenses against empathy. They convince us that we already know the truth, and don't need to ask any questions.

Empathy is different from sympathy, which is feeling sorry for someone. In sympathy, we are absorbed in the other person's injured feelings and helplessness, while ignoring their power or ability to do something to alleviate or resolve their problems. With sympathy, there is a kind of consensual boundary violation that turns the other person into a powerless "victim" who is often left feeling less secure and self-confident than before. In a strange way, sympathy *ignores* people by turning them into casualties, saying "Poor you, I feel sorry for you." Sympathy places them in a power-down position, in need of help from someone with greater strength and ability, allowing us to feel superior and encouraging us to become their rescuers.

Empathy is locating the other within the self. It is trying to understand what another person *might* be feeling, then asking questions to find out whether we are on the right track. It is recognizing other people as separate, unique, complex individuals whose ideas, feelings, and experiences can never be fully known or understood. It is walking a while in their shoes, understanding their ideas, feelings, and experiences, and resonating with them inside ourselves. Empathy is realizing that we all share human frailties, strengths, desires, and expectations.

Creating Empathy Through Role-Reversing Dialogue

The best way to practice empathy is by consistently following the "golden rule," by speaking as though *you* were the one being spoken to and acting as though what you are about to do were done to you and not to some faceless, crazy, mistaken opponent.

To practice empathy as a strategy in resolving conflicts, try the following exercise. Think of someone with whom you are in conflict or have been in a dispute in the past, and complete the following steps. You can also do this exercise orally by shifting from one chair to another and acting both parts. Or you might role-play your opponent and ask a friend to role-play you, and then:

1. Write or say what you would most like to say to this person
2. Respond with what you would want to say if you were the other person

3. Reverse positions and state your response to what "they" wrote or said to you
4. Continue searching for deep places where meaning wells up
5. Consider what it would take to bridge these two sets of statements and make them into one
6. Create a single, internally consistent, composite version that captures the essence of both experiences

Now look at what you came up with and ask whether you honestly expressed both sides of the conflict and presented them equally. If so, what did you learn? If not, start over again. To make the exercise more powerful, ask your questions in real life by initiating an open conversation with your opponent. You might even suggest that your opponent take your side in the argument for a few minutes while you argue his position, just to see what it feels like to be on the other side.

By practicing empathy you will travel deeper into yourself and discover the internal places where you recognize and understand others. Even if you feel anger, fear, or pain in conflict, you can discern what lies beneath the surface in your relationships by considering what would lie beneath their surface for you.

Empathy can be a powerful tool for organizations as well. An information technology organization we consulted with was in turmoil, with staff members engaged in conflict with a business unit over what they perceived as unrealistic demands. In turn, the business unit complained about IT bureaucracy, unreasonable rejections of their requests for help, poor quality of customer service, and chronic miscommunications.

We asked both groups to participate in a problem-solving session at which they agreed that several staff members would exchange work locations and departmental reporting relationships to better understand the conditions, priorities, and demands in each other's work and allow them to interact "up close and personal."

In the business unit, several people were assigned to work in IT offices and several IT staffers were assigned to the business unit to act as liaison. All staff who exchanged places got a "feel" for what it was really like to be in the other department and began to appreciate the pressures and rewards of the people who worked there.

After a year, the conflicts between the departments were almost completely over, and the employees who changed work units asked to remain in their new locations so they could continue coordinating the delivery of services. They reported that they had enjoyed walking in each other's shoes and really understood what their colleagues were trying to do and what they were up against in their efforts to make it happen.

As their empathy increased, they were able to develop a powerful, integrated strategic plan. They chose to focus on the company as a whole and were able to design a number of collaborative ventures that reduced conflicts across the company and provided vastly improved service for customers.

Empathy can be increased in organizations by using reverse role plays such as the one described above, or others in which titles, status, and positions in the organizational hierarchy, or sides in a dispute, are reversed. For example, try letting the person who ordinarily runs staff meetings sit quietly while someone who normally sits quietly runs the meetings. Afterward, debrief the exercise to see what was learned. The results can be as profound as in the organization we described, and participants can come away with lasting empathy for each other's roles.

The Connection Between Empathy and Honesty

Empathy alone may not be enough to resolve aggressive, long-lasting, or chronic conflicts. Once we successfully place ourselves in another person's shoes and discover inside ourselves what may be important to him, we require the courage to honestly communicate what we learned. Empathy that is not combined with honesty becomes sentimental, placating, and ineffectual; whereas honesty that is not tempered with empathy becomes brutal, aggressive, and judgmental.

If empathy consists of discovering others within ourselves, honesty consists of communicating what we discover so they can consider whether it is accurate. This can be done by asking questions and offering responses. Honesty means not turning away from what we see, but speaking openly, fearlessly, yet empathetically so others can learn the lessons that lie hidden in what they have *not* communicated.

In this way, empathy and honesty are intertwined. To reach a deeper level of honesty and successfully communicate what is taking place beneath the surface of any conflict, deeper and more profound levels of empathy are required. As new levels of empathy are reached, deeper levels of honesty are needed to communicate them.

Honest communication is not easy. Most of us have learned to "play it safe" in conflict. We may even be participating in a "conspiracy of silence" with our opponent based on an unspoken agreement to communicate superficially and avoid honestly facing what is true. If so, it is easy to guard communications, withhold critical information, and mistake internal conflicts for conflicts with others.

Worse, by not being honest, we may be cheating ourselves, our opponents, and our organization out of opportunities for learning and improving by confronting a deeper set of issues and recognizing what we or they actually think and feel.

There are huge risks connected with the use of honesty as a conflict resolution strategy. Yet honesty is what differentiates *resolution* from suppression, avoidance, and mere settlement. Indeed, when we settle disputes without reaching or resolving the underlying reasons that gave rise to them; or maintain distance through denial, defensiveness, and self-justification rather than risk honest self-examination; or allow the downward spiral of rage and shame to block our ability to communicate authentically, we accept the inevitability of safe, static, meaningless, and shallow relationships.

Conflict suppression and avoidance occur when we are afraid to hear or tell the truth. Settlement takes place when we want to avoid addressing the deeper issues that lie beneath the surface of our conflicts. Resolution, on the other hand, happens when we surface and bring into the open the issues that are driving our disputes and work our way through them.

Although honesty can give the impression that we are escalating or intensifying the conflict, it is nearly impossible to resolve the real reasons for a dispute without being honest. When we are deeply honest *and* empathetic with our opponents, we become more authentic ourselves and encourage our opponents to participate in problem solving. In the end, we are able to live more authentically and comfortably and improve the quality of our lives by facing and addressing the issues that are important to us.

Genuine honesty is difficult, however, and can easily backfire. In a single comment we can lose the empathetic connection that invites deep listening and improved communication. We can escalate the dispute to the point that it becomes more difficult to resolve. We can even convince ourselves that we are being honest when we are actually being brutal or aggressive.

It is especially difficult to be honest with those we dislike, or who dislike us, partly because superficiality, silence, secrets, and lies seem less risky and more powerful than vulnerability, honesty, shared responsibility, and open communication. Aggression and self-defense offer an *appearance* of honesty, and are more readily accepted in many organizational environments because they are instinctual, superficially honest, based on distrust, and easier to control.

By contrast, empathetic honesty requires vulnerability and *self*-honesty, which are opposites of aggression and self-defense. Moreover, aggression and self-defense end up leaving us weaker than honesty because they are reactive, self-protective, and based on the falsehood that our opponents are out to get us, as opposed to simply looking out for themselves. Most often, our opponents use *our* aggression and self-defense to avoid being vulnerable and defend themselves, exactly as we would.

When we hide our true thoughts and feelings from others, we condemn ourselves to silent suffering and self-doubt. In this state, we may repress our most vulnerable thoughts and feelings because they are too frightening or powerful to discuss openly. Often we externalize them, use them to characterize our opponents, and experience them from the outside-in rather than the inside-out. At the same time, our need for self-protection, sympathy, and uncritical support from others makes us less willing to take responsibility for our own aggressive or defensive actions, further reducing our self-esteem.

It is dangerous to be honest because that gives the other person the right to be equally honest with us. Hence, we are reduced to silence, banality, and nonengagement, fueled partly by a fear that honesty will not be held in check by the other side, or that we lack the willingness to be honest with ourselves, or that we do not have the skills to manage the chain reaction of anger that could cause our conversation to spiral out of control.

Honesty is difficult also because we want to avoid being blamed for conflict, and therefore make ourselves appear good and right by casting others as bad and wrong, because we want to be kind more than we want to be honest, because we want to protect ourselves and each other from the harshness of the truth, and because we want people in power to like us and are afraid that being honest will have a negative effect on our career. Yet the negative traits we attribute to others ultimately and inevitably return to us. If we make our opponents look and feel bad, or blame them for what went wrong, our relationship and communication will suffer, and we will both pay a price.

There is a deeper reason why honesty is dangerous. Sometimes we take deliberate steps to protect ourselves from the truth because we *know* it is true, and that serious consequences will happen as a result. We fear we will be forced to change our behaviors, redefine our lives and identities, or have to leave the comfortable—albeit dysfunctional—ruts we have created for ourselves. We know intuitively that honesty is a precondition for transformation.

Rationalizations for Not Being Honest

Most people at work are highly skilled at rationalizing dishonesty. They can easily present a list of perfectly good reasons for avoiding honest communication with their bosses, colleagues, family, and friends, not to mention their opponents in conflict. As a result, entire organizations accept cultural norms that justify dishonesty and encourage self-serving communications.

For example, in the sales and marketing division of a midsized corporation, staff members were so focused externally on customer sales targets that they communicated with unflagging, superficial, jovial banalities and never discussed their deeper ideas or honest reactions to what was happening on the job. They asked us to help them figure out why, despite their superficial camaraderie, there was such low morale in the organization.

Immediately, conflicts that lay hidden beneath the surface began to emerge. Staff began to realize that their need for honest communication had not disappeared, and their true feelings and reactions that had been hidden or suppressed actually became *more* powerful, making even minor conflicts more difficult to resolve. By creating "happy-face, have-a-nice-day" norms of communication, they had failed to address critical issues, solve real problems, improve morale, or ensure continued success.

Here are some rationalizations they used to justify keeping their communications superficial and not risking honest dialogue. As you review them, notice any that you use to hide honest feelings, or protect yourself from the risks that inhere in all open and honest interactions.

- "I don't want to hurt his feelings."
- "She'll misinterpret what I say."
- "He won't be receptive."
- "It will put our relationship at risk."
- "I will become open to retaliation or counterattack if I open up."
- "There's nothing in it for me because we can settle our issues without it."
- "It could escalate and I shouldn't increase the conflict."

- "I'll be out on a limb and won't be supported."
- "Nothing will change anyway."
- "I always take the risks, and this time it's her turn."
- "In the past, I haven't found it useful."
- "I could lose my job or the respect of others."
- "It's not me; he is the one who's stuck."

If any of these rationalizations has discouraged you from communicating honestly, ask why you bought into it. Have you been using it to defend yourself against a fear that could be better handled through open, honest communication and problem solving? Are your negative conflict experiences a result of being honest, or of not being sufficiently empathetic in communicating what you think or feel? Ultimately, where do you think avoidance of honesty will get you? Is that where you want to be? What impact do you think avoidance of honesty is having on the organization? What would happen if you abandoned these rationalizations and spoke honestly? What would it take for you to do so? What price have you and your organization paid for operating without honesty?

Rationalizations for Being Honest

For each rationalization listed above there is a counter-rationalization that is equally valid, yet encourages honest communication. For example:

- "It's possible for me to communicate honestly without hurting anyone's feelings if I do so empathetically."
- "It's possible for me to communicate accurately so there will be less possibility of misinterpretation."
- "She can't be receptive unless I offer her something important to hear."
- "Without honesty, there can't be an authentic relationship between us."
- "If I act collaboratively, he'll find it more difficult to respond defensively."
- "Through honest communication I'll increase my own self-esteem and skill as well as her opportunities to change."
- "The problem will get worse if I don't communicate honestly."

- "If it escalates, I can use conflict resolution skills or mediation to resolve the conflict at a deeper level."
- "If I risk being honest, the other person may take that risk also."
- "Things will begin to change when I communicate honestly."
- "I can't live with myself if I don't speak my own truth."
- "I could improve my job and gain the respect of others."
- "We will both remain stuck unless I do something to end the impasse."

Consider asking a colleague, coach, or mentor at work to give you feedback on how honest you are in your communications, or consider asking your opponents to be completely honest with you, and respond to any rationalizations they offer with counter-rationalizations and a request to be more honest in the future. You could also ask coworkers to identify the rationalizations they hear or use most often and use these rationalizations as a checklist to analyze the subtle, invisible messages regarding honesty that are being communicated in your organizational culture, and develop strategies to encourage empathetic and honest communications.

In the end, the reasons for honesty and empathy run far deeper than resolving conflict. They concern our integrity and authenticity, our values and ethics, our willingness to change ourselves, our ability to trust each other, our capacity to collaborate and live in community. They are what make us human.

STRATEGY 4

ACKNOWLEDGE AND REFRAME EMOTIONS

By embracing the inescapable, I lost my fear of it. I'll tell you a secret about fear. With fear, it's all or nothing, like any bullying tyrant, it rules your life with a stupid blinding omnipotence, or else you overthrow it, and its power vanishes in a puff of smoke.... I stopped being afraid because, if my time on earth was limited, I didn't have seconds to spare for funk.

— Salman Rushdie

How do you respond when your efforts to speak or listen result in intense emotional outbursts instead of calm and reasoned conversation? What options are available to you when you get caught up in negative emotions during a conflict and your efforts to communicate disintegrate or slip out of your control?

Emotions are complex. They can be expressed in ways that are constructive or destructive, pleasurable or painful, positive or negative, distorting or clarifying, escalating or de-escalating, collaborative or adversarial, reactive or preventative. They can blind us and offer insights that allow us to see others as they really are. They can energize us and leave us feeling exhausted. They can leave us hanging or bring us to closure.

Expressing, acknowledging, reframing, and integrating emotions can be a powerful positive force for problem solving, conflict resolution, and personal and organizational transformation, depending on how we decide to understand, approach, process, and express them. How we respond to our own powerful emotions limits our capacity to hear and respond to those of others, making us more or less available for communication and relationship with those who express similar emotions. It is therefore useful to think of emotions as requiring skill, or as teachers from whom we can learn, rather than as irrational experiences we need to suppress. Despite the ambivalence and uncertainty of the emotions we experience in conflict, we can all become more skillful in how we handle them, both in ourselves and in others.

Every conflict produces an emotional response, yet most workplaces and organizational cultures require us, either overtly or covertly, to "check our emotions at the door" or "leave them at home," and suppress them whenever possible. We can temporarily hold our emotions in check, but we cannot eliminate them or keep them permanently on hold, and trying to do so simply makes them surface somewhere else. What is worse, constraining our emotions keeps us from learning from them, integrating them, and using them to help solve our problems.

The primary reason for our repressive attitude toward emotions in the workplace is a general and pervasive lack of skill on the part of leaders, managers, and staff in handling intense emotional communications. Professor Daniel Goleman has called this ability to recognize, handle, and learn from feelings "emotional intelligence."

Emotional intelligence consists of a combination of self-awareness, self-regulation, motivation, empathy, and social or relational skills, as depicted in the following chart:

Components of Emotional Intelligence

	Definition	Hallmarks
Self-Awareness	The ability to recognize and understand your moods, emotions, and drives as well as their effect on others	Self-confidence Realistic self-assessment Self-deprecating sense of humor
Self-Regulation	The ability to control or redirect disruptive impulses and moods The propensity to suspend judgement, to think before acting	Trustworthiness and integrity Comfort with ambiguity Openness to change
Motivation	A passion to work for reasons that go beyond money or status A propensity to pursue goals with energy and persistence	Strong drive to achieve Optimism, even in the face of failure Organizational commitment
Empathy	The ability to understand the emotional makeup of other people Skill in treating people according to their emotional reactions	Expertise in building and retaining taltent Cross-cultural sensitivity Service to clients and customers
Social Skill	Proficiency in managing relationships and building networks Ability to find common ground and build rapport	Effectiveness in leading change Persuasiveness Expertise in building and leading teams

Source: Daniel Goleman, *Harvard Business Review,* November-December 1998.

Goleman argues that everyone can significantly increase their emotional intelligence, integrate emotional skills, and thereby improve even ordinary workplace decisions. We agree with him that "passions, when well exercised, promote wisdom, guide our thinking, establish our values, and help secure our survival."

Scientific studies have shown that expanding access to our emotions and not suppressing them dramatically increases the accuracy of our memory of what happened during an emotionally laden experience. Other studies have shown that those who can access the emotional processing centers of their brains and recognize emotions are able to make more accurate assessments of the meaning of words and phrases. In some instances, people who have experienced strokes or injuries to the emotional centers of their brains become unable to make even simple ordinary decisions, suggesting that emotions are an important element in problem solving and decision making in conflict.

In our experience mediating disputes over several decades, those who are able to respond skillfully to the negative emotions of others experience fewer conflicts and resolve them faster with fewer repercussions than those who are not skillful in handling their own emotions or those of others.

We invite you to look at your emotional responses to the conflicts you experience at work, how your feelings have influenced your perceptions, motivation, decisions, communications, and relationships, and how they have shaped your view of yourself and your opponent. Also consider how they may have limited or expanded your ideas regarding what you might do to resolve your conflicts and the underlying issues that created them.

Emotional Responses to Conflict

We all pay a heavy emotional price for unresolved conflict. This price includes not only irritation and aggravation, but physical pain and illness that are often triggered by the stresses of conflict. Howard Friedman, a psychology professor at the University of California at Riverside, has analyzed a hundred studies connecting people's states of mind with their physical health. He found that being chronically pessimistic, irritated, cynical, depressed, or anxious doubles your risk of contracting a major disease.

There are strong neurological connections between the emotional processing centers of the brain, the immune system, and the cardiovascular system. When stress hormones and brain chemicals produced during negative emotions flood the body, they hamper the immune system's ability to fight off disease, making us more susceptible to cancer, raising blood pressure, increasing cholesterol, and rendering us more vulnerable to diseases of all kinds.

Emotions are present in all our relationships, even when they do not appear on the surface or reveal themselves in obvious ways. These emotions produce diverse results, depending on how we regard them, and how we respond when they occur. Just as *experiencing* conflict routinely triggers negative emotions such as hatred, fear, shame, depression, and grief, *resolving* conflict routinely triggers positive emotions such as affection, courage, pride, elation, and joy.

Every emotion has a negative and a positive pole, making it possible for each of us to shift suddenly from anger to caring based on how the other person responds. Our feelings are not in a fixed state, but in constant motion, allowing us to move slowly or rapidly from one extreme to another and anywhere in between.

Because emotions are so deeply engrained in conflict, are so meaningful, and are constantly fluctuating, we become sensitive to small variations and our emotions become highly volatile. As a result, the most important questions from the point of view of conflict resolution are these:

1. Are we capable of acknowledging our emotions and the emotions of others in the midst of conflict?
2. Is it possible for us to learn how to respond more skillfully and intelligently in their presence?

The answer to both questions is an unqualified yes. However, it is important to recognize that there is a risk of opening a floodgate of repressed emotion whenever we communicate openly and honestly with our opponents or directly address the emotional issues in conflict. There are three fundamental ways of responding to any emotion, whatever the type of conflict, and whether the emotions emanate from us or our opponent:

1. We can give in to our emotions, express them in their pure form, *externalize* them, and risk alienating our opponent.
2. We can tighten up, suppress our emotions, *internalize* them, and pull away from our opponent.
3. We can relax, acknowledge, reframe, and express our emotions, *transform and learn* from them, and move closer to our opponent.

Suppressing, denying, avoiding, and giving in to negative emotions will lead us away from solving the problems that caused them to surface in the first place. If we give in to our emotions and express them without skill, or if we suppress or withdraw from them without transforming them, we will learn little or nothing about what gave rise to them, fail to experience them completely, and be compelled to experience them repeatedly because we have not learned how to respond to them skillfully or been able to recognize what lies beneath them.

Many people fear that if they relax, acknowledge, and express their emotions, they will sink into a morass of negativity, become angry or fearful, and retreat from resolution. Yet the opposite is true: relaxing, acknowledging, reframing, and expressing emotion helps unlock our conflicts, while moving away from them keeps us stuck. The object of acknowledging, reframing, and integrating emotions is to complete and release them, allowing them to inform the decision-making process without hijacking it.

Emotions are useful and important in dispute resolution, not only because they obstruct authentic communication, but because they also invite it, because they express what we actually feel, because they focus attention on the *meaning* of our conflicts, and because they allow us to learn how to communicate who we are and what matters to us in powerful and constructive ways.

If we combine emotional intelligence with skill and let go of our fear of expressing even our most shameful and negative emotions, we will be more successful in reaching closure, releasing ourselves and others from the grip of our conflicts, increasing the clarity and creativity of problem solving, and finding opportunities for learning, resolution, and transformation.

How Unexpressed Emotions Create Conflict

We were asked to mediate a bitter conflict in the payroll department of a large public sector organization in an atmosphere that was so angry, rude, tense, and hostile that over the last two years, *every* employee in the department had applied for a transfer! They had experienced intense negative emotions for *eight years,* and the price they paid was enormous.

We began the mediation by asking how the conflict started and were met with total silence. We waited. Finally Blanche said that eight years ago Frieda had made an insulting comment about her husband when he was dying of cancer. The anger, pain, grief, and guilt connected with her husband's death left Blanche so upset that there was no easy way for her to communicate her intense emotions. She felt the workplace did not allow her to express these feelings and, as a result, had slipped into a cold, punishing, seemingly irrational anger.

Frieda was visibly shocked to hear that this was the reason behind their enmity. She told Blanche that she had not known her husband, had not known he was dying of cancer, and had no reason or desire to insult him. We asked her, "Since Blanche believes you insulted her husband when he was dying of cancer, what do you want to say to her right now?" There is only one answer to this question, and Frieda immediately and sincerely said she was sorry.

We then asked Blanche, "Since Frieda did not know your husband or that he was dying of cancer, had no reason or desire to insult him, and has apologized to you, what do you want to say to her in response?" Again, there is only one answer, and Blanche also apologized, admitting she should have gone to Frieda and told her of the emotional pain her remark had produced. Both women started to cry, releasing their anguish and pent-up pain, and realizing the price they and their colleagues had paid for eight years of emotional miscommunication.

Everyone in the department was shocked and speechless at the realization that such an innocent mistake could have created such enormous anguish and pointless suffering. We asked the group, "Is there anything anyone else wants to apologize for, or any other mistaken communications you want to discuss?"

Since they had kept this conflict alive for eight years, they all had something to say. As they spoke about related incidents and apologized for their role in the conflict, relief began to spread. Several staff members apologized for having been complicit in spreading rumors and gossip, remaining silent, or supporting their friends and not telling others what they assumed was true. They were able to see that they had jointly created a culture of avoidance and emotional hoarding that prevented resolution and healing.

At the end of the session, the two former archenemies tearfully hugged each other, and everyone agreed to communicate more openly in the future. Within six months, the performance record of the department increased by 200 percent, and the staff was much happier. They became so united that they went on a "wildcat strike" together when management tried to change their work rules!

These women were not alone in their inability to express their emotions in conflict. Unfortunately, the unwritten policy of "no emotions allowed" in most workplaces is based on a false premise: that people can collaborate or function successfully while suppressing deep emotions over long periods of time. Successful work teams are defined in part by their ability to acknowledge and discuss emotions and support team members who are in distress. By contrast, in organizations where emotions are suppressed, so are creativity, open communications, problem solving, and morale.

More to the point, it is nearly impossible to resolve many of the conflicts that arise in the workplace without delving into the emotions of the participants, or discussing their feelings about the events that fueled their conflict. Most of us have difficulty expressing intense emotions because we are afraid we will not be able to communicate them constructively, or skillfully, or contain their destructive potential. Many of us feel inadequate listening to other people's intense emotions, fearing we could be hurt or lose control over our responses. Yet the result of not confronting these fears can lead to years of unnecessary pain and anger.

Unfortunately, managers who try to resolve conflicts between coworkers often get stuck in emotional responses and feel inadequate as conflict resolvers. This is not surprising because they have been asked to perform a task many are unable to perform in their personal lives, have not been trained to do, and are discouraged from attempting by the unwritten rules of their conflict culture.

By sweeping disturbing emotions and intense conflicts under an imaginary rug, these managers, employees, and organizations pay a steep price for avoiding conflict and suppressing emotional expression. They postpone authentic open communication, honest dialogue, and creative problem solving, often making the underlying emotions and conflicts worse, and encouraging suppressed rage, emotional withdrawal, and litigation as substitutes.

Many organizations discourage emotional expression and favor settlement over resolution because they are captive to traditional masculine notions that emotion reflects weakness, makes us appear vulnerable, and allows our opponents to seize the advantage and crush us. In truth, expressing emotions makes us stronger, more creative, and collaborative, and suppressing them makes us more fearful, conforming, isolated, and brittle.

Nobel prize–winning Japanese novelist Kenzaburo Oe has written eloquently about his own reluctance to face deep emotions and what finally lay beneath them. He wrote: "What was he trying to protect himself from . . . that he must run so hard and so shamelessly? What was it in himself he was so frantic to defend? The answer was horrifying—nothing! Zero!"

Instead of trying to protect ourselves and our organizations from emotion and suppressing their honest expression or avoiding them, it is possible to move toward, through, and past our emotions, and learn how to responsibly express them. We can give people permission to openly and constructively reveal their hidden feelings and develop skills in acknowledging, reframing, and integrating them, and encourage the application of emotional intelligence to creative problem solving.

To be clear, we are not advocating that organizations countenance out-of-control tantrums in the workplace. Instead, we are suggesting that the responsible, empathetic, honest expression of feelings, together with the strategic development of emotional intelligence skills, can help us break paralyzing impasses and lead to better problem solving, higher levels of resolution, and personal and organizational transformations, including forgiveness and reconciliation.

By creating work environments that reflect and acknowledge our true human natures, we allow people to be present in the workplace as whole human beings who have emotions as well as intellects. We believe it is possible to create organizational cultures in which employees express their emotions and clear the air without being destructive or losing sight of the main goal, which is to resolve and learn from their conflicts.

Killarney Clary writes eloquently in a prose poem about the impact of not being able to be emotionally present at work:

> Because the ones I work for do not love me, because I have said too much and I haven't been sure of what is right and I've hated the people I've trusted, because I work in an office and we are lost and when I come home I say their lives are theirs and they don't know what they apologize for and none of it mended, because I let them beat me and I remember something of mine which not everyone has, and because I lie to keep my self and my hands my voice on the phone because I swallow what hurts me, because I hurt them I give them the hours I spend away from them and carry them, even in my sleep, at least as the nag of a misplaced shoe, for years after I have quit and gone on to another job where I hesitate in telling and I remember and I resent having had to spend more time with them than with the ones I love.

Emotionally intelligent organizational environments support co-workers in constructively and skillfully expressing, acknowledging, integrating, and satisfying each other's emotional needs, increasing their ability to work together collaboratively and allowing them to solve problems more effectively, generate greater workplace satisfaction, and produce better results.

To learn how to achieve these ends, it is necessary to return to the cauldron where emotional responses and attitudes were forged: in our families of origin. It is here that we discover how and why we learned the emotional patterns that influence our responses to conflicts at work, and can identify the emotional skills we most need to develop.

Families and Emotions

We are born with an innate capacity to experience pleasure and pain, desire and repulsion, satisfaction and frustration. As young children, we steadily increase and limit our capacity to communicate specific emotions by closely observing and reacting to the emotional behavior of our parents, siblings, and peers while they model how to engage in conflict, how to express feelings, what roles emotion play in conflict, and what succeeds or fails in getting what we want.

These patterns are reinforced over time by relatives, teachers, and friends until they become nearly automatic, like the default setting on a computer, and unconsciously guide our actions. As a result, we become imprinted with emotional patterns that we carry with us for the rest of our lives and trigger our initial responses to conflict in the workplace.

For the most part, we communicate our emotional patterns to those with whom we are in conflict unconsciously, without responsibility or scrutiny, and accept these patterns blindly, without awareness, choice, or intelligence. Indeed, an entire generation can develop specific ways of expressing anger, fear, sadness, addiction, guilt, panic, manipulation, and withdrawal, and pass these lessons on to their children. This is especially prevalent to the extent that they are unconscious or unaware of them, inviting the next generation to do the same. In this way, the conflicts of the parents are visited on the children.

In families we learn not only how to express our emotions and engage in conflicts, but how to suppress and avoid them. In the process, we come to accept a set of ideas, myths, and assumptions about emotions that shape our responses to conflict. We use these myths and beliefs to justify our feelings about ourselves and others, and to create self-fulfilling prophecies—sometimes of inadequacy, paranoia, or victimization.

We learn to limit and expand our expression of different emotions, to construct intellectual defenses, rationalizations, and explanations that justify our behaviors, and to avoid honestly communicating and owning our feelings. We learn how to respond to a narrow range of conflict behaviors and little or nothing about how to respond to behaviors we did not experience.

Each of us brings these unconscious emotional patterns and conflict experiences into the workplace and acts out of them as though our coworkers were our parents or siblings, silently assuming they will produce similar outcomes and responses in others. We may even express emotions and behave in conflicts in an unconscious effort to elicit from others the emotional responses and conflict behaviors with which we are most familiar and comfortable from our families of origin.

Once we have developed a successful strategy for responding to an emotion in conflict, we tend to repeat it over and over again, and use it even when it clearly cannot be successful. We stop learning how to develop alternative, potentially more successful approaches and rely instead on what we perceive as our strengths. As a result, we ignore our weaknesses, creating the possibility that they will turn into tragic flaws.

Overlaid on this legacy of family responses are a set of strategies we learned in childhood from friends, peers, team members, and classmates. Here again, we accept these experiences for the most part without conscious choice, in automatic response to our school, neighborhood, and peer environments, and bring them into the workplace. Yet what we perceive as a successful emotional response or conflict behavior that worked for years can suddenly become a failure when we try it with our managers, colleagues, and team members.

One strategy for moving from impasse to resolution is to conduct a conscious, critical, but nonjudgmental examination of your emotional history and repertoire of conflict responses. In the process, it will be helpful for you to research your family history, cultivate a capacity to listen and learn from your opponents' strategies, make a determined effort to choose the right emotional path at work, and become responsible for your emotional life and conflict behaviors. The following assessment may be useful in helping you analyze the roots of your personal conflict style and responses to negative emotions at work.

Addressing the Roots of Emotions in Conflict: An Assessment

For this assessment, identify a workplace conflict that you recently experienced. It may be a conflict you are having with a coworker, boss, subordinate, or customer, or one that colleagues asked you to solve.

- In a few words or phrases express any feelings you have about this conflict and the individuals involved in it.
- What is the strongest feeling you have about the conflict, your opponent, or those involved?
- Is there an experience from your childhood or family of origin that evoked similar feelings? That exhibited similar behavior by others? That resulted in a similar response by you?
- How was that earlier conflict resolved? If it was left unresolved, how long did it remain unresolved? What price did you or others pay for your inability to resolve it?
- What can you learn from that earlier conflict and its accompanying emotions that could help you in your current workplace conflict?
- What emotional or conflict patterns have you taken from childhood that you are bringing to work or to your current conflict?
- What can you do differently to rid yourself of unproductive patterns learned from childhood?
- What can you do or say to your opponent that can help you resolve your current conflict by acknowledging that you have been stuck in the past?
- What can you say or do regarding the ghosts of family emotions and past conflicts to let others know you have learned from them and want to find new ways to resolve your disputes and handle your emotions?

Common Myths and Assumptions About Emotions

In every organization, whether as employees, managers, customers, or vendors, we encounter cultural myths and assumptions that profoundly influence how emotions are experienced and handled. In most organizations, these myths and assumptions encourage and reinforce others in suppressing emotions and avoiding conflicts. When they are unconsciously and uncritically followed, more and more issues and feelings get swept under the rug, causing people to periodically explode with emotions or shut down or leave.

Here are some commonly held myths and assumptions about negative emotions that may be influencing your organizational culture. As you review them, write in the space provided when you first heard this idea and who suggested it.

WORKSHEET

It's not proper to express emotions at work.

___

Emotions are irrational.

___

Emotions are negative.

___

Emotions can't be controlled and will escalate if released.

___

Emotions can safely be ignored.

___

Emotions are not helpful in making decisions.

___

Emotions are unnecessary.

___

(*continued*)

Emotions are for children, women, or the helpless.

Good, nice people don't express emotions.

It's okay to express emotions if I can justify my feelings logically.

I shouldn't feel emotions immediately but save them for later.

I'll lose control or go crazy if I express my emotions.

People will go away if I express my emotions.

Other people have no right to express emotions to me.

I'm responsible for fixing other people's negative emotions.

If I express my anger to someone, it means I don't love or respect them.

If they express their anger, it means they don't love or respect me.

Do these myths and assumptions sound familiar to you? Have they hindered your communication with people who are important to you? Have they supported or undermined your relationships at work? Have they affected your family or others in your life? What have you done to understand or counter them or keep from controlling your behavior?

Many new options become available when you are able to skillfully experience intense emotions in the midst of conflict and choose to overcome dysfunctional family patterns and cultural dictates when you experience negative emotions in the workplace. You can alter your emotional responses any time you choose by bringing a deep level of awareness and acceptance to your early emotional experiences, and dissecting and distinguishing the jumble of elements that constitute your feelings.

Distinguishing the Elements of Emotion

We often experience emotions as an overwhelming muddle and feel powerless to shape or control their force and power. As a result, we resist or repress their deeper meanings and are unable to learn from them. But if we can become more aware of our feelings and experience our emotions as separate, distinct elements that *combine* to produce what we feel, we can begin to acknowledge, integrate, and apply them to constructive purposes.

The first step in doing so is to *recognize and accept* your emotions, and experience them as fully as possible without resisting or suppressing them. This does not mean venting, dumping, or passing them on to others. It does mean paying attention to your feelings and allowing them to move freely inside you. When you block your emotions, they tend to congeal and harden, become camouflaged, and find a distorted expression. But when you accept them and experience them fully and completely, they tend to break up, become more manageable, and disappear.

The second step is to bring *awareness* to your emotional experiences and isolate and identify exactly what it is you are feeling. As you become more precise in your awareness of each separate element in your emotions, you will find it easier to observe their ebb and flow without feeling controlled by them.

As you consider the following list of emotional elements, drawn in part from meditation practices, reflect on the questions we ask after each element to help you gain insight into your responses, become more accepting of your emotions, and increase your moment-by-moment awareness while they are happening.

- *Quality:* Is the emotion you are feeling depression, anger, guilt, pain, shame, love, fear, or some other reaction?
- *Intensity:* Is it mild or intense? Is it barely noticeable or gripping?
- *Importance:* Is what happened important enough to get upset about? Is it worth communicating to others? Why?
- *Direction:* Are your feelings inner- or outer-directed? Toward a specific target or generalized toward no particular person or situation?
- *Duration:* Is your reaction momentary or long-lasting? Does it come in cycles? How did it start? How long has it lasted?
- *Location:* Where is the feeling located in your body? Where is its impact strongest?
- *Movement:* Is it a wave or a spot? Does it radiate? What is its shape? How is it moving?
- *Origination:* When have you felt this way before? What triggers or causes it? How is it linked to other feelings or experiences? What makes it disappear?
- *Resistance:* Is any part of you resisting the full expression of the emotion? What part of you is doing so? Why are you doing so? What are you afraid will happen if you let it go? What makes you think that will happen?
- *Meaning:* What does the emotion mean to you? Why does it have that meaning? Where did you learn the meaning? What else could it mean?
- *Awareness:* How aware are you of each of these elements? Can you detect subtle movements in each? Are you blocking or impeding your awareness of some elements? If so, why? What would happen if you didn't?
- *Change:* How often and easily do your emotions change? Are they increasing or decreasing? Are they fixed or flowing? Can you change them by will?
- *Patterns:* Take a few moments to review your emotional responses. Do they fit together in a pattern? How might you consciously alter their patterns of expression?

Stages of Emotional Response to Conflict

You may have noticed that your emotional responses extend over time. If you watch the flow of your conflict emotions carefully, you can discern a number of discrete triggers and stages in their formation. You may also notice that some of these stages are over within seconds, even as others last months or years. It is possible to intervene consciously at *any* point to transform what you are feeling and open the possibility of resolution by moving to a different stage in the process.

As you review the following stages in the development of emotion, reflect on whether they fit your experience, on the times and circumstances when you have lost awareness, on your ability to choose the right emotional response during conflict, and on the times when you have slipped into "automatic pilot" and resorted to old patterns.

- *Triggering action or event:* An action or event takes place and is communicated to you, becoming a fact in your life.
- *Perception of emotional tone or intent:* You perceive an underlying adversarial intention, perhaps through body language, tone of voice, quality of action, context, or style of communication coming from your opponent.
- *Stimulation of memories and subjective associations:* Your perceptions of an action or encounter trigger and connect with conscious and subconscious memories and associations with other conflicts that have their own emotional content.
- *Interpretation or attribution of meaning:* You attempt to explain or interpret the action or event and its emotional tone in an effort to make sense of your experience according to your emotional patterns and prior experiences with conflict.
- *Rise of an emotional response:* Based on the meaning or interpretation you have given to what happened, you begin to feel fear, anger, sadness, shame, guilt, hate, grief, or similar emotions.
- *Suppression, repression, intensification, and neutralization of response:* You become uncomfortable with your own emotional response, suppress or repress it and push it down—yet, in doing so, you also reinforce and intensify it, and if that doesn't work you try to neutralize or turn away from it.
- *Action or inaction based on emotional response:* You then respond to whatever triggered the emotion by taking or not taking some action.

- *Internal consequences of the action or inaction:* You experience internal consequences and feelings that reflect your perception of whether you acted or failed to act properly, and how you feel about yourself as a result.
- *Reflection and reinterpretation:* You reflect on what happened, what you felt and experienced, and what you did or did not do in response. You then reinterpret the experience after the fact to fit what the experience *felt* like, and reconstruct it so you can integrate it into a coherent pattern of emotional responses.
- *Learning and transformation:* As a result of what happened, you may learn from your emotional experiences, or from your opponent and the conflict. Your response patterns may be transformed as a result and you may become more skillful in processing your emotions in future conflicts.

As you reflect on these stages of emotional response to conflict, consider the following questions: Are these the stages you go through in responding emotionally to conflict? If not, where and how do you differ? In which stage do you first get stuck responding to conflict? What happens to you, your opponent, and the conflict as a result? What keeps you from having a complete experience of your emotions? What would it take to be able to learn and become more skillful in your conflicts?

In organizational conflicts, these stages are frequently distorted by past experiences with conflict and unspoken cultural messages regarding the expression and experience of negative emotions. Conflicts can be transformed into sources of learning, change, and transformation in organizations only when there is permission within the culture to discuss and express the stages of emotional formation and there is a high level of emotional awareness, skills, and intelligence among executives, managers, and employees. Conflicts can also be transformed when emotions are acknowledged and when ways of responding more skillfully to the reasons for emotion are clarified through training, dialogue, coaching, mediation, and informal problem solving.

Human resource managers, leaders, coaches, mediators, and other conflict resolvers can use these elements, stages, and techniques to refocus emotionally difficult conversations, encourage the expression of feelings and identify more skillful ways of responding to emotionally charged events. By acknowledging the human character of emotional experience and openly and honestly addressing emotions, conflicts can be unlocked and reoriented toward creative problem solving.

Reframing Emotions

In many organizations there are undercurrents of intense emotion hidden just below the surface that powerfully shape people's relationships and color their communications, processes, and interactions. These undercurrents accumulate over time as colleagues store away and hoard deep emotional injuries they can neither express, release, nor resolve.

When intense emotions accumulate, the pressure to release them can become so strong that people feel they cannot do so safely, or that doing so will trigger consequences they are not prepared to face. When opportunities for release suddenly arise in the midst of conflict, the desire for release may be so great that the emotion emerges with far greater power than if it had not been suppressed. An outsider who only witnesses the release and does not understand the accumulation of injuries behind it may interpret the resulting explosion as an overreaction or irrational response.

Yet emotions are not irrational or illogical. They are *non*-rational and *non*-logical, or rather, they are successful evolutionary adaptations we have developed for reasons we do not entirely understand. They are shaped by our experiences in the families, organizations, societies, and cultural systems in which we grew up, and are *strategies* that at some point succeeded in getting us what we wanted or needed, even at the expense of pride, self-esteem, and love. And they are useful sources of information about the world that, when integrated and communicated positively, can assist us in solving a wide range of problems.

In organizations, expressing emotions in conflict is often seen as reducing the chances for resolution. Yet when we are aroused and our most intense emotions are triggered, we are finally able to say what we *really* think, feel, and need, and to become more authentic. Expressions of negative emotion can clear the air, allowing people to move beyond ancient grievances. But they can also prove destructive, trigger escalations and counterattacks, keep people trapped in the past, and end in impasse. Simply expressing emotions without altering the *way* we express them may only reinforce and strengthen them.

In our experience, it is possible for people to constructively express intense emotions, even in the workplace. They can channel the destructive potential of their emotions in collaborative directions by shifting from destructive "venting" and "dumping" to constructive forms of owning and acknowledging feelings, discovering their deeper meaning and encouraging empathy with others.

One method of doing so is reframing, in which we make "I" statements rather than accusations, explain our emotions rather than exhibit them, and ask questions that move the emotion in the direction of problem solving, as in: "What would you like me to do differently in the future?" We can ask questions that turn emotion inward toward increased vulnerability, as in: "What would you like me to know about you that you think I do not adequately understand?" We can ask questions that reframe the emotion by pointing to what is underneath it, as in: "Are you angry at me because you feel I don't respect you?" We can ask for feedback, as in: "What did I do that caused you to feel that way?" And we can request direction, as in: "What is one thing I can do to let you know I do respect you?"

Reframing is a powerful method for clarifying emotional communications, encounters, and conflicts. It consists of using empathy to find a fresh word, phrase, or statement that includes the most important content or meaning of what was said, while avoiding mistaken impressions created by poor choices of words. For example, you can

- Reframe statements to express what you want from the other person rather than judging their attitude or behavior.
- Reframe issues so they cannot be answered with a simple "yes" or "no" and their deeper meaning is expressed.
- Reframe problems as questions or issues rather than as statements of fact or opinion.
- Reframe issues so that multiple solutions are possible.
- Reframe issues to separate people from problems and depersonalize the problem.
- Reframe issues so that they are seen as jointly shared problems.
- Reframe issues in terms of future relationships rather than past guilt or innocence.
- Reframe issues so the person has the ability to make a decision and implement it.
- Reframe issues in a manner that does not threaten anyone's self-esteem or dignity.
- Reframe issues in an objective and neutral manner.
- Reframe issues to make them explicitly subjective by using "I" statements.
- Reframe issues in specific rather than general terms.

- Reframe broad or complex, multilayered issues into more easily handled subissues.
- Reframe issues so as to encourage creative problem solving.
- Ask the listener to confirm that you framed the issue accurately.

Reframing can help your opponents manage and communicate their emotions by modeling a different way of expressing them. For example, by reframing and asking a series of calm, empathetic, and poignant questions, you can give someone who is expressing anger permission to experience what they are feeling completely, become more observant and accepting of their feelings, discover their sources and causes, realize they can communicate their needs or wants without yelling, and plumb their feelings for information that can help solve the problem.

Simply by asking the right questions, you can subtly shift your opponent's focus away from the emotion-processing parts of the brain and toward the parts that observe, accept, and analyze experiences. If your opponent is able to accept his feelings nonjudgmentally, become aware of what he is feeling, and experience those feelings as useful sources of information, he will be able to release his emotions and make the transition to collaborative problem solving without becoming overwhelmed by their intensity.

For example, in a conflict resolution session between a female manager and her male subordinate, we noticed a pattern in the words and phrases he was using to describe her: she was "controlling," "punishing," "a bitch," and "bossy." He was unable to solve problems because "she won't let me," "I have to ask for permission," and "she micromanages me."

When we read these words back to him and asked if they described anyone else he knew, he immediately said, "Oh my god, it's my mother!" In that moment, the conflict literally disappeared. This insight allowed him to recognize his subconscious family patterns and enabled his manager to recognize that she was unknowingly behaving like his mother. They were then able to reach a number of agreements on how they could work together in the future and successfully freed themselves from the grip of ancient, seemingly irrational emotions. They reached a resolution—and a real transformation—by moving *through* their emotional responses to an analysis of their origins.

Often what upsets us has little to do with the other person, but flows from anger we have toward ourselves, or is connected with unresolved issues from the distant past. Through a deeper understanding of why these emotions are so powerful we can uncover strong indicators of conflict patterns we have not yet fully recognized or resolved.

In a different organization, the director requested feedback on her leadership skills by asking staff to provide her with anonymous feedback on three-by-five-inch cards. When she read their responses she felt attacked, became angry and defensive, and tried to figure out who wrote which comments. We spent considerable time listening to her pain and anger, and asked whether she felt she was in the right job. She immediately started to cry and told us she knew she was in the wrong job and could not seem to do anything to please her staff or her superiors. Her tears revealed her hidden sadness, loneliness, and shame. She admitted she had chosen the wrong career, was desperately unhappy, and resented having had to move from a city she loved to take this job in one she intensely disliked without any friends or comfort from the stresses of work.

Once she was able to reveal her true feelings, rather than being defensive and angry toward her staff, she thanked them for their honesty and admitted that they had accurately described what she was feeling. We reviewed several ways she could manage her strong, misplaced emotions while she looked for a new position, and she was able to drop her anger and defensiveness and quiet her emotional responses.

Immediately, her conflicts began to dissipate or were quickly resolved and a problem-solving process was initiated that resulted in her being offered a more appropriate position in the same organization in the city she loved. She became happy when she learned she was going to return home, and her staff grew in understanding, courage, teamwork, and emotional intelligence as a result of watching her work through her emotions and the underlying problems which they had helped her uncover.

Behind the Mask: Hidden Markers in Emotional Communication

As conflicts escalate, emotions tend to spiral out of control, so much so that one of our clients, describing the intensity of his boss's anger, said that listening to him was like "trying to drink from a fire hose." If we can learn to manage our intense emotions, minimize angry outbursts, and respond more skillfully when they happen, we can sidestep powerful streams of emotion and let them pass around or even through us. We can see who is really behind the fire hose, where it is twisted or kinked, why the stream is emerging now with such force, and how we can act more strategically by using its energy to promote problem solving and resolution.

When we are confronted with intense emotions, we tend to lose track of what is going on beneath the surface. Indeed, one purpose of intense emotional outbursts is to distract us from deeper and more revealing problems. When we feel stunned, frightened, or trapped in an emotional drama and unable to see what is going on behind the other person's mask, we get distracted by the bluster and intensity and fail to notice what our opponent has carefully hidden.

Many people express intense emotions because they are afraid of being seen as they really are, and that their true, intimate, shameful feelings and inadequacies will be exposed. In this way, anger and sadness can be used as diversionary tactics, like a mother bird who feigns injury to draw a potential predator away from her nest.

To help you discover the hidden messages that significantly differ from the ones being presented, we offer the following glimpse behind the emotional masks people sometimes wear. See if you can recognize the masks you wear, and identify those worn by your opponent. To do so, use the questions below to search behind the facade for what is really happening emotionally:

- *Accusation as confession:* It is often the case that those who feel guilty about something they have done accuse others of having done it. This is a way of diverting (and sometimes attracting) attention to an issue they would like to hide. Have you ever accused others of something you did yourself? How did it feel? Why did you do it?
- *Insult as jealousy:* Every insult is a choice that says more about the insulter than the one being insulted. For example, if X says that Y is lazy, it is likely that X is hardworking and does not give *himself* permission to take time off or relax. The insult, therefore, is more about the jealousy of X than the character of Y. Think of the insults you have used to describe your opponent, or vice versa. What do these insults reveal about the one who used them?
- *Anger as caring:* Anger is partly a request for communication or connection based on something the person deeply cares about, and partly an effort to create distance or boundaries because their caring is too great, and threatens their need for stability.

Both are a result of being extremely vulnerable, either to the person, the issue, or the message. Do you ever express caring as anger? Are you vulnerable when you are angry? To what and whom? Why? What might you do instead?

- *Defensiveness as egoism:* People often become defensive when they mistakenly assume the conflict or disagreement is directed at them, or are unable to separate their ideas from their identity. Have you ever thought someone meant something personal, only to discover it was not about you at all? How can you take responsibility for your role in conflict without making it be about you?
- *Withdrawal as rage:* Those who withdraw from conflict may do so to silence their own uncontrollable rage, based on an assumption that they cannot communicate what they deeply want to get across. They see no alternative other than withdrawal. Have you ever withdrawn in a silent, punishing rage? Can you think of a safe way of communicating what you deeply want without withdrawing?
- *Passivity as aggression:* Public compliance often masks private defiance. Passivity does not always mean agreement, but may instead signal an aggressive form of inaction, or a decision to use inertia to block momentum or consensus. Sometimes the victim role is used to disguise a power play. Have you ever played the victim? Have you ever used passive behavior to gain power over others? Has this created a satisfying relationship? What might you do instead?
- *Attack as smoke screen:* Sometimes people attack others to draw attention from their own failures. Children sometimes initiate arguments or make blunders to draw their parents' attention away from conflicts with each other. Have you ever used an attack as a smoke screen to hide your failures or vulnerabilities? Why not admit your failures instead? What would you gain by doing so?
- *Apathy and cynicism as hurt feelings:* Apathy and cynicism sometimes "protest too much," revealing injured feelings as a result of deep caring, or a sense of pain and frustration that so little has been accomplished, thus causing the person to give up. Have you ever been cynical when what you really wanted was the opposite? Have you ever given up when you really cared? What would happen if you became vulnerable and showed you cared instead?

There is often a strong connection between intense emotional energy that is opposed to some person or idea, and a secret attraction to the very thing that is being fought against. As novelist Thomas Mann noticed, "We are most likely to get angry and excited in our opposition to some idea when we ourselves are not quite certain of our position and are inwardly tempted to take the other side."

When we look behind these masks, we observe managers who get angry and accuse their employees of "goofing off," yet would secretly like to goof off themselves. We see employees who are strongly opposed to their supervisor's arbitrary use of power, but would secretly love to exercise it themselves. We watch people become highly emotional and argue dogmatically over an issue when they secretly know there is something true in what the other person is saying.

Take a look at the masks you use in conflict. How have these masks helped or hindered you in creating authentic conversations, engaging in problem solving, negotiating collaboratively, and resolving your disputes? What would it take for you to drop them completely?

Taking Off the Masks and Revealing Hidden Emotions

When our masks hide our true desires and intentions, we send distorted, contradictory, double messages to others and it becomes more difficult for them to hear or understand our innermost voice, or respond to our requests, or understand what we actually mean and who we really are.

We often don masks or engage in distorted behaviors because we are afraid we are not good enough, or that others will not like or accept us, or because we believe we need a thick skin made out of ego to protect our deepest vulnerabilities. Once we adopt a mask, we become accustomed to its safety and, after a while, we begin to think it is who we really are. We cannot remove it then without creating confusion within ourselves and in others, and must keep it in place at all times and at all costs. As Oscar Wilde observed, "the penalty for having a mask is that you have to wear it."

Jim, a manager with a brusque, blunt style almost like a street fighter had a quick wit and willingness to call things as they were. He asked his organization to become more empowered and self-managing and told his staff he was willing to give up his top-down, command-and-control management style. But his frustration with the team process increased as his staff expressed their fear of accepting responsibility and "stepping up to the plate." As a result, he yelled at people, telling them to "get it or get out." He raised his voice to a fever pitch and delivered ultimatums, shouting that if they did not get empowered they would be fired!

After a devastating meeting in which he blew up and yelled angrily at everyone, we gave him some tough feedback and told him he was sending mixed messages. We said we knew he clearly cared deeply about the team process, but his angry ultimatums were unlikely to encourage staff to do what he wanted and he could not force them to be empowered. He listened carefully to what we said, but did not respond.

A week later, we received a call from a team member who was in a state of shock. Jim had called a special meeting of the entire staff to apologize for his angry outbursts and statements. In a softened, gentle voice, he told them about his passion for what they were doing, his fear of letting go, and his desire to do exactly that so he could move on to more challenging work.

Jim's anger was simply a mask for his caring. He was projecting his own fear that he and his staff would fail if he released control over all the details he had been managing for years. By opening up and becoming more vulnerable, he communicated his desire to give the teams more direct control of their own work. His willingness to take off his mask set the tone for what followed. His staff took the reins and designed a series of meetings for the leadership group, then for the entire organization, that helped make sure everyone was on board and there were no failures. This initiative dramatically shifted responsibility for leadership, decision making, and results to the teams. Jim played a key role in these meetings, acting as an equal participant and fellow team member, but also as an empowering leader rather than a controlling boss.

Jim was able to give up his mask and break through his anger by using "I" statements instead of "you" statements and accusing "them" of misdeeds. The use of "I" statements helps communicate that strong emotions *belong* to the person who is speaking, rather than to the one who accidentally or intentionally triggered or inspired them.

There is a vast difference, for example, between saying "You are a filthy slob!" and "I feel you don't respect me or my need to work in a clean environment when you leave dirty coffee cups in the lunch room." Or "How about if we both commit to keeping the lunch room clean—are you willing to help?" Each of these statements expresses authentic emotion, but the second opens the door to negotiation, dialogue, and possible solutions, and the third invites collaboration.

The first statement simply dumps the speaker's frustrations onto someone else, triggering denials, counter-accusations, and defensiveness. "You" statements may sometimes get the listener to wash the cups, but also trigger negative responses, undermine self-esteem, stiffen resistance, and encourage defensiveness, perhaps leading to broken cups and placing the whole relationship at risk.

Using "I" statements provides opportunities for the speaker to *own* their emotions and be released from feeling controlled by them. It allows the listener to hear how their behavior affected the speaker without feeling compelled to respond defensively or aggressively. It encourages everyone to put their cards on the table and not scatter them chaotically, or attribute blame for what they are feeling to others. It invites everyone to take responsibility for their emotions and search for joint solutions to shared problems.

Behaviors That Trigger Anger

Anger is often difficult to fathom, partly because people often use it as a mask to hide deeper emotions, and partly because others respond to it instinctively, immediately get plugged in, and become unable to recognize its actual source or respond skillfully to it.

For example, the manager of a small entrepreneurial company was well known among his staff for getting angry and disgruntled, quickly raising the temperature of his responses and becoming more and more enraged for reasons no one could identify or attribute to anything that happened recently.

As his conflict coaches, we initially tried to communicate with him by responding logically to his anger, but paradoxically, logical behavior sometimes produces increased anger. We tried to uncover the source of his anger, but he would not reveal it. Finally, we told him we could not continue working with him if he was not willing to make an effort to explore and control his anger. Once we set clear limits, he relaxed and calmed his voice.

We gently probed to discover the source of his anger and he recited several incidents in the company that had left him feeling isolated, besieged, unappreciated, and like a complete failure. We asked him, "Then who is the one you are really yelling at?" He recognized instantly that the anger he was directing at others was actually anger at himself, that it was a mask for his own feelings of inadequacy.

In response, we initiated a group conflict resolution process with the leadership team to agree on a set of ground rules for their future interactions, identify what was not working in their communications and relationships, and jointly focus on rebuilding the company.

In the ground rules, they agreed to begin each team meeting by acknowledging their successes; to stop yelling at each other; to offer honest, supportive feedback to anyone who continued to yell; and to assess a yelling penalty of $20 to purchase pizzas for the rest of the team. As a result, the yelling completely stopped. The fine for yelling was minor, but it gave them an enjoyable excuse to stop behaviors that were not satisfying, even to those who were doing the yelling.

It is inevitable that people will engage in behaviors that push your buttons and trigger your anger. But anger is always a choice. They are *your* buttons, you own them, and you are ultimately responsible for how you react when they get pushed. As a result, no one can "make" you angry. You can choose instead to ask people to agree on ground rules, or ask questions that reveal what is behind the mask. Becoming angry ourselves merely reinforces the anger and encourages others to think we are the problem.

Instead, by surfacing the manager's anger and allowing him to express his discomfort, we helped him calm down. We could then ask him respectfully what upset him, listen empathetically while he spoke, and bring his colleagues together to discuss the underlying issues and agree on ground rules they all wanted, allowing them to make plans for improving their relationship in the future.

Reasons for Anger

There are many excellent reasons for getting angry that are legitimate and understandable. For example, it is reasonable to become angry when our personal space is invaded and we feel violated, when our needs are not recognized or met by others, or when we are treated disrespectfully. Anger creates a protective boundary that surrounds us, commands people's recognition, and even encourages their respect.

Anger toward others, as in the previous examples, can be merely a projection of our own low self-esteem, anger at ourselves, or pain over our false expectations of others. When one of these reasons is at the core of our anger, instead of openly and honestly communicating what we are feeling, we more commonly suffer silently or blame others and use our anger to make *them* feel bad.

At work, when someone is fired, he may use anger or anger-creating behaviors as a way of releasing the pain of losing his job, surrendering his false expectations about a future career, processing his grief and shame, and avoiding responsibility for his failure. Paradoxically, anger is sometimes a way of giving someone permission to leave a dissatisfying job when she would not otherwise have the courage to do so. Whenever anyone involuntarily leaves a place where they have worked for many years, anger and emotional distancing are likely to occur.

Employees who have been disciplined or terminated often feel mistreated, misunderstood, and betrayed, and may blame the organization for being unfair and forcing them out, their colleagues for not supporting them, and managers for being out to get them. They may even be right about these conclusions but also have a deeper underlying problem that is masked by their anger.

These employees may feel better by transforming their pain, grief, shame, and loss into anger, which feels safer, more acceptable, and powerful. Yet they pay a hidden price for not honestly expressing their emotions, critically examining their own skills and performance, accepting responsibility for what they did or did not do, and acknowledging their own silence or complicity in what occurred. As a result, it will be difficult for them to learn from their experiences, act responsibly, or continue growing and improving their emotional intelligence.

One powerful motivation for anger is that it generates intensity and intimacy. Anger strips away our masks and forces us into the present moment. It demands our attention, and though it is a deeply intimate emotion, it produces only *negative* intimacy, which is frequently preferable to indifference when positive intimacy becomes impossible.

Another motivation for anger arises when we feel bad or worthless and try to relieve our misery by reassuring ourselves that we are no worse than others. As a result, we may subconsciously try to get them angry with us so we will feel less guilty and seem more righteous. Sometimes, when we speak judgmentally about others, it is because we have already judged ourselves, cannot accept the negative opinion we have formed, and want to bring others down to our level so they can directly experience and understand our pain and frustration.

In the workplace, anger can be a way of pointing out what needs to be improved within the organization, introducing a new paradigm, or indicating something that is not working for someone. Sometimes we use anger to gain attention, recognition, acknowledgment, affection, and other outcomes we feel unable to obtain through achievement.

Anger can be a substitute and compensation for feeling underpaid or treated unfairly, and is routinely used to create alliances, friendships, and cliques at work. In place of sharing positive interests, which requires us to become open, vulnerable and risk being rejected, we may instead use gossip, rumors, and anger against others to cement alliances, under the theory that "the enemy of my enemy is my friend."

Anger can be a distorted expression of fear, guilt, shame, or humiliation. For example, when children do something dangerous, their parents often respond initially with anger, as a way of forcing the child to pay attention to safety, instead of frankly acknowledging their own fear. Thus, beneath anger lies fear, and beneath fear lies their desire to avoid feeling pain, loss, and guilt, if something terrible happened to their child. And beneath all of these lies love and caring, which is the true point of origin for their anger.

These feelings lead to four fundamentally different conversations. For example, we can yell angrily at our child who is in danger of hurting himself, "Don't do that!" But we can also speak from our fear, saying, "That scared the heck out of me!" Or we can speak from our perception of the possibility of pain, guilt, grief, or loss, saying, "I would feel terrible if anything bad happened to you." Finally, we can speak from love and caring, saying, "I love you so much I would feel awful if anything bad happened to you." While these conversations are different, they are also essentially the same, yet elicit vastly different emotions in the person to whom they are directed.

Anger is sometimes a cry for help, or a need to be heard when no one is listening. Getting angry can be a useful tactic in trying to get one's own way. Aggressive negotiators, for example, use it to throw the other side off balance, and command-and-control managers use it to secure their subordinates' compliance, or to divert attention from their own failures.

Anger can also feel cleansing. It can help release negative feelings and the shame of victimization, either by expressing them constructively, venting them, or dumping them destructively onto others. It can make us feel more powerful in the face of our perceived powerlessness or victimization, and cleansed when we feel besmirched or dirty.

Unless the true reasons for anger are recognized, acknowledged, and addressed, it will prove more difficult to discover or solve the underlying problem that gave rise to it. Moreover, until we address these underlying reasons, surrendering anger will feel like surrendering our issues and the right to respect. This will make it more difficult to resolve the reasons that gave rise to our conflict, encouraging it to spiral out of control or remain at impasse.

We encourage you to explore your anger, including the triggers or flash points that stimulate it. Doing so will allow you to say to yourself,

"This is a trigger for my anger. I don't need to react immediately. I have a choice. I can choose to respond by discovering the reason for my anger, which I may be able to communicate successfully to the other person without becoming angry, use it to clarify and develop solutions to the problem I need to solve, and become more skillful in expressing anger in the process."

Just as anger creates intimacy it also creates boundaries. Just as it focuses attention on problems it is destructive, leaving greater problems in its wake. Every positive payoff that anger produces can be achieved in a more skillful, lasting, and constructive way without it. We recognize that there is a dark, destructive side to anger and can refuse to surrender to it. Our challenge is to find ways of gaining people's attention, achieving results, creating intimacy, and resolving conflicts by asking directly for what we want and need.

Once we understand the reasons for being angry, we can identify the behaviors that are triggering it. We can then communicate to our opponent the feelings that lie beneath our anger—such as fear, pain, or caring—along with a request for changed behavior and a proposal for how we might jointly solve the problems that gave rise to it. As we do, our anger will begin to dissolve automatically, and our conflicts will turn into sources of learning and change.

Subconscious Beliefs and Assumptions About Anger

Behind the many reasons for angry responses in workplace conflicts lie a set of largely unexamined subconscious beliefs, feelings, and assumptions. As you consider the underlying issues fueling your anger, ask whether you are willing to give up the assumptions on which they rest, question their validity, or alter the conditions that created them.

For example, you may become angry because you believe a coworker or manager treated you unfairly or unjustly, and feel your unfair treatment was not natural, inevitable, or a result of your own actions, but reflected a conscious choice on their part. Their actions will then seem wrong to you, because if they had a clear choice to treat you fairly and did not, it must be because they harbor a hostile intent.

If they claim they do not understand why you are angry or how they caused or contributed to your problems, you can easily assume they are lying, or that if they really understood or cared about you, they would have acted differently. You may even assume that because they didn't, they are ignorant, insensitive, or evil.

Yet it is equally possible that the people who treated you unfairly are simply obeying orders or conforming to the mandates of the organizational culture or context in which they are working. By understanding the culture and context in which the dispute arose and using empathetic and responsive listening techniques to explore your opponent's underlying experiences, assumptions, emotions, and realities, you may discover that your assumptions are false, one-sided, or unwarranted. You may find your opponent did not have a choice in how he responded, or the choice may not have been apparent, or may have flowed from a different set of interests, experiences, or feelings that have been not been understood. You may find the organization's structures, systems, culture, and context are driving the conflict, offering few choices in how to act.

When we assume others are acting deliberately against us, we get angry as a way of helping them understand by *direct experience* what it feels like to be treated unfairly. Anger is an effort to communicate what we feel, encourage others to change their behaviors, and mitigate or correct their unfair assumptions. Yet, by getting angry we treat them unfairly and re-create the very behavior we find objectionable. We rarely use anger to honestly communicate our objections in ways the other person can hear.

We often assume we can't express anger to someone who is superior to us in an organizational hierarchy. Therefore, when we express anger, we indirectly and subconsciously communicate that the other person is *not* our superior, but an equal or inferior to us. If our opponents express anger back at us, they descend to our level and reinforce our assumption.

Most of us assume that anger emanating from our homes and families should not intrude into the workplace. But if we are angry at a spouse, partner, or family member, or at life in general and have no other means of communicating our emotions, we are likely to find covert, subconscious ways of releasing them. For example, we may engage in gossiping to coworkers, sabotage the success of a project, undermine the reputation of an opponent, or get angry over trifles.

We may assume we have no right to express our anger to others, or believe they have no right to express anger to us because there is not enough intimacy or reciprocity in our relationship. If they cross this invisible boundary, we become angrier, marking our subconscious perception that our boundaries have been violated and signaling to others that we reject, or perhaps desire, their attention or affection, even as we drive them away.

Anger tests our relationships, deepening, solidifying, or breaking them apart. We therefore subconsciously assume that if others accept us they will also accept our anger, and their anger toward us confirms the importance of our relationship to them, and shows us they care. The closer the relationship, the more we assume we have a right to get angry without breaking the relationship apart. Yet we also use anger to drive away the people who care about us—especially if we are afraid we will be hurt—but in the process, we do not see how much we have hurt them. Thus, anger is a barometer of caring and as long as anger is present, so is caring.

If we are in a relationship that is in the process of ending, most of us would rather the other person feel anger toward us rather than indifference, because anger shows he still cares. But once the relationship is over and we've met someone new, we no longer prefer the other person to feel anger and no longer want his caring. But as long as we feel angry, a caring connection continues to exist between us. When we stop feeling angry, we release ourselves from caring.

When we feel powerless or helpless or that we have no right to express our anger directly, we assume it is acceptable to find indirect, ambiguous ways of expressing it. Edgy jokes, satire, emotional withdrawal, passive-aggressive behavior, resistance to change, and noncooperation are all ways of expressing anger without admitting to it. Each of these indirect methods communicates the anger while blocking our ability to address the reasons that gave rise to it.

When we are angry, we receive attention from others, and sometimes they give us what we want. We then feel powerful because others have changed their behaviors in response to our angry feelings. Our anger subconsciously makes us feel righteous and important, justifying our pain and diverting attention from our faults. It allows us to express our pain and fear indirectly without becoming vulnerable in the presence of someone we do not trust. It blinds us to the price we pay, and to the ways it renders us less effective in achieving our goals.

These subconscious beliefs and assumptions fuel our anger, yet few of them have anything to do with the *person* with whom we are angry. We may become angry, for example, at people who engage in behaviors we would secretly like to engage in ourselves, or behaviors we do not like in ourselves, or behaviors we would like to discourage ourselves from engaging in. Or we may get angry at ourselves for tolerating their continued disrespectful behavior toward us. All of these are reasons to let go of anger.

Reasons for Letting Go of Anger

Just as there are many reasons for anger, there are an equal number of reasons for giving it up, letting it go, and using more effective tactics. Here are some important reasons for giving up your anger:

- Anger is a form of ongoing connection with someone you dislike, distrust, and probably don't want in your life.
- Anger is a double-edged sword that injures both its target and the one who wields it.
- Anger is often just externalized anger at yourself, and forgiving the other person means forgiving yourself.
- Anger creates the "other-as-enemy" and does not allow for empathy or the "other-as-friend."
- Anger converts the person who uses it from a victim to a perpetrator and undermines the sympathy that would otherwise be due as a result of the original injury.
- Anger can be released without giving up what we want; all we surrender are ways of getting it that are destructive to ourselves and others.
- Anger is paradoxically a reflection of weakness and vulnerability to others. When we develop our internal strength, others' actions needn't bother us.
- Anger creates a barrier against our own vulnerability, a defense against the most intimate and important parts of ourselves.
- Anger undermines successful collaboration among team members and blocks efforts to reach consensus on important decisions.
- Anger in organizations forces bystanders to take sides for fear of being injured themselves. It promotes the formation of cliques and factions that fuel the conflict and keep the anger flowing.
- Anger is sometimes used to force changes, increase productivity, and attack the competition, but ultimately erodes well-being and corrodes the results that flow from building unity, morale, and trusting relationships.
- Anger is a kind of energy that lives in us, destroying our souls from the inside.
- Anger saps the energy we need to live in the present, plan for the future, and be available for change and personal transformation. This energy is reclaimed when we let anger go.

Releasing our anger feels better than keeping it locked up inside, or turning it against ourselves and possibly destroying us. Expressing anger directs our pain outward; yet can end up hurting us as well as those we care about or want to reach. In the process, we can fail to realize that we *always* have an alternative, which is to release our anger without inflicting it on anyone.

Methods for Responding to Anger

In organizations, anger nearly always destroys trust, reduces morale and motivation, undermines collaboration and team relationships, sabotages strategic planning, and creates a culture of shaming and blaming. It turns customers away, increases employee turnover, fuels grievances and litigation, obstructs creative problem solving, deepens frustration, and adds to the already enormous cost of unresolved conflict.

Being able to be aware of, constructively express, and release your anger is an important life skill that can help you dissipate its destructive effects and move toward resolution. Here are some techniques you may find useful in managing your anger:

- *Own it.* Don't blame anyone else for your anger. Be responsible for your own intense feelings and for openly and constructively expressing them.
- *Discover the underlying reasons for it.* Ask yourself why you are angry, what triggered your emotion, when your anger began, and what deeper emotions or prior experiences are connected to it.
- *Share your feelings and perceptions nonjudgmentally.* Drop all the self-justifications, defenses, stories of wrongdoing, accusations, and judgments you are using to support your anger. Avoid statements like "you're wrong" and instead indicate what the other person *did* that led you to get angry. Use "I" statements, report your feelings constructively, and identify what triggered your emotions.
- *Ask questions to discover whether your perceptions are accurate.* Without making judgments or fixing blame, ask questions to find out more about what happened so you can get to the bottom of what caused your anger. Ask if the other person meant to treat you disrespectfully and, if so, why.

- *Focus on solving the problem rather than blaming others for it.* Define the problem as an "it" rather than a "you." Brainstorm solutions with your opponent. Take a problem-solving approach to the underlying reasons for your emotional response to the conflict.
- *Avoid responding defensively.* Don't fall into the trap of defending your behavior. Consider the possibility that you may have been wrong, or that you may be both right and wrong at the same time. Explore these possibilities openly. At the very least, if the other person doesn't understand, recognize that you didn't communicate your feelings skillfully.
- *Ask clarifying questions.* Ask the other person (keeping your own tone nondefensive and avoiding hostility) to clarify what she meant to communicate by her comments or behavior. Ask if your assumptions are correct and allow her to explain. Listen more carefully if you were not right the first time, then summarize and ask if you are correct.
- *Clarify your expectations.* State specifically and in detail what you expect and why. If the other person cannot meet your expectations, you can always negotiate more realistic expectations so that he will be clearer next time about what you really want.
- *Take a time-out.* Step away from the interaction for a few moments to reflect on whether it is getting out of hand. Determine whether it is possible to say the same things in a way that the other person can hear.
- *Ask for help.* Ask a third person to mediate or facilitate the communication. People often tone down their anger and are more polite when company comes to dinner.
- *Apologize and start over.* An apology is merely a declaration of responsibility for whatever is not working and a request for improved communications and a better relationship. Apologizing is a way of overcoming impasse and returning to collaboration and problem solving by reversing the arrogance of anger with humility.

As you consider these methods and ways of using them to soften your conflicts, notice which ones are hardest to practice. Look at the ones where you balk or require more long-term focus and dedicated effort.

Ways of Apologizing

One way of defusing anger is to apologize for any misunderstandings or miscommunications you engaged in, and any discomfort your opponent may have experienced as a result of your anger. A little apology can go a long way. An apology does not have to mean you were wrong or a bad person. It can mean you understand what the other person experienced and are sorry for whatever you may have done that contributed to their pain or discomfort.

An apology is simply a way of saying, "I value our relationship more than I value being right." It signifies a willingness to accept responsibility for your behavior and what you contributed to the conflict. Your acknowledgment of responsibility will encourage your adversary to follow suit, which may lead to a resolution of the conflict and a melting away of the anger that kept it going.

What would it take for you to apologize to the other person in your conflict? What do you think would happen if you did? Here are a number of different ways of apologizing, along with representative phrases from which you can choose:

- *Make your regrets about what happened completely clear.* "I am very, very sorry for what I did." Include specifics.
- *Take full responsibility for what happened.* "It was totally my fault."
- *Specify the behaviors that were wrong or offensive.* "I really apologize for having . . ." Again, be specific but neutral. "I'm sorry I embarrassed you in front of your staff" is a statement that works; "I'm sorry I let everybody see what a jerk you are" does not.
- *Focus on the events and results you regret.* "I'm sorry you weren't told about this in advance. It must have upset you."
- *Indicate your understanding that there was an alternative.* "I should have handled it differently."
- *Acknowledge the feelings that resulted.* "I'm sorry for the pain this must have caused you."
- *Ask for forgiveness, then wait until you receive it.* "Can you forgive me?"
- *Indicate what you wish you had done to prevent the problem.* "I wish I'd spoken to you before this happened."
- *Recognize the positive results of the error.* "This has been a real learning experience for me."

- *Make good on your promises quickly so the other person can see an immediate result.* "I will make sure your name is put on the distribution list today so this doesn't happen again."
- *Ask what they need from you.* "What can I do to make it up to you?"
- *Negotiate an agreement for future forgiveness.* "What would it take for you to forgive me?"

Once you choose a method, consider why you chose it over others. Then ask your opponent to rate your apology on a scale of one to ten, with ten being highest in authenticity, caring, humility, and forgiveness. If you did not choose an apology that was a ten, ask yourself why, and what it would take to make it a ten.

Transcending and Integrating Emotions

The only way out of an intense negative emotion is to experience it fully and own it. By running away, suppressing it, or blaming others, we create internal knots that sap our energy, keep us focused on the past, and diminish our capacity to live in the present or plan for the future. We get locked into behaviors we do not like in ourselves or others, and feel unable to transcend. We become stuck in conflict.

The primary purpose of working through our negative emotions is not to settle or resolve them, but to accept, acknowledge, integrate, and thereby *transcend* them so they become our teachers and release us from their grip.

Transcendence means no longer being dominated by our emotions, but *integrating* them into a coherent, constructive part of who we are. It means using our emotions to expand our awareness and the awareness of others. It means directing our emotions, in conjunction with logic and analysis, to solving our problems. Fundamentally, it means overcoming, rising above, and becoming greater than the sum of our problems.

As Milton Glaser has eloquently written, transcendence is the principal task we are given in life:

> All life is about transcendence. If you're ugly you have to transcend your ugliness; if you're beautiful you have to transcend your beauty; if you're poor you have to transcend your poverty; if you're rich you have to transcend your wealth.... You get nothing at birth except things to transcend.

STRATEGY 5

SEPARATE WHAT MATTERS FROM WHAT GETS IN THE WAY

Plantagenet: The truth appears so naked on my side
  That any purblind eye may find it out.
Somerset: And on my side it is so well apparell'd
  So clear, so shining and so evident
  That it will glimmer through a blind man's eye.

—SHAKESPEARE, *King Henry VI,*
Part 1, Act 2, Scene 4

When we are in conflict, there is one thing we *always* share with our opponents: we both know we are right, and that the truth is on our side. We assume there is only one truth, that it is ours, and that it is so clear it will be apparent to every unbiased listener. Yet our opponent somehow has no difficulty rejecting our truth, any more than we do rejecting his, despite the fact that we're both *completely* convinced we're right.

The British playwright Harold Pinter had it right when he reminded us, in his Nobel Prize acceptance speech, that there are no "hard distinctions between what is real and what is unreal, or between what is true and what is false. A thing is not necessarily either true or false; it can be both true and false." He added:

> More often than not you stumble upon the truth in the dark, colliding with it or just glimpsing an image or a shape which seems to correspond to the truth, often without realising that you have done so. But the real truth is that there never is any such thing as one truth. . . . There are many. These truths challenge each other, recoil from each other, reflect each other, ignore each other, tease each other, are blind to each other. Sometimes you feel you have the truth of a moment in your hand, then it slips through your fingers and is lost.

When we apply these insights to conflict, instead of claiming our experience is "The Truth," and trying to invalidate our opponent's truth, we can recognize that our experience, while true for *us,* is not necessarily true for everyone else. Each of us experiences life differently and therefore perceives slightly different truths. What we see, recognize, and comprehend is always a *combination* of the truths we all see, along with the angle of our vision, what we feel and think about what we are experiencing, our history and relationships, and our emotional state, personality, and attitude.

In conflict, even our own truth shifts dramatically as a result of small changes in our frame of reference, including our ideas, emotions, attitudes, assumptions, expectations, and relationship to what we are observing. Truth in conflict is therefore not solitary but *composite,* allowing us, by combining and integrating our diverse perspectives, experiences, and ideas, to discover a vastly greater, more universal, and far more profound truth than would have been possible by affirming any single truth standing alone. Here is why.

Positions Versus Interests

The idea that our experience in conflict is the sole and solitary truth leads us to formulate and advance a *position,* consisting of *what* we want, and to advocate it as the only solution, based on competitive, subjective assumptions about what is true. On the other hand, the idea that there are multiple truths leads us to identify *interests,* consisting of the reasons *why* we want it, and to engage in dialogue about diverse solutions, based on collaborative, intersubjective assumptions about what is true.

Interests allow us to combine separate individual truths and create a composite perspective. When we transition from assuming a single truth to permitting multiple truths, we alter the potential outcome in our conflict from one of win-lose inevitability to one of win-win potentiality. We shift our process from one of *debate* over who is right to one of *dialogue* over creative solutions that satisfy everyone's interests. We transform our relationship from one of competition to one of collaboration and a search for common ground.

For example, a group of thirty sales representatives at a large commercial bank began to organize into self-managing teams. Prior to working in teams, everyone had been rated monthly on their individual sales performance. These ratings influenced bonuses and were published throughout the organization, stimulating intense, aggressive, frequently destructive competition to see who could achieve the highest score.

The newly organized teams wanted to eliminate these *individual* ratings and recommended reporting only *team* results to encourage their transition to a collaborative team process. But the head of the organization refused. He wanted to keep the individual ratings in place to motivate higher results. In a strategic planning session, a conflict flared between a woman who spoke in favor of team-based ratings and the head of the organization who defended individual reporting. Neither would budge from their positions because they were both certain they were right.

When we shifted the focus of the discussion from positions to interests, their process automatically changed from debate to dialogue and their relationship was immediately transformed from one of competition over who was right to one of collaboration over how they could come up with the best solution that would satisfy both sets of interests.

They discovered that the head of the organization wanted individual results reported because he was afraid they would use their newly formed teams to slack off, become irresponsible, and blame other team members for their poor performance. Everyone on the teams understood and acknowledged the legitimacy of these interests, and responded with alternative suggestions that might satisfy their shared goals.

It took the manager some time to recognize that the reason the teams wanted to be judged on team results was to motivate their members to achieve *more*—not to provide room for them to slack off, become irresponsible, or blame others. They wanted to support each other in making their team effort succeed and to dramatically change the culture of the organization by encouraging greater collaboration. The head of the organization then saw their interests as legitimate and realized they all shared similar goals at heart.

As a result, the manager and the teams negotiated a compromise reporting system in which, in the beginning, team *and* individual results would be listed, together with an agreement that they would assess the sales each person produced in the following quarter and interview each other to see which approach worked best. This decision motivated the teams to produce extraordinary results. On average, they produced 130 percent of their departments' annual goals in just six months!

By being willing to listen to each other, separate what mattered from what was in the way, and acknowledge the truth of each other's interests, they were able to discover a higher, more creative truth that would support collaboration and teamwork, acknowledge the need to make sure individuals did not slack off, and focus on producing outstanding results.

Another example of the damage caused by being certain of The Truth of one's own position occurred during a strategic planning process with senior staff in the office of the mayor of a large U.S. city. The mayor's staff and city council were at loggerheads with each side not only knowing it was right, but also convinced that the other side was mistaken and operating from a hidden agenda.

One staff member expressed the mayor's point of view: "The city council is our main obstacle. They've decided to defeat the mayor's programs so he won't get credit. It's an irrational power struggle." A city council staff member saw it differently: "There is an ideological war between the mayor and the city council. There is also an issue of respect, both politically and in terms of behaviors. We are criticized for not being consensus-oriented in our relations with the mayor, but the mayor's office is far more isolationist than the council. We don't have an independent way to accomplish our goals, and we need each other but they are too arrogant and don't want to work with us."

Everyone in this conflict was frustrated at their inability to reach agreement but continued asserting their positions and refusing to acknowledge the other side's point of view. When each group realized it could not achieve what it wanted without the cooperation of the other, a change began to take place. The mayor's office created a task force and assigned a staff member to work with each council member to build a closer relationship. His staff agreed to stop acting unilaterally, coming in with fully developed plans and demanding instant approval. Instead, they committed to develop programs in partnership with the council.

On both sides, committed protagonists were locked into positions they were prepared to defend to the death, if necessary, because they knew they were Right and the Truth was on their side. Argumentation and debate solidified each group's stance and prevented them from listening to the truth of the other group or even trying to meet their reasonable and legitimate interests. What was needed—as in every conflict—was for each side to listen closely to the other side's "truth," and use it to separate what might be useful in resolving the dispute from what was not and was getting in the way.

Separating the Issues in Conflict

When we are in conflict, we tend to lump all the issues that upset us into a mass of indistinguishable complaints that are intertwined and difficult to understand, negotiate, fix, or resolve on their own. As strange as it may seem, simply creating distinctions or separations between the core issues in conflict can produce a significant shift, allowing us to approach them constructively.

Separating issues, elements, and problems can transform our attitude toward conflict from negative, reactive, and powerless to positive, proactive, and strategic. It can signal our readiness to transition from listening and emotional processing to problem solving and collaborative negotiation. With these separations, seemingly monolithic issues can be broken down into easy-to-handle, bite-sized bits, revealing solutions and increasing both sides' willingness to implement them.

The framework provided in the following list delineates a number of "separations" that can profoundly influence our conflicts, clarify what is preventing us from reaching resolution, identify strategies for tackling each one separately, and transform our understanding of the dispute as a whole. We can, for example, in any conflict, separate

- Positions from interests
- People from problems
- Problems from solutions
- Commonalities from differences
- Future from past
- Emotions from negotiation
- Process from content
- Options from choices
- Criteria from selection
- Yourself from others

Although these separations may seem obvious, there are complexities, nuances, and subtleties implied by each, and it is easy forget to separate them when you are caught up in a conflict. In an ultimate sense, nothing in conflict can be completely separated from anything else. By focusing on separating things that are actually inseparable, it is possible to lose sight of their underlying unity and what they have in common. For example, the deepest truth is that there *is* no separation between ourselves and our opponents, other than the illusion that what separates us matters and is unbridgeable.

When we discover that there are commonalities as well as differences between ourselves and our opponents and that we can unite elements we previously thought of as separate, we can see ourselves and our opponents as parts of a larger whole. In these moments, we realize that every conflict is actually an expression of some deeper, underlying unity.

Yet it is important to begin by recognizing these separations, in order to later arrive at a place where we recognize their underlying unities, which are far more difficult to grasp when we are confused by artificial adversarial assumptions. To understand the distinctions between them and apply them successfully, we will discuss each in greater detail and provide questions to aid you in clarifying the separations and unities in your conflicts.

As you proceed, remember that our goal is to move beyond merely *settling* disputes to fully *resolving* the underlying reasons that gave rise to them, and ultimately preventing and transcending the sources of our conflicts so they do not resurface later under a different guise.

Separate Positions from Interests

Recall that positions are *what* we want, while interests are the reasons *why* we want it. Positions are competitive, based on the perception that there is not enough to go around. Interests are collaborative, based on the realization that diverse needs, wants, desires, and feelings can be mutually satisfied.

If we can shift our dynamic in conflict from debating over positions to engaging in dialogue over interests, not only will our process change, but the substance of our communications and the nature of our relationship will automatically begin to change as well.

Roger Fisher and William Ury, in *Getting to Yes,* their classic book on collaborative negotiation, develop the idea of interest-based negotiations, and Ury, in *Getting Past No* and *The Power of a Positive No*, describes ways we can use interests to resolve disputes in collaborative ways that help people avoid getting stuck in mutually exclusive, positional arguments.

Here is a simple example: Imagine you are meeting in a room with several colleagues and that some of them want the air-conditioning unit turned off while others want it left on. If we assume that the air-conditioning unit can only be on or off, there are only three fundamental ways we can resolve this dispute:

1. *Power:* If we resolve the air-conditioning dispute on the basis of power, whether by applying physical force, mental coercion, money, status, position, organizing ability, or political connections, each side will be pitted against the other, inevitably producing winners and losers and dividing the group against itself. The most powerful faction will be able to turn the air-conditioning on or off at will regardless of what the powerless faction wants, permitting the winners to abuse their power. When accumulated power is used to gain personal advantage or to protect a small group's privileges, it inevitably results in tyranny, corruption, instability, contempt, divisiveness, and perceptions of unfairness, creating chronic conflicts. These actions encourage the powerless to use negative forms of power to prevent abuse, increase systemic fairness, and get their

needs met. When this dynamic continues, those in power begin to look down on those who do not have it, resulting in stereotyping, prejudice, discrimination, fear, hatred, and systemic oppression.

2. *Rights:* If the air conditioner dispute is resolved on the basis of rights, as through lawsuits, voting, or adversarial contractual negotiations, there may be a compromise in which, for example, the air-conditioning is on from 10 A.M. to noon and off from noon to 5 P.M. If people vote or litigate there will still be winners and losers, though it is rare that victory and defeat are as absolute as when disputes are resolved using power.
   With rights, corruption, oppression, and abuses of power are reduced in severity, but continue to exist along with a new problem that rarely appears when power is used: namely, bureaucracy. Rights are preferable to power, especially among minorities and the powerless, yet people are divided, negotiations are still adversarial, communications are blocked, relations are distant, conflicts are endemic, and no one is able to resolve the underlying reasons for the dispute.
3. *Interests:* If the dispute is resolved on the basis of interests, we begin by asking *why* people want the air conditioner on or off. If they want it off because they are unable to hear as a result of the noise it creates, we can use a microphone or speak louder. If they want it on because they need fresh air, we can open a window, or take a break. If they want it off because they are cold, we can bring in blankets, exchange sweaters and jackets, or find a directional heater. If they want it on because they are having trouble breathing and feel stuffy, we can find a fan.
   In the end, everyone is able to feel like they won, no one loses, there are no *necessary* abuses of power, tyranny, bureaucracy, or oppression. Instead, negotiations are collaborative and the group feels united. In short, there is no fundamental reason why *anyone* has to feel stuffy so that someone else will not feel cold.

For thousands of years we were governed by absolutist monarchies and resolved disputes primarily on the basis of power, prompting Lord Acton to remark that "All power corrupts, and absolute power corrupts absolutely." For the last several hundred years, representative democracies have shifted from power to rights-based processes relying primarily on law, or policies and procedures. Rights are therefore *limitations* on the exercise of power. Indeed, every word in the U.S. Constitution can be considered a limitation on the power of an absolute monarch to do exactly as he or she wishes. Nonetheless, rights originate in and depend on power. As a result, we only have the rights we are willing and able to enforce.

Only for the last few decades have we begun to shift toward deeper forms of direct, participatory democracy and create diverse mechanisms for making decisions on the basis of interests. Interest-based approaches such as creative problem solving, collaborative negotiation, dialogue, and mediation define an arena within which there is an equality of power and rights because decisions are voluntary and based on consensus.

Although interest-based approaches are superficially the most time-consuming of these processes, this is only true in the short run if we ignore the time otherwise wasted in arguments, petty squabbles, and emotional tirades; the time spent resolving chronic conflicts that are generated whenever power- or rights-based processes are implemented; the time spent overcoming resistance; the time wasted on gossip, rumors, and being unproductive; and the time saved by increasing motivation, caring, and unity within the group.

The easiest way to separate positions from interests in conflict is to ask our opponents why they have taken a given position, or why a given issue is important to them. Here are some questions to elicit your opponent's interests or reveal your own:

- "Why does that seem like the best solution to you?"
- "If you could have any solution, what would you want?"
- "Help me understand why that is important to you."
- "Why do you care so deeply about this?"
- "What concerns do you have about this?"
- "What's the real problem here?"
- "What would be wrong with . . . ?"
- "Why not do it this way . . . ?"
- "What are you afraid would happen if we . . . ?"
- "What would you do if you were in charge?"
- "What are your goals for the future?"
- "Why not just accept my [or their] proposal?"
- "What would your proposal be if I was willing to meet your interests?"
- "What would it take for you to give up that proposal?" "Here's what it would take for me . . ."

- "What could I do to make my proposal more acceptable to you?"

Simply asking these questions will automatically shift the assumption that there *has* to be a win-lose outcome to the assumption that both of you can win. By identifying interests, you make it possible to consider multiple options that are not mutually exclusive, do not result in anyone's defeat, and seek to satisfy everyone's legitimate needs.

Consider the conflict between Jim and Helen, who worked at the same level in a large accounting organization. Helen started at the company fifteen years before Jim and spent most of those years working for Sarah, who was senior vice president for the unit. Jim arrived only two years ago and also worked for Sarah, who hired him and recently recommended him for promotion. The division moved to new headquarters and each person was assigned a cubicle. Everyone was expected to move in and immediately start work. Sarah arrived on Wednesday morning, expecting to find all fifteen of her staff members settled in their new office spaces, putting photos of their family members and pets on their desks and arranging their files.

To her surprise, she found Helen in her office in tears and Jim outside her door demanding an immediate conference. Perplexed and annoyed at facing two disruptions so early in the day, she invited them into her office, hoping she could take care of the problem quickly.

Sarah quickly learned that a conflict had arisen between Jim and Helen over their new workspaces. Through a misunderstanding or mistake by maintenance, Helen and Jim had been assigned the same cubicle. When the movers realized their error, they offered to move one of them to a double space that was available across the hall, but that solution was not acceptable to either of them.

As it happened, the cubicle in dispute was next to Sarah's office, and Jim and Helen both insisted on having it. In her haste and annoyance over their "childishness," Sarah decided to take the cubicle away from both of them and assigned them to occupy the double cubicle across the hall, telling them to "share it until you get over this silly argument and learn to work together."

As "the boss," Sarah clearly solved the problem, but what did her decision teach Helen and Jim about conflict resolution, leadership, and how to collaborate? With hindsight, Sarah was able to see that by accepting Jim and Helen's positions at face value and failing to identify their underlying interests, she had missed an opportunity to create a win-win solution and improve her department. Worse, her action communicated the following subconscious lessons to them about how they should go about resolving disputes in the future:

- You do not have the ability to resolve your conflicts yourselves.
- Therefore, you need someone to intervene and solve them for you.
- The person who will solve them for you will be someone in a position of power or authority.
- That person will not care what your real interests are.
- As a result, you will at best get only half of what you really want or need.
- This result will be imposed on you as a kind of punishment for standing up for yourself or getting into an argument with each other.
- Conflict is therefore dangerous and pointless.
- There is no reason to think you can satisfy both sets of interests.
- There is no reason to think you can collaborate and both get what you want.
- There is no way to talk about and resolve the deeper conflict that is driving this one.
- There is no reason to think you can learn from your conflicts.

An alternative scenario would have been for Sarah to ask Helen and Jim to find out from each other *why* they wanted the cubicle near her office. If she had done so, they might have learned about the deeper conflict that was simmering just beneath the surface and been able to discuss and resolve it.

When we were called in to meet with Helen, Jim, and Sarah, we started by asking them why they each wanted the cubicle. Helen told us she had worked with Sarah for a much longer time and needed to have daily contact with her to do her job. She felt Jim was trying to push her out and take her job. Jim responded by denying Helen's allegations and accusing her of trying to block him from communicating directly with Sarah and wanting to make him look inefficient. He felt the other cubicle was too far from his staff, which would make his job more difficult and take longer.

We asked Jim to tell Helen why he was *not* trying to push her out and take over her job. He said he had no interest in replacing her and was looking for promotion to a position in a different department. In fact, he said he thought Helen was doing a great job. We asked Helen to tell Jim if she was trying to block him from communicating with Sarah or make him look inefficient. She said she felt hurt and jealous and may have done some of the things Jim mentioned, but actually admired his work, was pleased to hear that he did not want to take over her job, and promised to stop getting in his way in the future.

They saw that their conflict raised issues that were deeper than who would get the cubicle, and not really about it at all. We asked them to brainstorm solutions that would allow them to satisfy both their interests. As a result of our earlier conversation, Helen suggested that Jim take the cubicle since he needed to be closer to his coworkers. Jim, on the other hand, suggested that Helen take it since she needed to communicate on a daily basis with Sarah. Once each person let the other know they recognized and appreciated their interests and wanted them to have what they needed, they began to appreciate each other a little more.

As they continued discussing how to solve the problem, they realized that Jim's coworkers could easily move across the hall, which would allow him to have the double-sized cubicle for himself and use it for team meetings. Both were extremely pleased with this solution, which would not have emerged if their conflict had not revealed the issues they were struggling over in silence.

Clarifying and communicating honestly and empathetically about these issues made it possible for them to reach a far better outcome than any that had been proposed before, and to resolve the underlying reasons for their dispute by simultaneously satisfying both their interests. It allowed them to see that by seeking to satisfy not just their own interests, but those of their opponent, they increased their ability to resolve their disputes in the future. The solution sent a different set of lessons from those listed previously, including:

- You do have the capacity to resolve your conflicts yourselves.
- Therefore, you do not need anyone to intervene to solve them.
- You can rely on yourselves rather than on someone in a position of power or authority.
- The way for you to do so is to ask each other a "why" question, or some other question that identifies both persons' interests.
- It is possible for both of you to get what you really want or need.
- You can feel good about yourselves and each other, and create a successful partnership.
- Conflict can be creative, useful, and a source of learning and improved outcomes.

- It is possible to satisfy both of your interests.
- It is possible to collaborate and get what you want.
- It is possible to talk about and resolve the deeper conflicts that are driving this one.
- You can learn from your conflicts.

If Jim had continued to be upset that Helen ended up with the cubicle he wanted, Sarah could have asked him why he was so angry, in which case he *might* have said, "Helen has been here longer, she's part of the 'old guard,' and I never get a chance as the 'new kid on the block' to be included, appreciated, or have access to informal information that would help me do my job and be successful. In addition, because you and Helen are both women, you seem to share information and news and have a friendship that makes me feel excluded."

If so, Sarah could have helped him recognize that the conflict was actually about the deeper problem of inclusion and exclusion in the informal network of the organization, and about her own leadership style and failure to provide sufficient acknowledgment and access for Jim to the information he needed to do his job, or about her playing favorites with Helen. Now, at least, they would be discussing the *real* conflict.

If Sarah had pursued her questioning further and asked Helen why she had such a high level of emotion connected with the cubicle issue, she might have discovered a deeper level of tension in her as well. Helen might have complained that she had been with the firm for fifteen years and been a dedicated staff member and loyal supporter of Sarah, but had never been promoted, while Jim, who had far less experience, had been promoted to the same level and received Sarah's recommendation for future promotion. This line of questioning would have led Sarah to realize that she needed to reevaluate Helen's skills and possibly consider her for a promotion or acknowledge her contributions.

By imposing a solution and denying both of them the cubicle, Sarah had quickly settled the superficial issue, but simultaneously pushed the deeper issues underground where they would have festered and emerged in an endless series of petty new disputes until they were finally addressed or ended by someone quitting, suing, or transferring to another location.

By separating positions from interests they were able to begin talking openly, honestly, and empathetically about their real problems and identify much better solutions than any of them could have imagined.

Indeed, Sarah might have gone still deeper and asked questions that would encourage their future collaboration, such as:

- "Now that you've identified the real problem, what deeper solutions do you suggest?"
- "Helen, could you put together a portfolio of your accomplishments so I can review them and possibly consider you for a promotion?"
- "Jim, I'd like you to accompany me to a conference next month with the manager you want to work for. Could you check the dates and let me know if you are available?"
- "I'd like both of you to work together to develop a plan for how we should assign space in the future. Would you be willing to present it *together* to a meeting of the leadership team next week?"
- "Now that you've solved this problem, what others do you think you might tackle?"
- "I'd like to take you both out for lunch to celebrate what you just did! How about it?"

Shifting from positions to interests automatically reduced their perception that they needed to compete aggressively in order to satisfy their needs. It helped them realize that they could collaborate and still get what they wanted. It allowed them to address the issues that lay beneath the surface of their dispute, woke them up to what they really cared about, and let them know there were much more important issues at stake.

As a result of their exploration of each other's interests, they were able to improve their communication skills, feel acknowledged by Sarah, make their relationship more collaborative, create better solutions for Jim's team, become more motivated, develop new leadership skills, improve teamwork, and save time and energy in the process.

By separating interests from positions, you may be able to do the same and transform your conflict. Consider asking the following questions to help clarify your interests and those of your opponent in any conflict you are facing:

- What is my position? Why do I want it? What are the facts that I feel demonstrate I am right?

- Why have I taken this position? Why is it so important to me? What are my deeper interests?
- What is your position? What do you want? What are the facts that you feel demonstrate you are right?
- Why have you taken this position? Why is it so important to you? What are your deeper interests?
- Is there anything about either of our interests that would actually prevent us from satisfying both our interests?
- If not, what could we do to satisfy both our interests?
- What are some ways we might both win?
- Have we gained any deeper insights by having this conversation?

When positions are not clearly distinguished from interests, solutions may be forced on others who feel resentful because their basic needs have not been met. Brainstorming and creative problem-solving techniques often allow much better solutions to be found. If they can't be created to each person's satisfaction, the separations described in the following section may be successful in resolving the conflict and revealing optimal solutions for everyone.

Separate People from Problems

Whenever we demonize our opponents, we label, stereotype, and prejudge them, sincerely believing they have evil in their hearts and are unjust, dishonest, disagreeable, untrustworthy people or personalities. We personalize their behaviors toward us, even when their actions have more to do with *their* perceptions, emotions, and unresolved issues than with us.

It is rare that people actually *intend* to harm each other. More often, they are focused on their own personal goals and simply ignore others' interests, and in trying to get what they want end up inadvertently harming others. While the harm we experience is the same, the motivation is different. We do not need to take their actions personally or demonize their intentions in order to put a stop to their actions and get what we want.

If you can separate the people with whom you are in conflict from the problems their actions or behaviors created, you will be able to focus your energy and anger on the issues you can actually resolve. Doing so will encourage you to recognize that your opponents—no matter how despicable their behavior—have redeeming human qualities that you should be able to recognize and appreciate. If you cannot, you will start behaving toward them as they behaved toward you, demeaning yourself and making it more difficult to find solutions to your problems.

The logic of personal hostility is circular, and always ends up aggravating conflict. It works like this: if others direct their hostility toward you, sooner or later you will become aware of it. When you detect their hostility you feel hurt, distance yourself emotionally, start to see them as your enemy, act aggressively in return, and become less willing to listen to their perceptions or negotiate collaboratively. When they detect your hostility, they do the same in return, causing the cycle of conflict to continue. When you feel personally insulted, you naturally withdraw, which they interpret as hostility, causing them to naturally withdraw from you. You see their withdrawal as rejection, retroactively justifying your earlier withdrawal, and vice versa, and the conflict becomes a self-fulfilling prophecy.

Only by recognizing your opponent as a multifaceted human being and by refusing to accept or condone the part of what he or she is doing that is harmful can you open pathways to resolution, learning, and transformation. Moreover, if we take separating people from problems to its logical conclusion, we inevitably reach a place of forgiveness and reconciliation—not for *what* your opponent did, but for the human being who did it.

The truth is, no matter how terrible a person our opponents may be, we cannot solve the problem of who they *are*. The only problem we can solve is what they are *doing*. The first step is to separate them from the problem, the second is to be soft on them as fellow human beings, and the third is to be hard on the problem, defined as an "it," instead of as a "you."

When we identify the problem as their *behavior,* as opposed to their personality, we are able to act more powerfully and effectively. We will then listen more effectively, which will encourage our opponents to listen to us in return. We can give each other honest, empathetic feedback without provoking a counterattack or defensive response and learn ways of responding more skillfully in the future.

In resolving organizational disputes, there are a number of practices, interventions, and techniques that can help you achieve these results. For example, you can

- Organize a meeting with your opponent or opposing group and agree on common goals for your working relationship.

- Create a vision for your work together.
- Define a set of ground rules for your communications and improve the way you solve problems.
- Develop a set of shared values you both agree to live by in the future.
- Ask questions that may make them seem more human to you, and you to them.
- Discuss why you both originally wanted to work for the organization.
- Compare and find commonalities in what you both feel most passionately about in your work.
- Ask what experiences you've each had that led you to care so deeply about the issues over which you are in conflict.
- Talk about the hopes and wishes you both have for the future.

Engaging in these conversations will remind you of some of the things you share and highlight qualities you can genuinely appreciate in each other. It will reveal that your opponent probably has the same fears and desires as you have. All our personal dislikes, personal attacks, and factional infighting start to melt away when we talk about our concerns and agree on what is important.

Paradoxically, you can be much harder on the problem by being softer on the person. If you do not dedicate your passion and determination to solving the problem but use it instead to blame or attack the person, your natural empathy and compassion may cause you to be softer on the problem so as not to unduly hurt the other person's feelings, leaving the problem unresolved. Or, it may cause you to be harder on other people than you have to be, feel guilty as a result, and lead you to suppress your empathy and compassion, alienate them, and make the problem worse.

Try answering the following questions to identify the human qualities of your opponent. Notice which questions you find most difficult to answer, try to determine why, and consider how you might respond to your opponent's difficult behaviors more skillfully in the future.

- What do you like most about your opponent?
- What are three admirable qualities your opponent possesses?
- How might you bring these qualities into your communication and relationship?

- What do you want or expect from your opponent? Why do you want it?
- Are you comparing yourself with your opponent? Why? Are you really comparable to each other?
- What is your opponent doing that is bothering you?
- How do you respond when your opponent engages in this behavior?
- Is your opponent's behavior succeeding? How?
- Has your response been successful in changing your opponent's behavior? Why not?
- Are you in some indirect way rewarding behaviors you do not like?
- What are three things you could do differently to respond more skillfully to your opponent's behavior?

The fundamental premise behind these questions is that we are all responsible *both* for our own behaviors and for how we respond to the behaviors of others. By separating people from problems and personalities from behaviors, we can shift the locus of responsibility from "me" versus "them" to "us" versus "it," in relation to how the conflict started and to how we go about resolving it. Doing so encourages us to take 100 percent responsibility for resolving our conflicts, make clear commitments, collaborate in finding workable solutions, and learn more as a result.

Separate Problems from Solutions

When we are in conflict, we are so busy focusing on disagreements, bolstering our positions, and searching for quick solutions that we fail to listen closely enough to what is taking place at a deep level within our conflict, and collaborate in a search for creative long-term solutions that meet everyone's needs. As a result, we propose solutions to the wrong problem, or our solutions are received with suspicion and distrust because both sides did not participate in proposing them. Thus we become locked in mountainous disputes over molehills, unable to find creative solutions without replicating the very problems that got us stuck in the first place.

When we stop for a moment, listen carefully, and analyze or try to understand the problem before starting to solve it, we find much more effective solutions. It is nearly always better to discuss the problem in detail with our opponent before coming up with proposed solutions. We can begin by trying to reach agreement on how the problem started, what caused it, whether it is linked to similar related problems, and the extent and nature of its effect on us and others, before deciding what to do in response.

Research on problem solving reveals that the effectiveness of solutions increases by 85 percent once the real problem has been identified. If you spend most of your time identifying and analyzing the problem, resolution often emerges effortlessly. In analyzing your conflict, try to answer the following questions:

- What exactly is the conflict about? Why is it about that?
- When did the conflict begin? Why then?
- Who does it impact or involve? Why them?
- What kind of conflict is it? Why that kind?
- What aspects of the conflict have been overlooked? Why those?
- How has your understanding of the conflict changed or evolved over time?
- What specific actions or inactions do you think caused or aggravated the conflict? What does your opponent think? What do your colleagues think?
- How would you analyze the conflict? What type of conflict is it?
- Can you break the conflict down into separate parts?
- How would you prioritize these parts?
- What might you or others have done to prevent the problem from occurring?

It may seem counterintuitive *not* to implement a fast and easy solution to the problem, but stay with it and resist the temptation to solve it quickly. In some organizations that are stuck in conflict, there seem to be a bewildering, endless array of overwhelming problems. When this is the case, we often ask people to divide into small teams and identify, define, analyze, and prioritize their problems without trying to solve them.

After a few minutes, we often find them laughing cheerfully and working collaboratively while analyzing five or ten difficult and significant problems. When we ask them why they are enjoying themselves, they say they feel relieved to finally be able to talk openly about what they know is happening, but have been unable to discuss with each other. They feel relieved just to talk with others who have the same problem and excited because discussing their problems automatically increases the possibility of finding solutions.

We then ask them whether, while discussing their problems, they actually experienced *any* of the ones they listed during their meeting. Rarely does anyone say yes. We then ask, if their problems are so deep and all encompassing, how could they *not* experience even one of them in their teams? They begin to recognize that their problems grow less weighty when they are faced honestly, openly, and together, without blaming anyone for causing them or feeling compelled to immediately implement a solution.

Our problems become easier to solve when we include our opponents in our efforts to define, analyze, and prioritize them, and come up with possible solutions. They also become easier to solve when we facilitate the problem-solving process, when we work in teams and set clear process rules, when we create identifiable goals and operate by consensus, and when we talk openly and honestly about the causes and nature of our problems without feeling they are failures and desperately try to solve them.

Separate Commonalities from Differences

When labor and management teams work together to resolve grievances or collective bargaining disputes, improve interdepartmental relationships, or develop skills in negotiating, we often ask each group to meet separately to identify their goals for their relationship with the other side. Even the most antagonistic and rancorous groups discover they have many goals in common and want the same kind of relationship.

Afterwards, we ask them to meet separately again, this time to identify what they or their opponents are doing that is undermining their ability to achieve these goals. Again we find that both groups are nearly always in agreement. We then ask them to meet together in small, bilateral teams to reach consensus on what they might do instead, and how to make their goals a priority in their communications and relationships. Afterward, they are able to discuss their conflicts and disagreements without feeling angry and overwhelmed.

Conflict causes us to focus on how different we are from our opponents. Although it is important to understand and work through our differences, focusing exclusively on them makes it difficult to remember what we have in common. We share multiple interests as human beings, and if we cannot bring them to mind in the midst of our conflicts, we can at least recognize that we care about the same issues.

It is paradoxical, yet true, that at the very moment we find ourselves poles apart, we become linked and inseparable. Our conflicts point out not only how we are different, but also how we are similar, and reveal that we care deeply about many of the same things. Simply recognizing that there is a human bond between us and allowing our awareness of this bond to grow makes it easier to discuss our problems and negotiate collaborative solutions.

This does not mean you should eliminate or understate your differences. Your conflicts are important sources of diverse perspectives and ideas, and therefore of learning, improvement, change, and of richer and more creative solutions. If you can discuss your differences while recognizing what you have in common, you will speak or act with awareness of this connection, and improve your ability to collaborate in finding and reaching solutions.

The following questions can help you define a *context* of commonalities in which to surface and discuss your differences:

- What are three things you have in common with your opponent?
- If you were reluctant, resistant, or unable to identify three, what was it inside of *you* that made it difficult to do so?
- How much do you actually know about your opponent? What is one thing you do not know but would like to find out? What questions could you ask to learn more about your opponent?
- What are some things you have assumed about your opponent without trying to find out whether they are true or not? How have these assumptions influenced your choices? How have they influenced your responses and reactions?
- What are three values, beliefs, goals, or principles that you think you and your opponent may have in common?
- What are three solutions to your conflict that you both might be willing to accept?

To highlight what you both have in common, try identifying your core values, ask your opponent to do the same, then share your values with each other. Probably there will be several that you have in common—no matter how different your cultures, languages, and experiences—and these can be used as criteria to judge your future interactions and discourage behaviors you do not like. This does not imply forgiving what your opponent did, but simply denying yourself permission to do the same in return.

An enemy can be defined as anyone you give yourself permission to speak or act toward in ways that do not reflect your core values. Identifying what you have in common with your opponent can therefore be transformational—not only because you will begin to see her differently, but because doing so will make *you* more powerful in solving problems and encourage you to surrender the idea that your conflict can be defined in terms of "good" and "evil" or "either/or," and instead focus on your commonalities and alternatives that are based on "both/and."

Separate the Future from the Past

The world has been embroiled in countless bloody conflicts throughout history, most of them fueled by an accumulation over generations of past grievances and the mutual exchange of pain, anger, humiliation, revenge, and retaliation. In this way, the carnage of centuries survives, and is passed on to succeeding generations.

The heavy price we pay for present conflicts often derives from our failure to distinguish past from future. If, in previous conflicts, the combatants could have agreed on a vision for their children, or their hopes for their future, or had been able to let go of what happened in the past and decide to create a completely different kind of future, they might have found a path to resolution and not allowed their conflict to continue.

In every conflict, the past weighs heavily on the present and the future. This is especially true in organizations with cultures of conflict avoidance, in which differences and disputes are routinely suppressed, denied, partly settled, or incompletely resolved. In these organizations, conflicts are allowed to fester and multiply, or are isolated, shunned, compromised, and sidelined. Most often, they are passed on to others through gossip and rumors and are nursed or hoarded, sometimes for generations.

Disputes were handled this way in a school where the faculty had forced three principals to resign in less than six months. Divisiveness among the staff was so intense that even the factions had factions and their anger and bitterness at one another made the entire educational community angry, frightened, and miserable. No one knew what to do.

We began an intervention by asking the faculty, staff, and administration to introduce themselves and to offer one suggestion on how they could make this the best school for student learning in the state. We wrote their ideas down on flip charts and posted them around the room. We then asked whether anyone disagreed with *any* of these ideas. No one did. We congratulated them on reaching complete consensus on the kind of school they wanted, and their goals for student learning, and they were stunned to find themselves in complete agreement.

We then asked them, "What would you rather spend your time on today, proving you were right about the past, or working on your ideas for the future and making this the best school in the state?" The response was unanimous. *Everyone* wanted to let go of the past and focus on the future. Of course, we had to spend time addressing the underlying issues and cleaning up problems that remained from the past so they would not leak into the future and undermine their consensus.

We ended the day with optimism, energy, and enormous enthusiasm for their ideas about the future and possibilities of working together to improve the school. And they did just that. Their results, based on an evaluation by the state accreditation commission, verified that in one year they had vastly improved in morale and student achievement.

When people are stuck in conflict and arguing bitterly with their opponents, we sometimes ask: "Will you *ever* convince each other you are right?" They always say no. It is rare that we ever succeed in convincing our opponents that we are right and they are wrong. This is partly because we are describing what is right *for us* and we do not include or care as deeply about what is right for them; and partly because we blame them either for who they are or for what they did in the past, without considering what we both want for the future.

We can disagree forever about what happened in the past, or who said and did what to whom, or who did it first, or who is most at fault. We each have our own stories to tell based on what we perceive and filter through our emotions, preconceptions, and needs. We sincerely believe our stories are true because if they were not, we might see ourselves as wrong or bad or at fault, and ultimately, none of it really matters. The only healthy, intelligent thing to do is let it go.

Recall a conflict in your workplace and how radically people's stories differed from one another. You might have wondered whether you were working in the same organization! Everyone in conflict recalls completely different facts, draws different conclusions, and identifies different people as heroes and villains. Everyone sees each other through subjective lenses and perceives events differently based on their diverse vantage points, needs, and roles, and comes away with vastly different memories that they feel passionately about, even years later.

In short, you will be far more successful in resolving your disputes when you stop debating endlessly over who is to blame for past transgressions and instead focus on how to solve shared problems in the present and create a mutually desirable future. Consider the following questions regarding the role of past, present, and future in your conflicts:

- What are some issues regarding the past about which you have been unable to agree?
- Are your disagreements about the past concerned with who is to blame for what happened?
- Is it likely that you will ever succeed in resolving these issues or that the other person will ever agree with you?
- If not, what would it take for you to give up your efforts to convince your opponent that you're right?
- What would the consequences be for either of you if you could agree on the present or the future?
- What might you have to give up? What might you gain?
- What are your mutual goals for the present?
- What are your goals for the future?
- Why not focus on these instead of on the past?

Focusing on the past and seeking revenge for your pain and suffering can keep you from letting go of it. Holding on to a painful past merely draws it into the present, reduces the likelihood of creating a different future, and denies you resolution, closure, and inner peace. Creating a dialogue with your opponent over what you want in the present or how you see the future can give you a framework for communicating your present realities and exploring your hopes and dreams with each other.

Separate Emotions from Negotiation

As we are naturally emotional beings, suppressing our emotions in conflict does not make them disappear, but causes them to submerge and reappear elsewhere, preoccupying our conscious and unconscious attention. These unresolved emotions distract us, making it difficult to focus our attention on finding logical or strategic solutions to our problems.

At the other extreme, when we vent destructively or dump our emotions onto others, we escalate our conflicts and are unable to identify or focus on our real priorities. We fail to perceive opportunities for resolution and have difficulty remembering what is actually important. As a result, we behave destructively and find it difficult to negotiate acceptable solutions to our problems.

It is important not to suppress or negotiate emotions, and it is equally important not to negotiate emotionally. Emotions should be acknowledged—not negotiated—then released so problem solving can take place without being grounded in emotional needs or temporary issues that will not provide long-term benefits. Emotions are useful as guides, even in the most important decisions. Justice William O. Douglas comments: "At the Supreme Court level where we work, 90 percent of any decision is emotional. The rational part of us supplies the reasons for supporting our predilections."

If you are unable to express your emotions you may also find it difficult to be free of them. Repressing deep feelings forces you to focus considerable energy on holding them in check, and prevents you from paying attention to what is happening around you. In this way, internal blindness leads to external blindness, to the "truth" becoming distorted and incommunicable, and to the ongoing self-fulfilling prophecy of emotional retribution.

If your opponent is more emotionally expressive than you are, it will be difficult for you to communicate your emotions and feel heard. Inviting both parties to constructively verbalize their feelings and validating their subjective responses will encourage acknowledgment, dialogue, and grieving to take place.

The following questions can help you identify the emotional issues in your conflicts, support you in expressing your feelings constructively, and encourage you to say or do whatever is necessary so you can take responsibility for your feelings, let them go, and negotiate nonemotionally.

- What emotions are you experiencing in your conflict?
- What do you need to say or do to let go of them?
- Have you tried communicating your emotions to your opponent? If so, what was his response? If not, why not?
- How could you express your emotions more constructively or skillfully and not produce the responses from your opponent that you do not like?

- Do you know what your opponent is feeling emotionally? What have you done to find out? Has that been successful? What might you do instead?
- What level of permission have you given your opponent to express emotions to you?
- What would it take for you to give your opponent greater permission?
- What could you do to encourage your opponent to communicate his or her emotions, let them go, and negotiate more logically?
- What might you lose by doing so? Would it be possible for you to initiate an emotionally honest conversation with your opponent and not lose anything in the process?
- How could you initiate an honest conversation? What would it take to do so?
- Have your emotions gotten in the way of your ability to negotiate logically?
- Have your opponent's emotions gotten in the way?
- How have they blocked your ability to have a constructive conversation?
- What could you do to get them out of the way?

Separate Process from Content

Conflicts that concern content—the accuracy of information, data, facts, chronology, precise recollections, and similar matters of substance—are difficult to resolve when we cannot communicate to convince the other side of the accuracy of our information. On the other hand, conflicts that concern process—*how* we go about working together, talking to each other, reaching agreements, and developing respect for one another—can be defined more flexibly and provide both sides with sufficient common ground to reach agreements over content.

In international negotiations, process is enormously important. In the talks that ended the Vietnam War, the parties argued seemingly endlessly over the size and shape of the negotiating table, who would be entitled to speak, how many days of discussion would take place, what issues would be on the agenda, and what would be communicated to the press. Yet both sides understood that if they could reach agreements on these process issues they would create a starting point for agreements over the content of the peace accords.

In workplace disputes as well, reaching agreements over process issues can help pave the way for agreements over content. Many corporations, schools, nonprofits, and government agencies have negotiated their differences and improved their communications simply by developing detailed ground rules and process agreements. Process agreements have the following advantages:

- They build arenas of trust between people who do not otherwise trust each other.
- They create boundaries around conflicts that safely contain disputed issues.
- They allow people to settle the rules of debate or dialogue and establish how they will operate within procedural boundaries.
- They eliminate small, petty conflicts that would otherwise get in the way of resolving larger ones.
- They encourage a sense of order and predictability about how things will happen.
- They provide a sense of fairness and equity.
- They encourage a feeling of ownership of the process and buy-in regarding commitments.
- They help people identify the key issues that need to be solved or negotiated and in what order.
- They normalize talking about what is not working in conflicted relationships.
- They encourage a constant monitoring of process issues and continuous improvement in negotiation skills.
- They help avoid miscommunications and future misunderstandings based on false expectations.
- They create small experiences of collaboration that encourage optimism about resolving the remaining larger issues.

In mediation, the first agreements are often about ground rules or process, making people clearer about *how* they will talk about substantive issues. In addition, ground rules encourage everyone to feel responsible for process and continual improvement. They allow deeper, more constructive and collaborative content to emerge in the negotiations and joint problem solving that follow.

Here are a number of common process agreements and ground rules from which you can select those that are most helpful. We have listed several that may not apply to your situation. Before beginning your next conflict conversation, negotiation, or mediation session, consider proposing that all parties reach consensus on at least a few of the following ground rules.

Possible Process and Ground Rules

We, the undersigned, hereby agree

- To be present in a spirit of good faith and problem solving
- To be as open and honest as we can with each other and address real problems
- To act with courtesy at all times and not engage in disruptive behavior
- To reach all substantive decisions through consensus
- To publicly support all consensus decisions made by the group
- To maintain a "cease-fire" during these sessions [alternatively: To agree on a list of actions that will be avoided by both sides while these meetings continue]
- To agree on when and where we will meet
- To agree on how many will participate on each side
- To agree on who will facilitate and record the sessions
- To agree on time lines for each meeting and when we will take breaks
- To begin and end the meeting and return from breaks on time
- To attend each scheduled session
- To agree on which issues will be discussed and in what order
- To keep all communications during these sessions confidential, except for those we expressly decide to share publicly [alternatively: To ask that no one's name be used in connection with any statement made during the session without their advance permission]
- To break into caucuses or separate meetings at either side's request

- To permit one person speak at a time without interruption
- To focus on issues, problems, and behaviors rather than personalities
- To sincerely try to listen objectively, openly, and nonjudgmentally
- To keep confidential whatever is said in caucuses [alternatively: To *not* keep confidential whatever is said in caucuses, unless the person speaking requests it]
- To not engage in retaliations or reprisals for anything said or done during these sessions
- To agree on who will issue and how we will respond to public announcements and press releases
- To agree on what will happen if confidentiality is breached
- To agree on what will happen if no agreements are reached
- To resolve all disputes regarding process, interpretation of these ground rules, or content agreements with a mutually agreeable mediator
- To agree on how we will select mediators or arbitrators, if needed

It is easy to reach consensus on most of these ground rules. If you run into difficulty, first decide whether you really need the disputed ground rule. If you do, try brainstorming alternative language that addresses your opponent's interests. If this fails, try reaching agreement on interim ground rules that will at least allow you to discuss the reasons the proposed ground rule is unacceptable and tailor a new ground rule to the reasons that are given.

In many disputes, content and process issues are difficult to separate, causing the parties to become confused as to what the real issues are and how to work through them. By separating process from content issues, they will be more successful in improving both. The following questions may help you sort process from content issues and discover how to create solutions for each:

- What role has process played in your conflict?
- How could the process you are using to communicate or make decisions be improved?

- How might changing the process affect the content of your communications or decisions? How might it change your relationship?
- Do the process conflicts you are having reveal underlying content issues? How? What are they? How might they best be addressed?
- Do your conflicts over content reveal process issues? What are they? How might they be addressed?
- Which of the process rules suggested above might be agreeable to you and your opponent? Which may not? Why?
- What could you suggest as an alternative if your opponent does not agree?
- What values do you believe should underlie your processes? What values does your opponent believe should underlie your processes?
- How might you develop process rules with your opponent that express your shared values?

If, at any time, you get stuck negotiating the content of your dispute, try shifting your focus back to process issues. If you can agree on a better process, the content of your dispute might be resolved more easily.

Separate Options from Choices

Before accepting or agreeing on a solution to our conflicts or problems, it is useful to first expand the range of potential alternatives and not assume our options are fixed. By playing with ideas, brainstorming alternatives, and considering all the possibilities, we can expand our chances of finding an even better method for resolving our disputes and revealing options that satisfy both sides' interests.

Options are not predetermined choices but creative possibilities, and the most effective way of generating them is to give your imagination full sway. Creativity automatically arises when we search together for new ways of solving problems rather than arguing over whose solution is best. This means *not* evaluating or rejecting anyone's suggestions until all the ideas have been expressed. It means encouraging wild, funny, and creative ideas. It means piggybacking on each other's suggestions and improving earlier proposals. Above all, it means going for broke—asking for everything you want. Here are some ways you can brainstorm options.

Impromptu Brainstorming

- Group members call out their ideas spontaneously.
- A recorder writes down the ideas as they are suggested.
- Afterward, these ideas may be discussed and prioritized, and one or more selected for in-depth research, more conversation, review by a different group or implementation.

Round Robin

- Each member expresses his or her ideas in turn.
- Anyone can pass on any round and not suggest an idea.
- The session continues until everyone passes and all the ideas are expressed.
- Ideas are recorded as they are suggested.

Secret Ballot

- Everyone writes their ideas on a slip of paper.
- The ideas are collected and organized.
- The ideas are exchanged, so that each person and group has some other person's and group's ideas.
- Each idea is discussed and prioritized by a new person or group, and all the prioritized lists are presented to the group as a whole, discussed, and reprioritized.

Subconscious Suggestion

- Each person thinks of words that may seem unrelated but can be used to generate new ideas about the problem.
- Or, everyone forgets about the problem entirely and tries to solve a dramatically different problem, then comes back to the problem to see which of those solutions apply, if any.
- Or, someone picks an object, and everyone describes it in terms that could be applied to the problem.

Guided Meditation

- Everyone closes their eyes, relaxes, and meditates on the problem.
- A leader may guide the meditation by asking everyone to visualize a time when the problem is solved, then asking how it was solved.
- People may be asked to imagine solving it in some incredibly creative way.
- Afterwards, everyone reports on their imagined solutions and the group transitions into problem solving.

Each of these methods has advantages and disadvantages. Impromptu brainstorming is spontaneous but has the disadvantage that a few vocal individuals in the group can dominate the conversation while others remain silent. Round robin, on the other hand, involves everyone but takes longer to complete. Secret ballots are useful when there is a high degree of distrust, but allow people to take cheap shots and not own their criticisms or ideas. Subconscious suggestion is extremely creative, but can strike some people as a diversion or too "touchy-feely" for practical problem solving. The same is true for guided meditation.

The object of these methods is to help you identify creative alternatives. After doing so, the following questions may help you identify creative solutions that lie somewhere between the ones you want and those your opponent wants:

- What creative options could you use to resolve your conflict that you have not fully imagined? (List everything you can think of as quickly as possible, without considering whether you think your ideas are realistic or acceptable to your opponent.)
- What are the top three among these options?
- What are three silly, outrageous, completely ridiculous, or impossible options? How might they be reframed to apply to your problem?
- How is the problem like an object you see in front of you? What options can you derive from this list?
- What words would you use to describe the problem? What are the opposites of these words, and could they lead you to solutions?

- What ideas might your opponent suggest for resolving your dispute that you have not considered?
- What do you think would happen if you searched for solutions together?
- Close your eyes and imagine coming up with the perfect solution. What was it? How might it be possible to do something like that with your opponent?

You can imagine many more potential solutions by initially disengaging from whether the solution is practical, or will ultimately succeed, or will be acceptable to the other side. There will always be time to analyze your choices and communicate them. We suggest you use these questions to consider all the options you possibly can before editing, analyzing, or proposing them to your opponent. If you and your opponent are able to meet together and *jointly* generate options, you may increase your respect for one another and find more solutions to your conflict.

Separate Criteria from Selection

Another way to resolve difficult disputes is to agree on criteria for successful outcomes *before* selecting or deciding on a solution, making it easier to judge whether a solution will be effective. The criteria may consist of the elements that would make up a perfect solution, or what it would take to satisfy everyone's interests, or what is required to achieve your common goals, or what approach would provide the greatest benefit to important third parties.

Many conflicts are not resolved because we are unable to agree on criteria or standards to use in prioritizing or selecting between multiple options. Some of the criteria we find most useful in resolving disputes include

- Equality of treatment or outcomes
- Agreed-on ethical standards or principles, such as fairness
- Jointly seeking the advice of an expert or professional
- A ranking or weighting of different priorities according to some agreed-on system
- The least costly alternative
- The least time-consuming alternative
- Bartering or exchanging one thing for another

- What the likely legal outcome would be
- Tradition or precedent
- What it would cost to buy or replace the current item
- An algorithm or agreed-on mathematical formula
- Chance (for example, a coin toss)
- Whoever has the greatest emotional commitment or investment in the outcome
- Letting each side take turns picking a solution based on subjective preferences
- Likely effect on third parties, such as customers, society, or children
- Impact on shared values, such as communication or teamwork
- Likely future effect, for example, on a strategic plan, vision, or mission

Conflicts can often be quickly unlocked by asking both sides to agree on what criteria they would like to use to decide which outcome is best. Fisher and Ury in *Getting to Yes* refer to "objective" criteria, but we believe there are a number of highly useful, mutually acceptable criteria that are entirely subjective, or even based on chance, such as flipping a coin.

Try answering the following questions to identify the criteria that you and your opponent can use to pick the best solution in your conflict:

- What are all the possible criteria you can use to select the best option for resolving your dispute?
- What would make any solution seem fair?
- How might you accomplish what you both want?
- How have other people solved the problem?
- What expert opinion might be useful?
- What would happen if you went to court? Why?
- What ethical or value considerations might influence your choice?
- Why do you think any particular criterion will not work? Do these reasons suggest a way of modifying the criterion so it will work?

- What would make you both feel that you won?
- What would yield the best results in terms of your future communications and relationship?
- What would provide the greatest benefit to your colleagues, customers, and the public?
- What insights about your conflict have you gained by making this distinction?

If you and your opponent can agree on criteria for selecting a fair solution, you will create a mutually acceptable framework for shaping the resolution process and increase trust between you, even if the end result is not exactly what either of you wants. As you generate options and test them against criteria, you will shift your communications from being about what is wrong, to being about what approach you can use to best resolve your conflict and improve your relationship.

Separate Yourself from Others

All conflicts generate identity confusions and boundary violations. We are confused, for example, by the difference between who we are when we are with someone we like and who we are when we are with our opponent. We are confused by the uncertain boundary between what we think and feel and what our opponent thinks and feels, between our anger and our compassion, between what the other person does that touches us and what we absolutely cannot fathom or accept, between our values and our conflict behaviors.

The adversarial emotional exchanges that take place during conflict paradoxically end up blurring the lines that separate us from our opponent, causing us to lose sight of who we actually are, what is rightfully ours, and what belongs to our opponent or to both of us. We lose track of what we know is right, and are confused by what our negative emotions tempt us to do or say instead.

Simply by arguing only for our own solutions, we may communicate that we are trying to control our opponent, or telling him what we believe he ought to think, feel, or do. And when he argues back, we may feel he is trying to do the same to us. Thus, it is crucial in seeking to resolve our conflicts that we recognize who we are and what legitimately *belongs* to us, and who our opponent is and what belongs to him.

Here are some questions and statements that can help create a clearer separation between you and your opponent. They are phrased in terms that demonstrate your willingness to accept responsibility for your role in the conflict, and can be phrased to achieve the same result with your opponent:

- "What did I do that you are upset about?" "How could I fix that in a way that would satisfy you?"
- "Here is what I understand you are asking for: [specific statement]. Is that correct?"
- "What do you think I'm asking for?" "Would you like to know?"
- "Here's where I believe you're right, and here's where I think we may disagree." [Insert specific statements for each.]
- "Instead of using the word 'you,' would it be possible to make the same statement using the word 'I'?"
- "What do you see as the main differences between us?"
- "What do you see as our main similarities?"
- "Are there any values you think we share?"
- "What role would you like me to play in this conversation?"
- "I can hear that you feel I am [insert specific statement, such as being controlling]. Would you like to know what I'm really worried about or afraid of?"
- "Thank you for your ideas. I appreciate your concerns and hearing your point of view. Would it be okay if I think about what you said and let you know my responses tomorrow?"

If you want to model the highest level of clarity regarding the separation between yourself and others, it is important to be clear within yourself and in communicating with your opponent, regarding who you are, what you want, and why. It will be most effective if you first ask who they are, what *they* want, and why, then respond for yourself.

All of your communications need to be presented authentically and naturally. If they seem staged, your opponent may feel manipulated, insulted, or further betrayed. State your ideas directly and listen in the same spirit. Avoid making assumptions about what your opponent wants or thinks or feels. If these efforts fail, you can communicate more directly about your confusion regarding the boundary between you, perhaps by saying "I am getting confused here about how we are describing the problem, or what we each really want, or what our respective roles and responsibilities are—can you help me clarify that?"

Before getting to that point, consider asking yourself or your opponent the following questions to discover what you may need to do or say to separate yourself from others in the conflict:

- Do you feel there has been a boundary violation in the conflict? In what way? How did it happen?
- Have you done anything to encourage or give permission for this kind of boundary violation? If so, what and why?
- Have there been similar boundary violations in your past? If so, are they related to what is happening in your conflict now? How did you handle them then? How could you handle them better now?
- What might help define the boundaries, definitions, and distinctions between yourself and others in your conflict?
- What could you do or say directly to your opponent to more clearly define the boundaries between you?
- Are there confused roles and responsibilities between you? How could these be clarified?
- Is it possible that your opponent feels you have violated his or her boundaries? How could you find out?
- If you have, would you be willing to stop? Would you be willing to apologize?
- What might change in your conflict if you and your opponent were able to clarify your boundaries?

Asking these questions demonstrates that you are willing to take responsibility for your role in the conflict. It suggests that you are not interested in playing the victim, and that you are able to separate yourself from your opponent. Separating yourself from others finally means accepting the idea that you stand alone *together* in every conflict, making both of you capable of forming positive connections with each other. If this is not possible for you, it may be necessary to consider the methods suggested in later chapters, and to back away, move on, and adopt a more distant relationship.

Sometimes it is necessary to completely stop the conversation and say something like, "I'm sorry for interrupting, but I find it very difficult to listen when you make negative judgments about me. I am finding myself becoming defensive and angry right now, and don't want to be that way. I want to be able to hear what you have to say and would appreciate it if you could focus on the problem, or what I did, rather than on who you think I am. If you can't do that, I suggest we find a neutral person to help us continue this conversation."

As you become more skillful in separating who they are from what they are doing, you will cease feeling hostile and adversarial and become more balanced and authentic, both in your relationship with them and internally within yourself. As your stance and attitude shift from being a hostile adversary to being a curious listener and creative problem solver, you will also automatically shift from a *mode of being* that is preparatory and poised for impasse to one that is participatory and poised for resolution. Whatever actions you ultimately take will be based on what is really important to you in your conflict and who you authentically are in your life.

We all form alliances with others through love, acceptance, and affirmation, or through pain, rejection, and negativity. When we are in conflict, the fear of separating from others, of failing, of being less when the conflict is over, of being judged for what we have said or done, can become overwhelming and block us from reaching resolution. When we separate what matters from what gets in the way, we clarify our disagreements and become able to take committed, collaborative action to de-escalate and end them.

Every conflict *already* contains the seeds of its own resolution, and we are better able to find these seeds by separating what matters from what gets in the way. The secret is to center ourselves in what really matters, to unlock what gets in the way, and to discover the hidden opportunities that lie hidden in the places where we get stuck. We can do so only by listening for the profound, poignant, vulnerable moments in our conflict conversations, deciphering their cryptic signals, and unveiling their deepest meaning.

STRATEGY 6

SOLVE PROBLEMS PARADOXICALLY AND CREATIVELY

Getting hold of the difficulty "down deep" is what is hard. Because, if it is grasped near the surface, it simply remains the difficulty it was. It has to be pulled out by the roots; and that involves our beginning to think about these things in a new way. The change is as decisive as, for example, that from the alchemical to the chemical way of thinking. The new way of thinking is what is so hard to establish. Once the new way has been established, the old problems vanish; indeed, they become hard to recapture.

—Ludwig Wittgenstein

The first stage in resolving conflicts consists of opening them up, encouraging them to unfold, and seeing what lies hidden within. These are encompassed in the first set of five strategies. Once we have listened deeply to our opponent and discovered the hidden nature of our conflicts, the second stage, consisting of five strategies, begins with searching for creative solutions to the paradoxical problems we have uncovered; learning from difficult behaviors; leading toward resolution and transformation; exploring resistance, collaboratively negotiating and mediating solutions; and designing systems, structures, processes, relationships and cultures that can prevent chronic conflicts and enable us to transcend them.

Each of us has our own unique way of solving problems. For the most part, our approach is automatic and unconscious, and we rarely consider the possibility that a dramatic new way of thinking, such as the one described by Wittgenstein, might completely transform our problems. Yet by understanding the culture and dynamics of conflict, listening empathetically and responsively, searching beneath the surface for hidden issues, acknowledging and reframing emotions, and separating what matters from what gets in the way, we can significantly increase our ability to recognize and identify problems, allowing us to search in earnest for creative solutions.

Problem solving is a watershed point in every conflict, where the process shifts from expansion to contraction, from emotion to logic, and from large-scale exploration to practical implementation. It is the place where analysis yields to implementation, where leadership is required, and where the deeper meaning of our conflict turns to extremely practical questions, such as who is going to do what by when.

When we feel stuck in conflict, or that we have not been listened to or acknowledged, or that its deeper meaning has not been understood, our problem-solving efforts will seem premature and ineffective. This is partly due to a natural tendency to see our opponent as the problem and what *we* want as the only possible solution. As a result, our problem-solving efforts and ideas will nearly always be one-sided, superficial, self-centered, and adversarial, particularly in the eyes of our opponents.

If our goals are to resolve our conflicts without forcing our opponents to surrender, to engage in constructive dialogue over common problems, and to reach consensus on practical solutions, at some point it will be necessary to surrender our efforts to communicate what happened and to cease searching for emotional acknowledgment for the wrongs done to us.

What caused the conflict is now over, past, and done with. The only remaining question is whether we are willing to let it go in order to solve the problems that led to and resulted from it so as to move on with our lives; or whether we would rather that the conflict continue, if only to cause *others* pain, even though it undermines *our* future. It is necessary then to choose between being right and solving the problem.

To begin ending our conflicts, we have to shift gears and be able to calculate logically and practically what we actually need and can realistically achieve. This means ending the period of emotional processing and initiating the period of creative problem solving. It means releasing ourselves from rage, recrimination, and revenge, and substituting redress, restitution, and reconciliation, which permit us to transcend our conflicts and design alternative futures.

Conceptual Preparation for Creative Problem Solving

There are three important conceptual or attitudinal shifts in initiating creative problem solving. First, we need to put aside the assumption that ours is the only solution, let go of the need to punish our opponent, and realize that the conflict does not have to end in a win-lose outcome. This will create a positive attitude on both sides toward problem solving and will open possibilities for resolution through imagination and creativity.

Second, we need to recognize that problem solving works best when it is collaborative, open, and inclusive of everyone who is affected by the problem. Problem solving should not be a lonely, isolated process. Inviting others to join us enriches the pool of potential solutions with ideas that no single person could possibly envision.

Third, we need to accept that there is more than one truth in our conflicts, making both our problems and their solutions paradoxical. If we view our problems as complex and multifaceted, and approach them with a learning orientation, we will discover that the paradoxes, enigmas, riddles, and contradictions that can be found at their core will lead us to more creative, successful, multidimensional solutions.

This shift in thinking is perhaps the most powerful of all. Albert Einstein and his collaborator, Leopold Infeld, offer an approach to how we view intractable problems and solve them, which focuses on the way we formulate or describe them:

> The formulation of a problem is often more essential than its solution, which may be merely a matter of mathematical or experimental skill. To raise new questions, new possibilities, or to regard old questions from a new angle, requires creative imagination and marks REAL advances.

This conceptual and attitudinal shift leads to far more effective, creative problem solving and openings to transformation in the way we see our problems, our opponents, our organizations, and ourselves. As you begin the practical work of problem solving, reflect on what you might do to shift your attitude and reflexive problem-solving responses and see them from a new angle. For example, consider the following fundamental shifts in how we approach problem solving in conflict.

Shift One: Adopt a Positive Attitude Toward Problem Solving

A dramatic transformation occurred in the attitude of a college president who was widely respected for her strong leadership skills, but due to severe budget cuts, became embroiled in a number of bitter conflicts with faculty and staff. After being subjected to several angry, vitriolic public attacks, she was torn between responding in kind or simply giving up and leaving.

In the midst of this crisis, an accrediting association conducted an audit and found that if the parties to this conflict could not create a shared governance program and work together more collaboratively, the college's educational credentials would be in jeopardy.

The president chose to take this warning as an opportunity to shift her attitude from defensiveness and counterattack to creative problem solving with the representatives of opposing factions. She convened a working group that included all the warring parties, agreed to meet with them over several months to design a governance structure, and promised to support their recommendations before the board of trustees.

Once the working group began meeting, she was careful not to slip back into hostile or hierarchical attitudes but participated fully in their sessions, calmly and openly debated issues, humbly offered suggestions, and actively encouraged her opponents to participate and make recommendations. As the process evolved and solutions emerged, previously hostile participants shifted their attitudes from suspicion and resistance to optimism and support.

By reorienting her attitude, the president sent a positive message regarding her intentions and became a role model for others. As a result, a collegewide planning council was created to plan programs, make decisions, and encourage collaboration and problem solving among all constituency groups.

If you simply approach problem solving with a positive attitude and can regard your conflicts as opportunities, adventures, and challenges, you will avoid taking your problems too personally or seriously and be far more successful in solving them. Perhaps the greatest obstacle to adopting a positive approach is the persistence of negative emotions and adversarial attitudes directed at your opponent. If you can create a conversation with your opponent that is *only* about the problem, and no longer about negative emotions or past behaviors, you will discover improved solutions and feel better about yourself as well.

Your attitude is *always* a critical element in solving problems, and there are a number of personal attitudes that will help you become a better, more creative and successful problem solver. Indeed, these attitudes are *themselves* solutions and represent the highest form of success, because once you genuinely adopt them, they will generate more successes as you encounter fresh obstacles. As you review this list of attitudes, consider those you would like to apply or practice in your conflicts.

- *Excitement* about the existence and complexity of the problem
- *Appreciation* and *enjoyment* of paradox and contradiction
- *Empathy* or *compassion* for the person you see as the source of the problem
- *Openness* to all possible solutions
- *Optimism* about the chances for success
- *Balance* and *flexibility* in approaching the problem
- *Curiosity* about what caused the problem and your opponent as a person
- *Humility* regarding your own role in creating or sustaining it

- *Courage* and *audacity* in addressing difficult or dangerous issues
- *Relaxation* in the presence of impasse
- *Subtle awareness* regarding the problem that allows subconscious ideas to arise
- *Playfulness* and *intuition* to encourage creative thinking
- *Surrender* to other people's interests, and to the possibility of resolution

Each time you confront a problem you have a choice about how to respond, and the attitude you adopt will play a significant role in either escalating and reinforcing or solving and transforming the problem. As you search for solutions, think how you might express and encourage the attitudes you would like to emanate from your opponent.

Take a moment for introspection and ask yourself: When you face difficult problems, are you curious, relaxed, and playful—or defensive, stubborn, and argumentative? What could you do to encourage more positive attitudes toward problem solving, both in yourself and in your opponent? What might your organization do to promote these attitudes?

Shift Two: Approach Problem Solving as a Collaborative Process

A large corporation that was making the transition from a hierarchical, command-and-control bureaucracy to democratic, self-managing work teams offered a vivid example of collaboration and creative problem solving. One of the key teams was failing, responsibilities were falling through the cracks, morale was extremely low, and there was no effective team leader. Team members were blaming each other and escalating their problems, and the entire process had come to an impasse.

The head of the organization wanted immediate action, and forgetting the lessons he had learned about empowering others, called the team manager into his office and read him the riot act, including a veiled threat that if *he* did not solve the problem, his job was in jeopardy. This conversation took place at such a pitch that people down the hall could hear every angry word.

As a result, the team manager used the same inappropriate aggressive hierarchical managerial style with the team, barking out a series of orders about how to implement his solution to the problem. As a result, everyone felt even more frustrated, disempowered, and upset, causing their performance and problems to grow even worse.

After the teams complained bitterly about what happened, we met with the manager and head of the organization and suggested that they try to solve the problem using a team approach. We suggested they meet personally with the team, acknowledge and apologize for their mistakes, and work with them to collaboratively assess the problem, determine what went wrong, and find ways to fix it.

They took our advice, apologized to the team for trying to impose solutions, and asked team members to facilitate a collaborative analysis of the problem. They worked together for several days to understand the deeper roots of the problem and were able to reach consensus on a solution everyone could accept and implement. The active participation of team members allowed new ways of understanding and solving the problem to emerge. Mostly, however, it was their shift to a more constructive and collaborative attitude to problem solving that allowed them to discover better solutions.

In many organizations, fixed hierarchies and bureaucratic separations obstruct creative problem solving. If you were ordered to solve a problem that you did not participate in defining, or handed a solution you did not assist in creating, you would most likely react with resentment, apathy, cynicism, resistance, or rebellion. But if you participated actively in defining the problem, searched collaboratively for solutions, and agreed on a unified approach to implementation, you would be more likely to respond with enthusiasm and eliminate a significant source of impasse.

In most hierarchical organizational cultures, there is an unspoken understanding that the role of managers is to solve problems, leading to solutions that are unilateral, hierarchical, and bureaucratic, in ways that conform with existing rules and regulations. It is often assumed that any manager who cannot do so without help from below is incompetent. But the role of *leaders* is *not* to solve problems, but to increase the ability of employees to solve them collaboratively, with a minimum of managerial intervention and advice.

While hierarchical organizational cultures foster isolated, individual, and competitive problem solving, as Warren Bennis and Patricia Ward Biederman astutely observe in *Organizing Genius: The Secrets of Creative Collaboration,* the problems we are now required to solve, particularly as a result of globalization, international economic crises, and worldwide environmental changes, are increasingly complex and paradoxical, and require collaborative, integrative, multifaceted solutions:

> In a society as complex and technologically sophisticated as ours, the most urgent projects require the coordinated contributions of many talented people. Whether the task is building a global business or discovering the mysteries of the human brain, one person can't hope to accomplish it, however gifted or energetic he or she may be.... [T]here are simply too many problems to be identified and solved, too many connections to be made.... [I]n a global society, in which timely information is the most important commodity, collaboration is not simply desirable, it is inevitable. In all but the rarest cases, one is too small a number to produce greatness.

Shift Three: Solve the Problem of How to Solve Problems

After choosing to address our problems creatively and collaboratively, the next step is for us to focus on the *way* we are going to solve them. There are many approaches we can take to solving problems, but it rarely helps to approach them with the attitude that they are adversaries or enemies that need to be defeated or controlled, rather than as opportunities for learning and improvement that lead us to exciting journeys and adventures.

When we solve problems, we generally do so automatically, rarely stopping to consider our assumptions about how we ought to solve them, or how we could improve the way we go about solving them. In a report by Michael Maccoby in *Harvard Business Review* on the success of Japanese management techniques, it is clear that we can approach our problems more creatively if we think of them as opportunities for improvement:

> When I visited the Toyota assembly plant at Nagoya [Japan] I was told that there were an average of 47 ideas per worker per year of which 80 percent were adopted. I couldn't believe it; this meant almost an idea from each worker every week. The Toyota manager said, "I think you in the West have a different view of ideas. What you call complaints, we call ideas. You try to get people to stop complaining. We see each complaint as an opportunity for improvement."

Shifting our attitude toward solving problems and redefining complaints as opportunities for improvement can produce enormous transformations. If we redefine our problems as challenges, adventures, and ways of deepening and improving relationships; if we see them as sources of learning, growth, self-actualization, pride, and creativity, many new successful solutions will open up. We can begin by realizing that every complaint and problem is simply the negative expression of a dissatisfaction that can easily be turned in a positive, constructive direction by asking, "What should we do to solve this problem?" Or even better, "What can we learn from it?" and "How could we tackle it together?"

The traditional approach to problem solving used in most organizations is very different. It begins with a *control-oriented* methodology that leaves everyone other than ourselves out of the process. Instead, it uses power, hierarchy, and bureaucracy to control the process and limit potential outcomes; it forces or imposes solutions *on* problems; it drives people to solve problems before they are ready to be solved; and it views problems as enemies to be eliminated or defeated. This approach is widely used in hierarchical, bureaucratic, and autocratic organizations, producing results that often create more problems than there were before.

An alternative approach is to adopt a *learning-oriented* methodology that includes everyone who is impacted by the problem in the problem-solving process, including those who oppose our solutions. This approach elicits interests and shares control over process and outcomes; it listens to the problem and allows solutions to emerge without forcing them; it is able to wait until problems are ripe and ready to be solved; and it views problems as allies, partners, teachers, and opportunities, producing results that are more nuanced and multifaceted, and allowing people to learn from their problems.

Table 6.1 describes these two fundamentally different approaches to problem solving. Take a closer look at the consequences of each and pick the one you think will produce the most satisfying long-term results for your organization.

It is extremely difficult to overcome our natural desire to control outcomes and rush to solve our problems, yet we discover much more by living with them, learning from them, and trying to solve them only afterward. If we can take a moment to view our problems in all their complexity and understand their underlying paradoxes, contradictions, and polarities, we will immediately recognize that they

Table 6.1. Orientation to Problem Solving.

	Control Orientation	Learning Orientation
Goals	To assert sufficient control to ensure that problems as you define them are solved in ways you see fit	To maximize my opportunity to create alternatives and test whether they work or not
Assumptions	Other people can't be influenced	Other people can be influenced
	Problems can't be solved unless they are solved "my way"	I can be influence Constraints can be altered
Strategies	Unilaterally impose your solutions and act as though you are not doing so	Identify shared responsibility for problem definitions and for solutions
	Do not request feedback about your own ideas	Encourage others to react to your plans, and do the same for others
	Shoot down others and don't share reasons why	Experiment off-line with alternatives
	Reflect privately on results	Discuss results publicly
Consequences	Low team commitment and responsibility	Increased team participation
	Public "group think"	Higher team commitment and responsibility
	Private politicking and subterfuge	Increased willingness to raise problems
	Polarized group dynamics	More resources to tackle them
	High risk to raise difficult problems	More creativity and better solutions

Source: Adapted from Diana Smith's "Working Paper."

cannot be successfully resolved through simple solutions, or dealt with as "things" that need to be changed or conquered.

Rather, when our problems are understood as natural phenomena that we can explore, learn from, and accept for what they are, we discover ways of solving them more elegantly, subtly, creatively, and sustainably, and begin to learn the profound lessons they occurred in order to teach us.

Paradoxical Problem Solving

Every day in our personal and professional lives we encounter a seemingly endless stream of problems. There are problems so petty we hardly take notice of them, problems so huge we can't begin to comprehend them, and problems that take us to the very edge of our skills, wake us up, and transform our thinking. In fact, all of work can be seen not just as the creation of products and services, but the solving of an endless succession of higher- and lower-order problems.

Paradoxical problem solving consists of recognizing the multiple, typically conflicting truths that shape and inform our problems. Paradoxical problems challenge us to deploy higher-level skills and intelligence, to discern multiple truths and discover fresh ideas in the complex, contradictory nature of our problems. They invite us to create something brand new that did not exist before, and to turn dilemmas that presented themselves as problems into evolutionary imperatives and opportunities to reveal new paradigms.

Awareness, learning, growth, and change are common by-products of constructively recognizing, exploring, wrestling with, and resolving paradoxical problems. The most challenging aspect of paradoxical problem solving is not finding solutions, but maximizing the opportunity to learn from and transcend them.

A first principle in this approach is to recognize, along with the German philosopher Hegel, that people have a *right* to their problems. By stepping in and solving them too quickly in simple ways, we may cheat them out of owning important parts of their lives, learning from their experiences, and discovering that they are fully capable of finding solutions themselves.

Many of us are irresistibly drawn to solve other people's problems, and it may be useful to examine the source of our motivation to see if we are doing so because it makes us feel powerful and helpful, or because it is easier to solve their problems than our own, or because we are addicted to solving them, or because problem solving is much simpler when we do not have to live with the consequences. If we immediately jump in to solve every problem, it will be helpful to consider why we find it so difficult to live with the problem for a while in order to learn from it.

Here are five sets of questions, drawn from our book *The Art of Waking People Up: Cultivating Awareness and Authenticity at Work,* that you can consider in assessing your own motivation. These questions can help you identify possible sources of compulsion or addiction to solving problems, and think a bit more carefully about the approach you would like to use in resolving your conflicts:

1. You have learned countless ways of solving problems. How well have you learned *not* to solve them? How willing are you to live with paradox, riddle, polarity, and enigma? Do you understand that by solving your problems too quickly, you could cheat yourself out of learning from them?
2. You have solved thousands of problems and learned a great deal in your life. How open are you to discovering that what you have learned is irrelevant or wrong? How do you stay in touch with your ignorance? How good are you at *un*learning? How able are you to live in the present without being caught up in past problems or future solutions?
3. You know how to make things happen. Do you know how to let them happen naturally and fluidly on their own? Do you know how to not intervene? Can you let things happen to you, or simply watch them as they happen? Are you addicted to controlling the outcome or the process?
4. You understand a great deal about what is. Do you also understand what is not, and what could be? Do you see not only what, but who is in front of you? Do you understand that what you understand includes the nature of your own understanding?
5. You have developed a number of strengths and achieved successes. Do you recognize that for every strength there is a corresponding weakness? Do you understand that continued success leads to complacency, while failure leads to learning and change? Are you certain about what is success and what is failure?

In today's workplace, problems are increasingly complex and paradoxical, yet the ways of solving them remain simple and one-sided. By not oversimplifying the natural complexity of our problems but mining them for information about novel ways of improving the quality of solutions, we can turn problems into sources of learning, growth, and evolutionary transformation.

Paradox means living simultaneously with apparently contradictory realities, which is critical for people working in complex, team-based environments and for learning organizations. Paradoxical problem solving can make our workplaces more humane, user-friendly, collaborative, and effective.

For example, one of our most unusual assignments was to facilitate an intensive three-day planning process for a world-renowned science museum that wanted to create a national teacher-education center. The assignment was unusual because the museum's CEO did not want us to create a linear final plan as the outcome. Rather, he asked that the process capture and preserve all the paradoxes, dissimilarities, conflicts, and the variety of contradictory ideas that were generated by a diverse collection of staff, science teachers, and international representatives of the scientific, political, and educational communities who attended the session, and encourage them to critique their own ideas.

The planning process produced three completely different prototypes that the staff decided to live with, discuss, and review only after six months. They wanted to use these models as sources for a final design, but *not* to combine them into a single, ultimate plan. Instead, they wanted to leave the plan open to allow the teacher-education center to evolve organically, learn from trying different approaches, and not rush things, but allow them to change at their own pace. The paradox of moving in several entirely different directions at once created a much more powerful, successful, exciting, and admired program than would have been possible by agreeing on a single fixed design determined through a linear process.

Paradoxes, riddles, contradictions, enigmas, and polarities are an integral part of nature, and essential to creative thinking. It is impossible, for example, to "resolve" the conflict between up and down, light and dark, plus and minus, hot and cold, or inner and outer, without at the same time abolishing both. The same can be said of life and death, pleasure and pain, good and evil, right and wrong, truth and falsehood, conflict and resolution. It is impossible to eliminate one without simultaneously eliminating the other. The Italian novelist Umberto Eco described this idea in an interesting observation about the evolution of his own thinking regarding paradoxes and enigmas:

> In those halcyon days I believed that the source of enigma was stupidity. Then . . . I decided that the most terrible enigmas are those that mask themselves as madness. But now I have come to believe that the whole world is an enigma, a harmless enigma that is made terrible by our own mad attempt to interpret it as though it had [a single] underlying truth.

Our greatest teachers in learning to live with paradoxes, riddles, contradictions, enigmas, and polarities are the conflicts and problems that we encounter in our everyday lives. It is precisely in the most aggravating conflicts and intractable problems that we find our greatest challenge in life, which is to live life fully and at the same time be aware of the certainty that it can end at any moment. The most paradoxical problem we face is accepting death as a natural part of life while not surrendering to it, choosing to live fully every moment with the certain knowledge that it could end at any time.

Paradoxical solutions are always at least two-sided and contradictory. The adoption of paradoxical problem solving therefore requires a series of profound, far-reaching paradigm shifts in how we think about our problems and the ways we respond to them. Consider, for example, the following shifts and note the ones you want to apply to your own conflicts and problems:

- A shift from eliminating problems to discovering them
- A shift from avoiding and attacking problems to inviting and including them
- A shift from solving problems to learning from them
- A shift from blaming, cynicism, reactivity, and passivity, to responsibility, optimism, proactivity, and prevention
- A shift from adversarial to collaborative problem-solving processes
- A shift from single, uniform solutions to multiple, diverse options
- A shift from forcing or imposing solutions to eliciting or inviting them
- A shift from knowing the right answers to asking the right questions
- A shift from disempowerment and infantilization to ownership and responsibility

- A shift from hierarchical solutions to heterarchical ones, from bureaucratic processes to innovation and teamwork, and from autocratically imposing solutions to democratically selecting them
- A shift from managing to leading and from directing to coaching
- A shift from following models to creating pilot projects
- A shift from conforming to past practices to experimenting and innovating
- A shift from rule-driven values to value-driven rules

By accepting problems, learning from them, wrestling with them, and at the same time not rushing to solve them prematurely, we discover the deeper paradoxes they express. As we become aware of these paradoxes and do not try to reduce them to single solutions, we become more open to learning and allow the interplay of diverse contradictory realities to inform our problem solving. Doing so enriches our lives immeasurably, allowing us to learn from and transcend our deepest problems.

In another paradigm shift, Douglas McGregor's classic book, *The Human Side of Enterprise,* distinguishes two opposing theories of human behavior, each expressing a fundamentally different attitude toward problems in the workplace. In McGregor's "Theory X and Theory Y" we find a shorthand approach to thinking about organizational conflicts and the idea of creative and paradoxical problem solving:

Douglas McGregor's Theory X and Theory Y

	Traditional (Theory X)	Potential (Theory Y)
1.	People are naturally lazy; they prefer to do nothing.	People are naturally active; they set goals and enjoy striving.
2.	People work mostly for money and status rewards.	People seek many satisfactions in work: pride in achievement; enjoyment of process; sense of contribution; pleasure in association; stimulation of new challenges, etc.

(continued)

	Traditional (Theory X)	Potential (Theory Y)
3.	The main force keeping people productive in their work is fear of being demoted or fired.	The main force keeping people productive in their work is desire to achieve their personal and social goals.
4.	People remain children grown larger; they are naturally dependent on leaders.	People normally mature beyond childhood; they aspire to independence, self fulfillment, and responsibility.
5.	People expect and depend on direction from above; they do not want to think for themselves.	People close to the situation see and feel what is needed and are capable of self-direction.
6.	People need to be told, shown, and trained in proper methods of work.	People who understand and care about what they are doing can devise and improve their own methods of doing work.
7.	People need supervisors who will watch them closely enough to be able to praise good work and reprimand errors.	People need a sense that they are respected as capable of assuming responsibility and self-correction.
8.	People have little concern beyond their immediate, material interests.	People seek to give meaning to their lives by identifying with nations, communities, churches, unions, companies, causes.
9.	People need specific instruction on what to do and how to do it; larger policy issues are none of their business.	People need ever-increasing understanding; they need to grasp the meaning of the activities in which they are engaged.
10.	People appreciate being treated with courtesy.	People crave genuine respect from their fellow men.

McGregor's distinctions challenge us to approach the problem of problem solving with an open mind, and to shift our attitude in a more open, collaborative, and democratic direction. Even if we reject a control orientation and adopt a learning orientation and are able to see our problems as rich, complex, and paradoxical, there remain additional obstacles to successful problem solving in most organizations.

Obstacles to Creative Problem Solving

Many people who face problems in organizations ask: "If it ain't broke, why fix it?" It often seems easier and less confusing to ignore what is troubling and hope it goes away. Sometimes it does. But sometimes the conflict or problem grows worse because we have not been willing to fix it. Here are some reasons why, even if it "ain't broke," we should still try to fix it:

1. It may actually be broken and you haven't noticed.
2. The competition is busy trying to fix it.
3. When you stop trying to fix it, you stop caring about it.
4. It's not about being broken, it's about improving it.
5. Unless you try to fix it, you will grow accustomed to it not working, and new ways of fixing it will escape your attention.
6. Who cares whether it's broken, it's challenging and fun to try to fix it.

Once we reach agreement that our conflict or problem needs fixing, a number of obstacles to problem solving remain that are common in many organizations. The following list of additional obstacles is based partly on research by Bolman and Deal, in their book *Reframing Organizations:*

- *We are not sure what the problem is.* Our definition of the problem may be vague or competing, and many problems may be intertwined.
- *We are not sure what is really happening.* Information may be incomplete, ambiguous, or unreliable, or people may disagree as to how to interpret the information that is available.
- *We are not sure what we want.* We may have multiple goals that are unclear or conflicting or both. Different people may want different things but do not openly discuss them, creating political, value-based, and emotional conflicts.

- *We do not have the resources we need.* Shortages of time, attention, money, and support may make difficult situations even more chaotic.
- *We are not sure who is supposed to do what.* Roles may be unclear, there may be disagreement about who is responsible for what, or roles may keep shifting as problems come and go.
- *We are not sure how to get what we want.* Even if we agree on what we want, we may be unsure or in conflict over how to get it.
- *We are not sure how to communicate what we want.* We may hesitate to communicate what we want for fear of offending others, or not know how to reach them successfully.
- *We do not know what is possible.* We may not have explored all the options or disagree about which alternative to focus on first.
- *We are not sure how to know if we succeeded.* We may be unsure what criteria to use to evaluate success. If we know the criteria, we may be unsure how to measure them.
- *We are not sure what we did that was responsible for our success.* Once we succeed, we may be unsure whether our efforts were responsible and, if so, which ones.

Each of these obstacles can be successfully overcome and learned from. You can ask your opponent to identify the problems she thinks are most important and brainstorm solutions before arriving at a decision. You can observe the problem over a period of time and see how it changes. You can identify the key elements in the organizational culture that block understanding the problem and collaboratively solving it. You can broaden your definition of the problem or analyze what worked, what didn't, and why.

For example, the CEO of a small, successful consulting firm was angry because the leadership team had failed to generate adequate sales and produce enough revenue to keep the company going. In his view, the problem was that they were not doing their work and not committed to finding clients or selling business. As a result, his solution was to yell at them and tell them they had to bring in more business or else they were out.

The leadership team, on the other hand, defined the problem as the CEO's hostile, blaming, micromanaging behavior, and the fact that he was not supportive of their efforts. Everyone involved had a simplistic view of the conflict and therefore chose the wrong problem to solve. Rather than learning from the problem, finding out how to work better as a team, and achieving common goals, they blamed each other, believed that only their solution would work, and tried to control the problem-solving process.

We suggested they stop, back up, and reconsider the process they were using to define and solve the problem. They divided into teams and brainstormed answers to the following questions:

- In what areas have we been successful in generating revenue and selling business?
- In what areas have we failed?
- What do we need to do to be more successful?
- What is standing in the way?
- How do we get around it?
- How can we target and coordinate efforts to make our work more successful?
- What role can each of us play in this process?
- What are we each willing to contribute to increasing our business?

As they answered these questions, their entire attitude changed and there was a burst of commitment and creativity in developing strategies to solve the problem. They agreed on a new set of programs, incentives, and sales initiatives, and each member of the leadership team identified a number of personal contributions they would make to eliminating obstacles and improving business.

The team also created strategies for working more cooperatively and supporting one another. They delineated a time line, targeted potential clients and results, and affirmed their commitment to producing more revenue. The CEO agreed to stop yelling, blaming, and micromanaging. These solutions were owned by everyone and they were able to market the company in a more positive way, so that by the end of the year everyone's sales and bonuses had increased.

Five Steps in Creative Problem Solving

How can you implement these ideas and approaches and adopt a learning orientation to solve your problems? How exactly do you come up with creative ideas? In the middle of a conflict, how do you invent options and alternatives that can satisfy both sides' interests and open up possibilities of resolution and transformation?

One definition of conflict is simply "being stuck" in a problem and unable to figure out how to solve it, or trying various solutions, none of which has yet succeeded. To improve your problem-solving process, you may want to break it down into discrete steps, each consisting of a series of substeps.

Step One: Admit You Have a Problem, Recognize It as a Problem, and Accept It as Needing to Be Solved

- Step one means overcoming denial, recognizing that the problem is having an impact on you, accepting responsible for solving it, and seeing that you can do something about it.
- Instead of saying your opponent is "the one who has the problem," recognize that any time you are in a relationship and the other party has a problem, you have one too.
- Clarify what is delaying or preventing you from solving the problem and what the continuation or cessation of the problem might mean.
- Specify all the short- and long-term costs of *not* solving the problem—to you, your opponent, your coworkers, and your organization.
- Choose to commit whatever time and energy may be necessary to solve the problem.
- Ask your opponent if she agrees there is a problem and is willing to discuss and work on it.

Step Two: Collaboratively Define and Clarify the Elements and Nature of the Problem

- The second step means working together as a team to define and clarify the problem so that you can better understand how to approach it strategically.
- Before meeting with your opponent, gather as much information as you can about the elements and nature of the problem.
- Define the problem with precision, separating it from the people and personalities involved in creating it.
- Write down a concise statement of the problem, and continue revising until you are satisfied that you have it right.

- Meet with your opponent and ask how he defines the problem. Then restate the problem incorporating elements from his definition.
- Jointly identify the barriers or difficulties that need to be overcome and the questions you need to answer to solve it.
- Jointly decide what information will help you identify the best possible solutions, who will be responsible for gathering it, and when you will meet to let each other know what you discovered.
- After completing these steps, redefine the problem again.

Step Three: Jointly Investigate, Analyze, Categorize, and Prioritize the Problem

- The third step means tackling the problem together, breaking it down into subparts, and prying it open to reveal its secrets.
- Meet with your opponent or a team to investigate, analyze, categorize, and prioritize the elements of the problem.
- Separate and define the emotional elements that may have distorted your perception of the problem. Discuss them separately and return to analysis.
- Break the problem down into smaller, bite-sized pieces, separate them from one another, and consider each separately.
- Compare the problem with others you have had in the past, notice their similarities and differences, and ask how those problems were solved.
- Identify the perfect state in which the problem no longer exists and work backward from the future to the present to discover solutions.
- Examine the ways the problem has been affected by the context and relationships that surround it.
- Consider the history of the problem and its evolution over time.
- Clarify any factual inconsistencies, hidden assumptions, false expectations, implicit value orientations, cultural myths, unexamined stereotypes, and clichéd ways of thinking about the problem.
- Search for the structural, systemic, contextual, and environmental sources of the problem.

Step Four: Invent Solutions That Satisfy Everyone's Interests Without Becoming Attached to Any Particular Solution

- The fourth step means generating options, assessing alternative criteria, and jointly inventing solutions that satisfy diverse interests, without deciding on or becoming attached to any single approach.
- Decide whether the information you have gathered is sufficient to solve the problem. If not, return to earlier steps.
- Jointly generate options through brainstorming.
- Incorporate objections, disagreements, and concerns into the solution.
- Develop appropriate criteria for determining whether you have been successful in solving it.
- Predict the probable costs, consequences, and impact of each proposed solution.
- Consult with experts, critics, coaches, and anyone affected by the problem or the solution to solicit feedback on alternative solutions.
- Search for solutions that include and are able to satisfy everyone's interests.
- Before selecting a solution for implementation, consider the merits of all possible solutions, without favoring any particular one.
- Reassess the solutions you rejected to see if some of their merits or advantages could be incorporated in the options that remain.
- Test your hypotheses or conclusions through a pilot project or test run, agree on the questions it should answer, and fine-tune the solution based on results.

Step Five: Jointly Act, Evaluate Results, Acknowledge Efforts, and Celebrate Successes

- The fifth step means taking specific, concrete, committed action to solve the problem, evaluating results, and giving each other feedback so you can learn from what you did and continue improving your problem-solving skills.

- Jointly create a strategy or set of goals, an action plan, and a time line for solving the problem, and identify targets, mileposts, and due dates.
- Make sure every action has someone committed to implementing it.
- Engage in committed action together to implement solutions.
- Periodically evaluate interim results.
- Give each other feedback on what is and is not working. Agree to stop doing what is not working.
- Ask critics and opponents of the solution to offer feedback, propose alternate solutions, and help evaluate the process.
- Make midcourse corrections.
- Summarize what you learned from the problem and how you solved it. Communicate what you learned to others.
- Identify ways of improving the problem-solving process.
- Pick the next problem and start over again.

Conflict Resolution, Problem Solving, and Strategic Planning

When we are stuck in a conflict or problem, it is easy to see it as personal and divorced from chronic sources within the organization. Yet our problems cannot be understood or solved separately from the organizational environments, including the systems, structures, processes, relationships, and cultures in which they occur. These environments have a direct impact on the problem-solving process, making it easier or more difficult to identify or implement solutions.

Moreover, many of the conflicts and problems we encounter in the workplace are not personal or isolated incidents, but chronic, predictable, and created or aggravated by the organization itself. What we experience as personal conflicts and problems are often actually organizational ones that are hidden, distorted, or disguised as personality or interpersonal issues.

Organizational conflicts appear to take place between people, while leaving the structures, systems, structures, processes, relationships, and cultures that created them invisible and in the background. These deeper sources of conflict become apparent only when we cease taking our disputes personally, analyze what took place from an organizational point of view, and realize that what we experienced is not unique, but is happening repeatedly and to others.

There are hundreds of sources of *chronic* workplace conflict, the most common being

1. Lack of agreement over values, vision, mission, and goals
2. Lack of clarity or buy-in regarding roles and responsibilities, policies and procedures, or rules and regulations
3. Lack of support for collaboration and participation in decision making over important issues
4. Lack of clear, courageous, and inclusive leadership
5. Lack of equality and fairness in the distribution of resources and pay

Through creative and paradoxical problem solving we can generate not merely personal or tactical solutions, but organizational, systemic, and strategic ones as well. Doing so increases the possibility of resolving the complex, chronic, and systemic sources of workplace conflict generated by dysfunctional organizational environments.

One of the best problem-solving methods for addressing these chronic sources of conflict is "democratic strategic planning." When strategic planning is conducted hierarchically, bureaucratically, or autocratically, it becomes an empty process that can recreate the very problems it is designed to solve.

In hierarchical, bureaucratic, and autocratic strategic planning, managers go through the motions, agree on a set of beautiful yet empty slogans, then "shine it on" and simply continue doing what they were doing before they began. Employees feel excluded from the decision-making process, blame management for glitches and mistakes in the plan, rationalize being apathetic and cynical, and either blindly obey orders, reluctantly go along with the plan, or quietly sabotage its implementation.

When this happens, people focus instead on short-term tactical problems that can be solved relatively easily. Their plans describe a future that sounds nice but is too simplistic, pathetic, or uninspiring, or uses grandiose words to restate the status quo, or is a complete fantasy. From this point of view, strategic planning appears to be unnecessary or a waste of time, and employees decide it is worthless, or that it is better to simply figure things out along the way. They may also feel that events are moving too fast to engage in any kind of planning, or that there is too much conflict in the organization to be able to plan strategically. As a result, problems remain unsolved and conflicts increase.

Democratic strategic planning, on the other hand, encourages people at all levels in the organization to participate in redefining their future—especially those whose participation is essential for any long-range plan to succeed. A simple democratic strategic planning model starts by empowering democratic, cross-organizational, cross-functional teams to define and drive the planning process. Everyone in the organization uses a collaborative, consensus-based, diverse, and inclusive problem-solving process to identify and answer foundational questions, possibly including these:

- *Values:* What are our ethical principles and shared values? What ideals do we want to stand for? What can we do to make sure we live up to them?
- *Vision:* Where do we want to go? What do we want to ultimately achieve? Why?
- *Mission:* Who are we? What are our main strengths and weaknesses? What do we do best?
- *Barriers:* What stands or might stand in the way of getting where we want to go?
- *Strategies:* How can we successfully overcome these barriers in a way that is consistent with our values and who we are? How do we get to where we finally want to go?
- *Goals or objectives:* What do we have to achieve in the next year to get where we want to go? How do we break our strategies down into achievable subparts?
- *Action plans:* Who is going to do what to achieve each one of our goals? What is our target deadline? What resources do we need to be successful?

It is useful to keep in mind that there are a number of erroneous ideas and ways of thinking that can easily undermine the planning process. Organizational theorist Henry Mintzberg has identified a number of fallacies in strategic planning, which we have modified to highlight the difficulties that individuals and organizations encounter in solving problems and resolving conflicts:

- *Prediction:* thinking we can actually know what is going to happen next

- *Reductionism:* thinking complex, nonlinear phenomena can be reduced to simple linear subcategories
- *Separation between planning and doing:* thinking planning can take place in the absence of implementation
- *Formalization:* thinking formal processes can alter informal realities
- *Personalization:* thinking personally or subjectively about systemic problems
- *Closure:* failing to "nail it to the floor," or thinking it will ever be over

To these, we can add two others, the first is what philosopher Alfred North Whitehead called "the fallacy of misplaced concreteness," meaning that we often perceive our problems as solid and exact when they are actually fluid and imprecise. The second is what we call "the fallacy of immutability," meaning that problems and conflicts in the workplace are often seen as fixed, but are actually in motion and changing from moment to moment. These ideas suggest that problem-solving and strategic planning processes need to be as agile and adaptable as the problems and conflicts we are trying to solve.

Democratic strategic planning consists not merely in finding solutions to problems, but organizing and facilitating constructive dialogues over important issues and continually working to improve problem-solving processes, skills, attitudes, and relationships. Yet simply by democratically addressing strategic issues and collaboratively planning our responses to conflicts and problems, we encourage others in the workplace to reflect on their experiences, become more responsible for their actions, own the results of their work processes, collaborate in responding to problems, reach consensus over critical issues, consciously plan their futures, and engage in coordinated and committed action.

In the process, we experience the pleasure of honest and open dialogue, passionate commitment, teamwork, camaraderie, self-fulfillment, enjoyable interactions and communications, deeper relationships, and an increased ability to solve our problems and resolve our conflicts. These outcomes are *at least* as important as coming up with useful strategies and solutions.

Problem Solving and Consensus Decision Making

Throughout these problem-solving, strategic planning, and conflict resolution processes, critical decisions are being made by participants regarding the attitudes, approaches, and methods they will employ in addressing the issues, the solutions they will implement, and how they will go about implementing them.

Many of these decisions are made *before* the problem has been solved in ways that can easily aggravate or replicate it. Unilateral decisions may consciously or unconsciously upset people, undermine relationships, escalate the problem, or trigger a fresh round of conflict. To avoid these outcomes, we need to solve the problem of how we should decide which solution to implement.

There are six fundamental decision-making processes from which individuals, teams, and organizations can choose in solving their problems. Rather than pick one as a template for all situations, it is better to become fluent in all six and select the one that will be most effective in each decision. These basic methods of decision making, followed by an illustrative phrase that expresses it, are

1. *Notification:* "The following decision has been made and will be implemented by Friday."
2. *Consultation:* "I would like your thoughts on this issue before I make a decision."
3. *Delegation:* "You decide, and I will support what you decided."
4. *Voting:* "The majority will decide."
5. *Consensus:* "I am willing to accept the wisdom of the group, can live with the decision, and feel it addresses my most important needs and interests."
6. *Unanimity:* "We are in 100 percent agreement."

In deciding which decision-making process to use, notice that in progressing from notification to unanimity, the time required increases, as does the degree of unity and ownership when we begin to implement what has been decided. The choice of which process to use will depend on the kind of problem we need to solve.

For example, rapid, unilateral decision making works well when the issues are clear, the stakes are minimal, and the time for deciding is short. Yet individuals and organizations that routinely make unilateral decisions and rarely if ever use consensus or unanimity generate higher levels of conflict and distrust than those that periodically take time to make sure that everyone is on board, in consensus, or unanimous regarding the decision.

It is most important to clearly communicate which method you intend to use and why, so as to avoid triggering future conflicts. For example, if some colleagues assume the process is one of delegation when it is actually one of consultation, they will work hard to come up with what they believe is a delegated decision and will be shocked when it is subsequently rejected, leaving them feeling disrespected, disempowered, and distrusted because the decision maker did not agree and thought it was merely a consultation.

Voting is widely considered the best form of decision making in a democracy, but significant problems arise whenever a minority loses an important vote. Voting is a "rights-based," "winner take all" process that can cause polarization and bad feelings, and undermine relationships. Because voting permits full participation, it is preferable to notification in many ways, yet can also be highly competitive, contentious, and unnecessarily adversarial.

Under these circumstances, voting is *less* preferable than consensus, which is grounded in interests, does not result in anyone winning or losing, invites participants to modify their ideas to meet everyone's needs, includes the useful ideas of dissenters and resisters, and encourages participants to own their decisions.

However, it is clearly inappropriate, for example, to use consensus to decide what someone else is going to eat for lunch, or what they will say during a meeting. It is equally inappropriate to use notification to decide what employees will do in teams, or vote on whether the majority in a group will treat their minority colleagues fairly and respectfully.

Each problem needs to be considered separately so that the optimal decision-making process is selected. It is critical that everyone involved in implementing the decision understands and accepts the *way* it was reached. It is therefore best to use consensus or unanimity in deciding important issues, and which decision-making process they should use for any given problem.

Consensus and unanimity are preferred methods for solving team problems and conflicts because they are naturally collaborative, include everyone regardless of their position in the organization, involve them in brainstorming and selecting options, promote understanding and ownership, encourage people to learn from dissent, and reduce the likelihood of sabotage after the decision is made.

Consensus and unanimity are also highly democratic and allow everyone to have an equal voice regardless of their status or place in the hierarchy, encourage differences of opinion to surface and be incorporated in solutions, increase overall unity, and give people the sense that they are moving in a common direction. Here are some typical statements that indicate that unanimity or consensus has been reached:

- "I can say an unqualified 'yes' to the decision."
- "I find the decision acceptable."
- "I am willing to support the decision because I trust the wisdom of the group."
- "I can live with the decision, although I'm not enthusiastic about it."
- "I do not fully agree with the decision and need to register my disagreement. However, I do not choose to block consensus."

You will know that consensus has been reached when every participant feels that the process was fair, that there was sufficient opportunity for them to influence the outcome, and that they are willing to live with what was decided and support it as though it were their first choice. A lack of consensus or unanimity, on the other hand, can be recognized in statements such as

- "I feel there is no clear unity in the group."
- "We need to do more work before I can reach consensus."
- "I feel I haven't been heard."
- "I do not agree with the decision and need to stand in the way of its being accepted."
- "I strongly (or repeatedly) disagree."

There is a common misunderstanding that consensus and unanimity require everyone to "be a team player" and surrender their criticisms to please the group. Actually, they require the opposite. There is a danger that consensus and unanimity will become a cover for coercion, or be used to suppress the open and honest expression of differences, or compel formal agreement, or only *appear* to solve problems collaboratively. When true consensus and unanimity are used, people refuse to compromise over principles, are determined to go deeper into what is blocking their agreement and make a strong effort to hold out for better solutions.

Regardless of which process is used, everyone should be clear about which one was chosen, feel free to express dissent, and avoid rushing decisions or asking people to decide before it is absolutely necessary. It is equally important to actively encourage honest participation, prevent anyone from dominating the process, and avoid acting unilaterally until it is clear to everyone that a unified decision cannot be reached.

While consensus and unanimity are the best forms of decision making in resolving conflicts and finding solutions that are acceptable and lasting, there will always be individuals, times, and places when it will fail. If, after ample time and effective support have been given for dialogue and a clear and committed effort has been made to work through differences, it is obvious that consensus and unanimity cannot be reached, consider taking one or more of the following steps to solve the problem:

- Use brainstorming and reopen options
- Expand the pie by including other issues and looking for trade-offs
- Separate issues over which there is no consensus to return to later
- Bring in a subject matter expert to provide advice
- Break issues down into separate pieces and seek consensus on each one separately
- Look carefully at objections to see if solutions can be created to each one individually while moving ahead with the proposal
- Create a small team of representatives from each side to brainstorm, prioritize, and recommend three to five possible solutions
- Take the decision to an expanded group for suggestions or additional problem solving
- Reach consensus on shared values, commonalities, principles, interests, or criteria; then develop procedures or guidelines for further problem solving that flow from them

- Return to agreeing on a common vision, mission, set of goals, barriers, strategies, or action plans
- Look for hidden issues or agendas and address them privately or, if that fails, publicly
- Refer the issue to a completely uninvolved group to develop compromise proposals
- Take a break and allow time for reflection
- Search for compromises
- Divide into factions and open a dialogue
- Table the decision or decide not to decide
- Take a straw vote
- Allow the minority group time to try and convince the majority to change its mind
- Vote and accept majority rule
- Bring in a mediator or facilitator to create consensus or resolve the underlying problems
- Prepare majority and minority reports and submit them to a higher level
- Allow the group's primary decision maker to decide

Our greatest challenge is not to solve the perplexing conflicts and problems we are busy fighting over, but to solve the problem of how we got stuck in the first place, what we can learn from the problem, and how we can improve our ability to solve problems in general. These introduce the possibility that we could not only learn better ways of solving them, but also ways of transforming and transcending them in a single stroke.

Transformation and Problem Solving

Sometimes, if we define something as a problem it becomes one, whereas if we do not define it as a problem it solves itself and ceases to demand our attention. Sometimes we magnify problems so we will have important work to do, in part because solving problems is more interesting, enjoyable, and challenging to many people than implementing solutions, and life without problems can become pretty dull.

Sometimes a breakdown, problem, or conflict is simply the precursor to a breakthrough, creative solution, and deeper level of resolution that is waiting to emerge. We can then see that our problem represents an emerging new understanding of what is not working in our organizations or our lives that has been perplexing us and holding us back.

Sometimes we think we are solving one problem when what we are actually working on subconsciously is a far deeper problem, such as who we are or want to be, or how we can improve our lives and be happier. Sometimes the problem is an outgrowth of our own false expectations or unrealistic assumptions regarding a conflict, or confusion about our lives. And sometimes, though we may not like to hear it, the real problem is *us*, and the attitudes or methods we have adopted in trying to solve the problem.

Thus, it occasionally happens that we do not actually solve our problems so much as learn from, transform, transcend, and outgrow them. We generally think of our problems as external; yet, for every external problem we face, there is a much more interesting and perplexing internal one that we may or may not be facing.

If, for example, we believe the problem is who the other person *is* or what she is doing, a far more interesting problem is who *we* are and why we are having so much difficulty responding skillfully to her personality or behavior. In this way, every *external* solution we identify and conflict we resolve corresponds to an *internal* one that is subtly demanding our attention.

If we consider our problems and conflicts as internal calls for growth, learning, and transformation that we have mistakenly assumed originated from outside, we will discover hidden opportunities for profound learning about ourselves, our organizations, and our lives. If we see our problems as ones we are capable of solving internally, we will gain a critical new perspective on them, which in many cases serves the same function as solving them.

The eminent psychologist Carl Jung brilliantly observed how it is possible to shift our thinking and understanding regarding the conflicts and problems in our lives:

> The greatest and most important problems of life are all in a certain sense insoluble. They must be so because they express the necessary polarity inherent in every self-regulating system. They can never be solved, but only outgrown.... What on a lower level, had led to

> the wildest conflicts and to panicky outbursts of emotion, viewed from the higher level of personality, now seemed like a storm in the valley seen from a high mountaintop. This does not rob the thunderstorm of its reality, but instead of being in it, one is now above it.

As we learn to solve each variety or type of problem, we make room for another higher, more advanced type of problem to take its place. As Buckminster Fuller accurately reminds us: "Once you solve your problems, what you get is a higher order of problem." Yet each new order of problem presents a new challenge and a fresh opportunity for learning and transcendence.

STRATEGY 7

LEARN FROM DIFFICULT BEHAVIORS

If you feel guilty, you invent a plot, many plots. And to counter them, you have to organize your own plot, many plots. But the more you invent enemy plots, to exonerate your lack of understanding, the more you fall in love with them, and you pattern your own on their model. You attribute to the others what you're doing yourself, and since what you're doing yourself is hateful, the others become hateful. But since the others, as a rule, would like to do the same hateful thing that you're doing, they collaborate with you, hinting that—yes—what you attribute to them is actually what they have always desired.

—UMBERTO ECO

In this passage, novelist and semiologist Umberto Eco reveals an essential yet hidden truth about our conflicts: we create our opponents in our own image, and are created by them in return. When we are in conflict and feel hatred, fear, guilt, or grief, we may externalize these feelings and attribute them to our opponents as intentions, assigning to them the actions, purposes, and motivations we imagine are responsible for what we have experienced.

By focusing on our opponent's cruel, hostile, or evil intentions, their plans suddenly turn into plots, their self-confidence into arrogance, and their supporters into coconspirators. Their determination becomes nothing other than bullying, and they are "always" or "never" doing something wrong or right.

This "conflict interpretation algorithm" allows both sides to externalize their pain, disappointment, and grief by turning them into anger, hostility, and betrayal, disregarding any empathy they may have for the other person, and dismissing the positive parts of their personalities, creative ideas, reasonable interests, and constructive intentions as ill-informed, pointless, and naive.

Yet by doing so, we lose sight of the real reasons for our conflicts, forget what we have in common, diminish our capacity for empathy and compassion, interpret even positive actions and statements negatively and personally, and become more frightened, angry, and defensive. This, of course, causes them to do the same, leading both sides to become increasingly inauthentic in the other person's presence, incapable of engaging in pleasant or effective problem solving, and gradually turn into people they both distrust and dislike.

Think of the most difficult person in your life. Yes, *that* one, the one who comes to mind immediately. Consider the possibility that by accepting the challenge of working through your conflicts with that person you could experience a profound resolution or transformation, not only in your conflict, but in your ability to resolve *every* conflict with every similar person in your life. It is our aim in exploring this strategy to assist you in discovering how to do so.

Defining the Problem *Is* the Problem

The way we look at, define, and think about our problems and conflicts has an immediate impact on the range and variety of options available to us in solving them, including what we are even capable of imagining as solutions. Some options for solving them will simply not occur to us unless we define the problem correctly.

There are four fundamental ways in which we commonly define problems when they consist of conflicts with people we view as unreasonable. These consist of identifying the problem as

1. A difficult person
2. A difficult personality
3. A difficult behavior
4. A difficult relationship

In the last chapter we will consider a fifth possibility, that it is a difficult system, structure, process, or culture.

It is common in many organizations for people to point their fingers at others and claim their opponents are difficult people, or crazy, or caused the problem, and to see them as the sole source of their problems. Staff members at a large county agency that had been involved in national efforts to reform organizational practices and "reinvent government" responded in interviews about their problems:

- My manager is the type who doesn't level with people. Giving a straight message is not part of how he does business. Things happen to people and they don't know why because there's no communication from the powers that be.
- We have difficulty as a management team working together as effectively as we should. There is too much discomfort among the personalities that are present.
- The majority of people are open to carrying on a dialogue, but one person has a strong personality. She either makes pronouncements or doesn't say anything. Socially, she's delightful, but when things are pushed or tense, it's very difficult to talk with her.
- He always thinks he's right and is not open to any other ideas.

These complaints identified important problems and pinpointed ineffective behaviors, but they also attributed problems to specific individuals based on their difficult natures as people or personalities. Their comments, however, clearly reveal that it is neither the people nor their personalities but their *behaviors* that are creating the problem, along with the interviewees' lack of willingness to accept responsibility for creating, aggravating, or rewarding the behaviors they complained about. They did not go to those they were accusing and offer them honest feedback, and once they labeled the problem as a difficult person or personality they could avoid critiquing their own behaviors and responses. Because of the way they defined the problem, there was nothing they could imagine doing to solve it. In response, we encouraged them to

- Shift the way they were defining the problem
- Instead of seeing the issue as one of difficult people or personalities, to see it as one of behaviors that were difficult *for them,* that they did not have the skills to handle successfully
- Focus instead on the actual statements, behaviors, and actions that other people were engaging in
- Develop alternative skills they might use in response, and in giving timely, honest, empathetic feedback
- Stop rewarding behaviors they did not want to continue experiencing

Many staff members had tried the strategies presented in previous chapters, but because their attention was drawn to the *person* whose difficult or unreasonable behaviors triggered their anger, their frustrations deepened, blocking their achievements and keeping them at impasse. More and more, they began to hope their opponent would just quit or disappear and their conflicts would be over.

In order to succeed in solving their problems, they needed to take responsibility for improving their *own* communications, rather than blaming others, giving up, or expecting someone else to solve their problems. By abandoning their attempts to change other people's basic natures or personalities, they were able to focus on behaviors and solve a problem that otherwise seemed insoluble.

To do so, even when you are in the heat of an argument or the throes of a conflict, consider these alternative ways of define the difficulty and find a more effective and powerful approach to people whose behaviors are difficult to understand, empathize with, or accept.

The Problem with Identifying the Problem as a "Difficult Person"

We commonly refer to those with whom we are in conflict as "problem people." We label them as "dishonest" or "negative," or describe them as "controlling," "mean," "manipulative," "lying," or "incompetent." When we are angry, we use even less pleasant words to label and diminish our opponents, or humiliate them in front of others, as we feel we were humiliated.

The effect of these words, however, is to shift attention away from what the other person *did* to who the person *is*. Yet by doing so, we make it more difficult to resolve our conflicts because defining the problem as a *person* means that the only remedy left is to fire him, demote him, or transfer him from the work unit.

These solutions are usually impossible or ineffective, especially in the long run, because they only succeed in transferring the problem somewhere else. In addition, it leaves us feeling powerless and frustrated when we confront similar behaviors in the future.

Worse, when we identify the person as the problem we automatically create a justification for acting against her in inhuman, antagonistic, and dismissive ways, just as we feel she has acted toward us. Ultimately, this gives us permission to annihilate her in some way, either by gossip or character assassination or, in extreme cases, by murder—because, by definition, nothing less will solve the problem if we have defined it as a person.

If we move to larger conflicts and consider the international and political consequences of this approach, when we define a *group* of people as the problem, we create a subconscious justification for genocide. Historically, genocide has always been preceded by campaigns of vilification and stereotyping directed against groups of people for the purpose of identifying the entire group as "the problem." Any statement that begins with the words "you people" or "they are" and adds the words "stupid," "lazy," "incompetent," "evil," "naturally inferior," or "brought it on themselves," automatically creates a justification for genocide.

It is precisely "the person is the problem" as a way of thinking that is responsible for producing malicious, revengeful, inhuman, murderous, and genocidal solutions to conflict. These assumptions and accusations are then rationalized by labeling the problem as personal, inborn, and unchangeable.

Another difficulty with this way of thinking is that we have all at some time or another been "incompetent," "difficult," or "problem" people who "brought it on ourselves." For this reason, there can never be a limit to our capacity for malice or revenge, or a barrier to our participation—if not in large-scale malicious behaviors such as genocides and acts of revenge, at least in small acts of malice and revenge and "mini-genocides" that take place every day in nearly every workplace against those who are perceived as difficult.

Conflicts between departments, divisions, and specialized functions in organizations often become personalized, causing the entire organization to turn adversarial. Each group then regards the problem only from its own point of view and blames those in the other group for having caused, aggravated, or tolerated it. They label their opponents as personally incompetent, untrustworthy, or stupid, and judge individuals based on the stereotypes they created for the group as a whole. This alienates the group being judged, creating a self-fulfilling prophecy of personal hostility and aggressiveness that blocks communication and collaboration, frustrates their ability to solve common problems, and makes it impossible to work as a unified team.

The attitude that the person is the problem, which can be found in some form in nearly every conflict, generates stereotypes that are nearly identical in form and consequence to those supporting deeper prejudices, such as racism, sexism, anti-Semitism, and homophobia. Stereotyping means turning people into caricatures of themselves by taking actual characteristics, exaggerating them out of proportion, ignoring the diverse ways they manifest themselves, collapsing individuals into groups or categories, omitting all the natural complexity of real human beings, grounding it in fear, and making it cruel.

When we stereotype our opponents, it is usually because we cannot find any convincing justification for the pain or fear we have experienced, presumably at their hands. Sometimes, paradoxically, it is because we are afraid they will retaliate for the injustices we have done to them, or because we are angry with them, if only for the pain they caused us by being on our conscience.

The logic of stereotyping in conflict is quite simple. If we are basically good and they intentionally hurt us, they must be bad. If we want to end the conflict and are unable to, it is because they are unreasonable. The value of this way of thinking is that stereotyping and labeling others lets us off the hook from improving our own behaviors, gives us permission to act aggressively against them, and allows us to claim the role of victim.

The Problem with Identifying the Problem as a "Difficult Personality"

If we define our problem or conflict not as a person, but as their difficult *personality,* we identify what needs to be solved as the product of inherited genes or decades of family and peer conditioning. But in that case, even long-term psychotherapy may not succeed in altering our adversary's personality, and again we are stuck. In essence, we have defined ourselves into a corner, believing that only skillful psychological manipulations and long-term remedies will allow us to escape injury at the hands of their malign personality.

Labeling our opponents' personalities as the problem or judging their character as defective gives us permission to permanently dismiss them. As a result, we are able to justify our refusal to listen or discuss our problems with them and withdraw or act in a manipulative, stubborn, or belligerent manner against them. It absolves us of responsibility for whatever we have done or failed to do that contributed to creating or aggravating the problem, while supporting our self-image as a powerless victim in the hands of someone who is crazy.

The real reason we prefer to believe that people and their personalities are the problem is that we simply do not know what to do to resolve our conflict. We are reluctant to listen empathetically or responsively, ask open and honest questions, acknowledge our opponent's emotions, discover their interests, or work collaboratively to solve the problem. If we reconstruct this chain of reasoning backwards, we can see that it offers a useful rationalization for throwing up our hands and doing nothing.

Part of the reason for our failure, however, is the way we have defined the problem. As long as we define the problem as a person or personality, it is *axiomatic* that there is nothing we can do to resolve it, other than wait for our opponent to leave, be demoted, move to a different department, or get bypassed in decision-making opportunities. And because they are the ones who started the problem, it is only fair that they should be forced to suffer rather than us.

When we are able to appreciate the human nature of our opponents and their personalities, willing to listen openly, honestly, and empathetically to them, or work collaboratively with them to find creative solutions to our problems and a real resolution takes place, we no longer view them as bad people or unreasonable personalities, and they immediately and inexplicably appear sane and human to us. How exactly does that happen?

If we critically examine the way we defined the problem, simple logic tells us it is not *them*, but our conflict and attitude toward them that creates the difficulty. We then realize that the entire set of assumptions, rationalizations, excuses, accusations, and mental constructs we created about who they are and what terrible personalities they have was fallacious and self-serving from the beginning.

In truth, we get into conflicts with people and personalities we call difficult because their *behaviors* are difficult for *us;* because their actions and statements triggered something in us that we have not resolved; because their behavior combined with our lack of skill causes us to feel powerless in their presence—in other words, because we have chosen a way of relating to them that is unskillful and unsuccessful, and we do not know what else to do or say. In this way, we become part of the problem. Once we discover that we can redefine the problem, the solution becomes clear.

We were asked to resolve a highly emotional dispute that had ravaged the board of directors of a large labor union representing thousands of people in the transportation industry. While the union was fully engaged in bargaining for a multiyear contract, the directors were spending an inordinate amount of time attacking one another. The secretary of the union had simply had it with the many personal attacks that were directed against her and began to respond in kind with dismissive, smug, challenging, and provocative statements about her opponents on the board.

As these exchanges grew more heated and tempers flared, they moved further away from addressing the real issues, which were increasingly obscured in a fog of recriminations, defensiveness, and retaliation. The real issues were the dysfunctional way the organization was operating, the failure of the officers to respond to messages from members on hot topics, a perceived lack of respect between members of the board, conflicts over who should lead the union in the next election of officers, arguments over styles and strategies for negotiating with the company, and significant differences in union philosophy over how militant or collaborative they should be.

All these issues could have been resolved by openly and honestly addressing them through dialogues, debates, and informal discussions, without engaging in nasty, vicious, and personal recriminations. The conflict was so far out of control that several directors refused to participate in facilitated informal problem solving until after the board officially reprimanded and punished the secretary for disobeying a board resolution. The focus of their attention was on punishing her for what they saw as her "hostile personality," rather than on working together to solve the problem. As a result, the bitterness increased and an opportunity for meaningful dialogue was lost.

What they could have done instead was to openly, honestly, and empathetically address the difficult issues in their relationship: first, by identifying the ways everyone was contributing to the deterioration of their communications; second, by agreeing to speak more respectfully to each other in the future; third, by targeting specific aspects of the secretary's behavior they perceived as disrespectful; fourth, by letting her know how her behavior was affecting them; fifth, by suggesting alternative ways of behaving that were more respectful; sixth, by treating her with greater respect; seventh, by indicating what they would do if she continued; and finally by refocusing their attention on high-priority problems in order to negotiate a satisfying contract and benefit the membership.

Identifying the Problem as a "Difficult Behavior" or Relationship

Rather than labeling the problem as a "difficult person" or "difficult personality," it is possible to view it instead as a "difficult behavior" or relationship. By shifting the way we describe the problem we can discover a number of more effective approaches of solving it, because everyone has changed their behavior countless times and can easily do so again.

By ceasing to identify the problem as a person or his personality, it is possible to acknowledge what we are each contributing to the problem without feeling we have to defend ourselves or counterattack. If what he is doing does not work for us, or the way we are acting or communicating has not been convincing, we can each recognize that we can be more successful by surfacing our separate interests or brainstorming options, without thinking of each other as bad people or flawed personalities.

As a result of this shift, our opponents will feel more respected, empowered, and responsible, both for the conflict and its resolution. They will become more skillful in handling our difficult behaviors and find it far more pleasurable, interesting, and effective than being personally attacked or feeling forced to defend themselves.

To begin addressing your opponents' difficult behaviors, start by answering the following questions:

1. Are their behaviors being rewarded by you or others in the organization? The chances are good that they have, if only by offering them the attention they have been craving and been unable to receive through positive behaviors.
2. Are their behaviors actually a coping mechanism or a way of surviving or adapting to a dysfunctional system? The behaviors you experience as difficult may also be a diversion to draw attention away from the fact that they are working beyond their capacity or skill, and are afraid of being fired.
3. Is it the people, their behavior, or the organizational system that is the real source of dysfunction? Perhaps they are being blamed for not fitting into a "shaming and blaming" environment that is not meeting their needs. Or perhaps the organization is not responding well to conflict and is avoiding or suppressing it, causing it to reemerge elsewhere in the form of difficult behavior.
4. How can I become more skillful in my responses without indirectly reinforcing the behaviors I experience as a problem? Your instinctive negative responses to difficult behaviors may actually be reinforcing or perpetuating them. In organizations as in families, "misbehaving children" and "squeaky wheels" receive the greatest attention. A more skillful response is to listen empathetically to them without supporting what they did.

Why People Engage in Difficult Behaviors

We frequently experience the difficult behaviors of our opponents as irrational, yet it is more often the case that they merely *seem* irrational to us because we have not taken the time or asked the questions that would reveal what is actually motivating them. Rather than labeling or stereotyping our opponents as irrational, we can try to discover why they are behaving in ways that appear senseless or irrational to us, and what rewards or benefits they are receiving in exchange.

Every behavior we find difficult suggests a "why" question we have not asked or answered sufficiently. Every honest, empathetic question we ask may lead to a more accurate description of the reasons they chose to engage in difficult behaviors. Every accurate description of those behaviors can help us develop a strategy for stopping or discouraging them.

A group of employees learned this lesson when they tried to reach consensus on a design for an employee coordinating committee charged with improving communications within the company. One person refused to go along with the consensus and adamantly refused to accept the design favored by the rest of the group. Her "difficult behavior" created considerable conflict and criticism, but she held firm, seeming to enjoy the conflict and smiling as she stood her ground.

By asking "why" and other open-ended questions, we discovered that her real issues had *nothing to do* with the design of the coordinating committee, but concerned her work team where she had been unsuccessful in raising or solving the problems.

We realized she was trying to draw attention to these issues in a roundabout way by discussing them in the large group and was hoping to embarrass her work team into facing them and solving them. We met with her privately and suggested she alter her behavior and raise the problems directly with the team. She agreed, and invited us to attend a team meeting where she apologized for discussing the issues publicly and asked the team for its help in addressing them.

The team finally understood what she was doing and said they were willing to address the issues that concerned her and work on solving them. Afterward, she accepted the design of the coordinating committee, met with the team, and solved most of their problems. Within a few months, she was chosen by her peers to lead the coordinating committee.

Sometimes, when coworkers engage in difficult behaviors at work, they are actually upset about personal problems at home, unfair criticisms from their manager, lack of respect from peers, actions of which they are ashamed, topics they are unable to discuss directly, poor self-esteem, repressed anger over past injustices, or they are feeling that no one likes them, and decide to reject others before being rejected by them.

If you are working with someone who is engaging in difficult behaviors, first consider: Have you asked him directly why he is behaving this way? If not, why not? If so, would the reason he offered motivate *you* to behave in a similar way? If not, is there a deeper, underlying reason that he may not have mentioned? Did you tell him how his behavior is affecting you and ask him to behave differently?

If not, what would it take for you to do so? Can you think of other questions you might ask that would help you understand the real motivation behind his behavior?

Stop Rewarding Difficult Behaviors

In any difficult interaction, you can take the initiative in shifting the focus from people or personalities to problem solving and change other peoples' difficult behaviors by altering how you respond to them. You can start by not blaming your opponent personally, not blaming their personality, and not rewarding their negative behavior but honestly calling attention to the difficulties it creates for you.

There are substantial payoffs for dysfunctional behaviors in most organizations. These include becoming the center of everyone's attention, being feared or placated, reprioritizing issues to focus on the ones you are upset about, controlling a group's decisions through negative power and influence, discouraging others from criticizing or confronting you, diverting attention from your mistakes, bringing everyone down to a lower level, and being promoted or transferred as a way of getting rid of the problem.

Take a moment to analyze how you and your organization could be rewarding behaviors you find difficult. Think of a person whose behavior causes problems for you and answer the following questions:

- What specific behavior are they engaging in that you find most disturbing?
- Why is that disturbing to you?
- Why do you think they are acting that way?
- Did anyone in your family of origin engage in similar behavior?
- How did you respond to those behaviors when you were growing up? Were those responses successful?
- How are you responding to the behaviors you find difficult now?
- Is that succeeding?
- Is your opponent benefiting in any way from your responses to their behavior?
- How might you change your responses to stop rewarding them for behaviors you find unacceptable?
- How are others in the organization responding to their behavior?

- Is anyone in the organization handling their behaviors skillfully, or not bothered by them? What are they doing differently?
- What organizational benefits are they deriving from their behaviors?
- Have you given them honest feedback about these behaviors? If so, how did they receive it?
- Has the team or work group given them feedback?
- What feedback have you *not* given them about their behaviors? Why not?
- What would it take for you to give them fully honest and empathetic feedback?
- What do you think might motivate them to change their behaviors?
- What would motivate you?
- How could you reward them for behaviors you find more acceptable?
- How could you support them in changing?

There are many people whose behavior is difficult for us to handle, who are labeled "crazy" because it is so difficult to understand them, reason with them, or respond to them successfully. Yet there is an enormous difference between being "crazy" and what we find more often, which is being "crazy like a fox." Most people we think of as crazy are actually conscious of engaging in difficult behaviors that, in some ways, work for them and produce many of the results they want.

Some people who are called crazy are simply—but unskillfully—using strategies that help them survive in what they experience as a hostile, dysfunctional work environment. If we believe this is the cause of their behavior, we may be able to help them find a more effective response or identify better methods for changing their behavior.

Methods for Changing Difficult Behaviors

By focusing on your opponent's behaviors, offering empathetic feedback, ceasing to reward their behaviors, and searching for collaborative solutions, it is possible for you to shift from feeling hopeless in your conflicts to being *strategic* about them. The methods that follow can assist you to become more strategic in your response to difficult behaviors.

We developed these methods to support the staff of a large U.S. government agency in changing their focus from defining their problems as difficult people and personalities to identifying the chronic behavioral problems within the organization and developing the skills they needed to address them. As a result, they were able to shift from reacting defensively to responding strategically, and became more successful in solving their problems.

- *Surfacing the conflict:* We began by interviewing the staff about their experience with conflicts in the workplace. We wrote down their comments verbatim and deleted names and identifying characteristics to preserve confidentiality. We summarized the main issues and distributed their comments to everyone without censoring or watering them down. In this way, we were able to surface and identify the difficult behavioral issues as perceived by most of the group. We turned these issues into a list of problems that needed to be solved and placed them on the table for discussion, negotiation, and problem solving.
- *Conflict coaching:* We coached the leadership team in the organization on how best to respond to conflicts and the difficult behaviors that created them, how to model openness to criticism, how to be strategic by not rewarding them, and how to reward honest, empathetic communications instead.
- *Teamwork:* In a group conflict resolution session, we assigned everyone to random teams and asked them to read through the comments from our interviews. We asked each team to reach consensus on the top five to seven behavioral issues that needed to change in order to create the kind of work environment they most wanted. Finally, we asked them to brainstorm five strategies for ending these behaviors or responding to them more effectively so that they would no longer be as difficult or dysfunctional.
- *Process awareness:* We asked everyone to identify the processes they could use to minimize difficult behaviors in the future. They suggested that group members regularly give each other honest feedback and discuss problems when and as they occurred. They then realized that they would experience fewer difficult behaviors if everyone felt heard and acknowledged, if goals were clearer, if leadership walked their talk, if they worked collaboratively to solve problems, and if they continued practicing and rewarding these techniques in the future.

- *Constructive feedback:* We gave them a checklist of the positive and negative behaviors they mentioned in our interviews and asked each person to identify the ones they wanted to do more of, less of, or eliminate for themselves. In rotation, starting with the leader of the group, they reviewed their own checked behaviors and asked each person present to give them honest feedback on the changes they needed to make. They thanked each person for the feedback they gave and stated what they would do in the future to improve their behaviors. In this way, everyone in the group assessed each person and received honest feedback from everyone, which resulted in increased open communication, decreased defensiveness, and a feeling on everyone's part that they could improve their behaviors and support each other in the process.
- *Problem solving:* As the group discussed ways each person could improve their behavior, the problem of respect for diversity emerged. Afterwards, the group discussed it in detail and agreed to hire more diverse staff members, and acknowledge people for having diverse skills, backgrounds, and personalities. They brainstormed strategies to increase respect for diversity both at the top and throughout the organization. We complimented them for successfully tackling a difficult problem strategically and discussing sensitive issues without slipping into difficult behaviors.
- *Shared responsibility:* When the group's leader heard identical feedback from all her coworkers, she suddenly became aware that there was a consistent pattern in her behavior, something that was perceived not only by those she saw as her enemies, but by her friends as well, and that she could no longer deny or minimize the negative impact of her behavior. When she recognized this, several people, including her principal opponent, replied that the fault was not entirely hers. They realized that no one in the group had given her empathetic feedback or supported her in changing her behavior. When she felt the responsibility was shared and not hers alone, her attitude toward the conflict and her opponent began to shift.
- *Support for change:* The leader asked the group to support her in changing her behavior in the following ways: she agreed to work with three people she respected, including her principal opponent, who volunteered to help her. These "on-the-job

coaches" agreed to meet with her every day to focus her attention on specific action items and help her adopt more skillful responses. She was able to modify her most difficult behaviors, reduce tensions, create more open and honest communication, encourage empathetic feedback, and increase collaboration.

- *Constructive attitude toward problems:* Everyone started out thinking that nothing could be done to change the negative behaviors in the group, especially at the top, but discovered that they were able to bring about significant changes by using these methods and approaching them with a constructive attitude, rather than with cynicism and apathy. The same results can be achieved in your conflict and your organization when you shift from blaming people to solving problems.

Difficult Behaviors Start in the Family

Your opponents' difficult behaviors probably began long before you entered their lives. Most difficult behaviors represent engrained patterns from childhood that are developed in response to unresolved issues or unmet needs in our families of origin and strengthened by repeated use in schools and workplaces.

Consider whether there are any hidden patterns in the behaviors you find most difficult, whether there is anything that connects all the people whose behaviors trouble you, whether these behaviors originated in your childhood, and whether you or your opponent may be responding to emotional patterns that have *nothing to do* with who you are, but are simply left over from the past.

Many difficult behaviors originate in our inability as children to get our emotional needs met, either because we were deprived and did not get enough of what we needed, or because we were smothered and got too much. In either case, we developed compensating behaviors that remain with us for the rest of our lives, or until we learn the skills we need to outgrow them.

As in tuning a stringed musical instrument, excessive tightness produces a high, shrill sound while excessive slackness produces a thick, dull one. Each of us is born with emotional needs and responses that get "tuned" in our families of origin. As we adapted to the difficult behaviors and conflict cultures in our families, we learned compensating behaviors that we carry with us to work, often without understanding why or where they originated.

If our parents, siblings, or peers responded to us in ways that we felt were inadequate or excessive, we may have developed compensating and limiting patterns of behavior that shaped our ability to participate in mutually beneficial adult relationships. Sometimes, we develop patterns of compensating behavior that are the exact opposite of the ones we learned, or engage in behaviors we are still struggling to overcome, or simply act in ways that elicit a parental response, or remind us of difficulties we had as children in getting our needs met.

If, for example, we sought affection as a child and did not receive enough, we may experience a kind of generic distrust of those who could give us the affection we need but do not. Later, as adults, we become unable to make commitments to our teammates, or develop close relationships with colleagues we unconsciously believe will disappoint us. Or, we may be plagued with fears that we will be rejected and our needs will not be met. As a result, we may become rejecting ourselves, or distant and overly defensive to feedback. On the other hand, we may respond in the opposite way and become clingy and dependent, excessively vulnerable to signs of rejection, or unable to tolerate clinging and defensiveness in others.

When conflicts occur, both sides may engage in behaviors their opponents find difficult to handle. Sometimes their reactions and responses have nothing at all to do with the issues, but are behaviors they learned as children from parents or siblings with whom they have been unable to fully resolve their differences.

As a result, the way we respond to our opponents' difficult behavior functions as a mirror, pointing our attention backward to our own unresolved childhood issues. Conflict can be defined as a relationship with someone whose behaviors we find difficult because they highlight issues we have not fully resolved in our own lives. When we face these issues, plumb them for fresh insights and fully resolve them, our opponents' behaviors cease to bother or entrap us. We become more skillful at handling their behaviors and regard them instead as idiosyncrasies.

For example, two women managers were asked to create a fast-forming team to develop a new product for a premier customer. Corporate management was about to pull the plug on the project because the managers became locked in conflict and unable to collaborate.

At one point, we privately asked April, the senior engineer, whether Sharon, the team leader, reminded her of anyone in her family. She began to cry and said that as a child she felt she had never been good enough to meet her parents' standards. They were distant and judgmental, and she felt she would never gain their approval. Not surprisingly, she had a similar complaint about Sharon. April felt that Sharon criticized everything she did, devalued her work, and communicated her judgmental attitude through personal distance, cool objectivity, and formal performance reviews. Rather than disliking Sharon, she grew increasingly defensive and emotional, and desperately sought her praise, support, and recognition.

Sharon, on the other hand, had an alcoholic father who filled her life with emotional uncertainty, stubborn defensiveness regarding criticism, lack of respect for emotional boundaries, and volatile instability. She complained that April was unreliable and defensive, never cleared plans with the team, always came up with unexpected reactions, and was too emotionally needy.

Rather than rejecting April, Sharon wanted her to stay with the team and change her behavior by being more contained, balanced, and predictable. When we asked them to share these personal stories with each other, they discovered the source of their conflict and began solving the problems caused by the behaviors each of them found difficult. Sharon agreed to be less distant and more acknowledging and April agreed to be less defensive and more collaborative, and both agreed to stop thinking of each other as a difficult parent.

Not every conflict ends like this. In many cases, difficult behaviors are too deeply engrained and too integrated with the person's history, identity, fears, anger, and self-doubts to resolve so quickly. In addition, in organizations with conflict-avoidant, emotionally averse cultures, considerations of privacy often discourage managers and employees from asking intimate questions about emotional patterns or early family life, or openly discussing their answers.

Yet it is possible for people in any organization—especially for outsiders such as mediators, coaches, and consultants—to create emotionally supportive team cultures that give people permission to explore family patterns and their role in triggering conflicts, misunderstandings, and poor communications. Resolution of deep, chronic, and engrained conflicts may then become easier, even in adversarial, avoidant, and resistant organizations.

It's *Your* Button

We all have emotional buttons that get pushed from time to time by someone's difficult behavior. Many of these buttons are obvious, especially when they are our own, and the people who seek our attention quickly learn where they are located. Others, however, remain hidden, or are convoluted, disguised, and less easily recognized. These are the ones we need to own and reveal or explain to those who push them.

For example, in a large corporate organization, an internal candidate was strongly favored for promotion to a marketing analyst position, but behaved insensitively to an interviewer who had pushed his buttons during the selection process and was now in disfavor.

At the interview, when she asked him about the pressures he expected to encounter on the job, he responded, "You're not looking for a marketing analyst, you need a psychoanalyst." And when she asked him about difficulties he anticipated in meeting the needs of their customers, he responded, "It's easy, you just give them Prozac."

As it turned out, the woman conducting the interview was deeply involved in psychoanalysis and taking Prozac. She first became hurt, then furious, and rejected him out of hand. Other members of the interview team thought his comments were flippant and silly, but still felt he was the best candidate and did not want to reject him. Their very different responses created a serious conflict on the interviewing team.

When other team members showed empathy for her upset reaction and did not defend his behavior, she agreed to go back to him and tell him how deeply hurt she had been by his comments. When he heard her response he began to cry and apologized sincerely for his insensitive remarks. She realized that he was genuine and sincere and had made the wisecracking remarks because he was nervous about being selected, and agreed to give him the job.

When we openly identify the specific behaviors that push our buttons and speak honestly and vulnerably about our responses to those who pushed them, we defuse them and become less emotionally reactive when someone pushes them again. We increase our balance, health, mental focus, integrity, and internal strength by finding the courage to speak openly and vulnerably about what upsets us, and can then suggest behaviors that will make them more successful in communicating and connecting with us in the future.

Often, what pushes our buttons are behaviors that *we* were not allowed to get away with, or were punished for engaging in, or would secretly like to engage in ourselves. These behaviors may reflect back some part of ourselves that we do not like, or that we believe we should have objected to earlier but did not, or that elicit emotions we have walled up inside, or that we lack the skills to handle.

Remember: even though someone pushes your button, it is *your* button, and you always have a choice in how to respond. Being skillful means choosing your response strategically from multiple alternatives, reducing your feeling that the other person can control you, and allowing you to achieve a greater sense of power in the relationship.

Attitudes, Approaches, and Techniques

You always have a choice about how to respond to difficult behaviors, turning every encounter into a test of your character and skills. You can respond to the behavior by blaming the person and washing your hands of responsibility for the problem; or by regarding it as a challenge and using it to practice increasing your capacity for awareness, empathy, and honesty.

Once you choose to take responsibility for your attitudes and behaviors, including those that trigger difficult behaviors in others, you will listen more empathetically to what your opponent is saying, better understand what is taking place beneath the surface of their behavior, and communicate honestly about what they are doing. There are a number of ways you can improve your skills in responding to difficult behaviors.

Learning successful techniques for responding to difficult behaviors is a lifelong process. Here are a number of attitudes, approaches, and techniques that will support you in responding to people who are engaged in behaviors you find difficult:

- Accept other people and their ideas and feelings about the issues that divide you as legitimate from their perspective. Don't question their character, personality, interests, or feelings.
- Don't try to unilaterally determine the process or how you will each communicate, but agree on ground rules and focus on their behavior and the deeper reasons it bothers you.
- Be willing to collaborate in defining what is wrong with your communication and relationship.
- Calm yourself and locate your center. If they yell at you, *lower* your voice rather than raising it and speak to them with a patient, yet confident tone of voice.
- Do not start by indicating how they should change their behavior. Instead, start with yourself, describe the issue as an "it," and use pronouns like "I," or "we."

- Take responsibility for what you contributed to what is not working between you.
- Express your curiosity about the reasons for their behavior and the sources of conflict between you. Do not assume you already know the answers.
- Search for a deeper, more empathetic understanding. Focus on the behaviors you are *least* able to understand. Ask yourself what would make you behave that way.
- Be willing to observe and release hostile feelings and judgments. Openly acknowledge your own lack of skill in responding to behaviors you do not like.
- Work collaboratively to find solutions. Start by thinking of something *you* can do to improve the situation.
- Tell the truth about your experience and express a desire to improve your relationship.
- Take responsibility for your own false expectations, and apologize openly for them.
- Ask questions to discover their interests, needs, and desires.
- Ask them what their goals are in communicating with you right now, and whether they believe they can achieve those goals by screaming, insulting, or engaging in aggressive behavior.
- Ask them if they would like some coaching on how they could communicate more successfully with you and be more likely to get what they want. If so, offer your responses and suggestions.
- Rigorously respect personal boundaries and differences, including your own.
- Accept the paradoxes, enigmas, riddles, and contradictions in other peoples' behaviors, as well as in your own.
- Strive for *perfect* integrity in your behavior.
- Keep an open mind and an open heart. Give the other person the benefit of the doubt, without conceding that what they are doing is right.
- Model the degree of openness, introspection, and feedback that you would like to receive from them.
- Be *unconditionally* respectful, courteous, acknowledging, and hospitable, regardless of their allegations and behaviors.
- Let them know that if they cannot communicate respectfully, you may temporarily distance yourself to regain your balance and perspective, or help them regain theirs.

- Hold on to your sense of humor, irony, and play, but do not direct it toward or impose it on them.
- Reach for completion and closure. Make your agreements, understandings, decisions, and responsibilities concrete.
- Follow up to make sure they are working, and if not, correct them.

Each of these attitudes, approaches, and techniques has a common core, which is to center yourself in who you are, act responsibly toward others regardless of how difficult they behave, cultivate your capacity for empathy and compassion, and be clear about what will you will do if their behaviors do not change.

As you become stronger and more skillful in your ability to ask for what you need in conflict conversations, you will become more open, honest, and vulnerable. You will be able to offer more powerful feedback about difficult behaviors, and coach or support others in being more effective and authentic in how they interact with you. As a result, you will start to transform the ways you respond, even to the most difficult behaviors, and use your new skills to change your life. These techniques take time to master, but the time will be well spent, particularly if you consider the time you've already wasted being upset about difficult behaviors and feeling powerless in responding to them.

Mediating Difficult Relationships: Bullying

Perhaps the most powerful technique is one used in mediation that explores difficult behaviors through questions by deepening our understanding and appreciation for the fact that every difficult behavior is a *relationship* that is not working for either person. This technique requires a high level of skill, particularly when used by someone who is a party to the conflict.

Consider, for example, the problem of bullying, which is common in many workplaces. Assume there is a dispute in which A says to B: "You are a bully." Many mediators will first reframe the insult by saying to A something like: "So what I'm hearing is that you feel bullied by B," to which A agrees, surfacing A's emotions and reframing bullying as something A *experienced*, rather than judging or labeling B's actions and intentions. This is a good start, but there are a number of additional questions that a mediator might ask to initiate progressively deeper interventions, such as

- "What specifically did B *do* that you consider to be bullying?"
- "What made that *feel* like bullying to you?"
- "What would you have *liked* B to have done instead?"
- "Why do you *allow* yourself to be bullied by B?"
- "How could B have made the same point, but in a way that would not have been *experienced* by you as bullying?"
- "What do each of you think are some of the reasons people in general bully others?"
- "What are some of the rationalizations people generally offer for allowing themselves to be intimidated?"
- "What do you think B wants to *get* through what you call bullying?"
- "If we talk about those issues do you think B will still feel the need to push so hard for what she wants?" "B, is that right?"
- "Can you think of anything A did that encouraged you to engage in what she calls 'bullying'?"
- "What could she do in the future that would encourage you to behave differently?"
- "Would you be willing to try that approach right now and see if it works?"
- "Why do you (B) think A felt intimidated by you?"
- "Was there anything you (A) did that encouraged B to think his behavior was acceptable?"
- "Why (A) did you do that?"
- "Why do you (B) think she felt that way?"
- "Did A do anything that made you (B) feel she consented to or accepted your behavior?"
- "Can you both agree that you could have a much better relationship if you did not engage in or accept bullying behavior?"
- "What are some of the ways your relationship might improve if you moved away from these behaviors?"

- "Was there anyone who was a bully or was bullied your family or in the neighborhood or school where you grew up?"
- "How did you respond to it then?"
- "Would you respond the same way now?" "Why?"
- "Can you agree as a ground rule for your future communications/ relationship that neither of you will act in ways that make the other person feel intimidated?" "Can you also agree that it is OK to refuse to accept bullying behavior?"
- "Can you agree that you will each listen to what the other is saying and not engage in or encourage bullying behavior?"
- "B, is it acceptable to you if A lets you know in the future if she feels intimidated by you?" "How would you like her to do that?"
- "A, is it acceptable to you if B raises issues for discussion and negotiation?" "How would you like him to do that?"

Similar questions can be asked of people in conflict regardless of whether the issue is bullying or any other unwelcome or difficult behavior. New openings for discussion will appear in response, leading to follow-up questions like: "What price have you paid for this behavior?" "What were you afraid would happen if you did/didn't do that?" "What would it take for you to give that up?" Remember that the object of these questions is to lead each person to *his or her own* answers, to encourage people to discover their own *authentic* responses, and help them be vulnerable with each other if they can.

Changing Difficult Behaviors in Organizational Cultures

Many organizations have cultures that foster and reward difficult behaviors and aggravate conflicts. Even when you improve your skills in responding to difficult behaviors or relationships and manage how your buttons get pushed, if your organizational culture does not support open, honest, and empathetic communications and collaborative forms of problem solving, difficult behaviors and chronic conflicts will continue to occur.

Every organizational culture includes a set of norms for behaviors that define what is acceptable and unacceptable. These include unspoken expectations regarding aggressive and collaborative relationships, guidelines for responsive communications, and implicit rules on how to work effectively together. Most often these norms are invisible, yet they shape everyone's thoughts, feelings, and interactions.

Nearly every organization has at least one member who ignores, disobeys, or challenges these rules by engaging in what those who follow the rules regard as destructive, dysfunctional, or difficult behaviors. Despite the damage these behaviors cause, they make it possible for people to recognize that they have the ability to change their culture by agreeing on the behaviors they want to encourage and those they want to discourage.

Often, when we want others to change, we give them personal advice or try to encourage or manipulate them into behaviors that fit our expectations and needs, but not necessarily their own or those of the organization. If you want to discourage difficult behaviors and increase opportunities for skill development, conflict resolution, and improved collaboration, it may be necessary to reshape your organizational culture to support these efforts.

One definition of organizational culture is that it is what everyone knows and no one talks about. But we can't change cultures we aren't allowed to talk about it. Indeed, every organizational culture defends itself against change, raises obstacles to new ways of thinking, and resists altering its core values. This is what gives culture its tremendous staying power. To change an organizational culture, it is necessary to reveal its norms and the ways it defends itself against change.

There are countless defenses against cultural change available to hierarchical, bureaucratic, and autocratic organizations. Perhaps the most common of these, described by nineteenth-century sociologist Max Weber, by organizational theorist Henry Mintzberg, and modified by us, are

- Rewards for competition, individualism, careerism, and selfishness
- Conditioned passivity and reactiveness
- Isolation, fear of being fired, and social fragmentation
- Separation into distinct professional, departmental, and hierarchical subcultures
- Reliance on formal rules, policies, and external forms of discipline

- Impersonal hierarchies of titles, offices, powers, and privileges that reinforce relationships based on superior and inferior status
- Fixed rules and consequences that reduce creativity, authenticity, and individuality
- Goals, processes, rules, and policies that are determined by others, disempowering those who actually do the work
- Separation of official from unofficial truth, resulting in rumors and gossip to fill in the blanks
- Loyalty to regulations and positions, rather than ideas or people
- Systems, structures, and rules that are regarded as superior to values, processes, and relationships
- Stability, tradition, conformity, and experience that are valued over change, innovation, criticism, and insight
- Personalized blame and impersonalized responsibility
- Secrecy and "need to know" that are used to withhold information and augment personal status and power
- Lack of support for candor, whistle-blowing, or anything that might reduce profitability
- Acceptance of stories of victimization and demonization
- Tolerance of covert behaviors, dysfunctional conduct, difficult behaviors, and unresolved conflicts
- Avoidance, aggression, and accommodation that are valued over listening, dialogue, and collaboration
- Conflict suppression and compromise that are valued over deeper forms of resolution and organizational learning

A powerful tool for initiating cultural change in avoidant or resistant cultures is simply to encourage open discussion of unspoken rules. For example, we may ask teams to identify the implicit cultural rules in the organization regarding how conflict or communication is handled in their current culture. We ask them to list the characteristics of their old culture and the characteristics they would like to see in their new culture, then brainstorm ideas on how they might overcome resistance and shift the rules to reinforce the new culture.

Another method is to identify the shared values, ethics, norms, or standards by which people in the organization want to live and ask everyone to agree to honor and promote them. By clarifying their values, ethics, norms, or standards, and committing to them, staff can redefine what behaviors are acceptable, which are not, and how they will respond to those they want to discourage.

To have a significant impact on organizational cultures that tolerate or reward difficult behaviors, it is necessary to openly discuss them and discourage responses that reward, reinforce, or legitimize those behaviors. Anyone, in any organization, can speak up when difficult behaviors take place, ask whether everyone in the group is comfortable with what is happening, and if not, how they would like to behave differently.

It is equally possible for anyone to say, for example, during a meeting, "I'm sorry, but this conversation is not working for me. Could we discuss this issue without yelling at each other?" Or at the end of the meeting, anyone can ask with complete impartiality if each person can make one suggestion on how they might make the next meeting more useful and effective.

It is possible for us to stop people before, during, or after they engage in difficult behavior, ask permission to give them honest feedback, and describe—calmly and gently, using "I" statements—how their behavior is affecting us. We can then ask what we can do to support them in behaving differently.

It is possible to ask our colleagues at work to write down what they feel is working and not working in their interactions, and list the behaviors they and others are engaging in that block or support their successful communications and collaborations. Each person then presents their list, receives honest feedback from others, and makes changes in their behaviors and in the culture as a whole. On the following page is a list of behaviors you can use to initiate this process. Feel free to add your own examples.

In team meetings, it is often useful to ask someone to be a process observer and report on how the team communicated, made decisions, and solved problems. Then the team can discuss what changes they would like to make in the next meeting to improve their process. They can also frame them as ground rules and ask team members to sign and review them before each meeting.

A more hard-hitting approach in difficult and intractable cases is to audiotape or videotape a meeting or conversation and, after watching it on tape, ask each person, starting with the group leader, to describe their *own* behavior, request honest feedback from others, state what they are willing to do differently next time, and indicate what support they would like from others to make sure they do.

WORKSHEET

Behaviors That Block Communication and Collaboration

Score each item from 1 to 5.

1 = Never; 2 = Rarely; 3 = Sometimes; 4 = Often; 5 = Always.

BLOCKING BEHAVIORS	SELF	OTHERS
1. Interrupts discussion	_____	_____
2. Starts side conversations	_____	_____
3. Makes sarcastic comments	_____	_____
4. Builds negative attitudes	_____	_____
5. Ignores others' comments	_____	_____
6. Is argumentative	_____	_____
7. Makes negative facial gestures	_____	_____
8. Dominates discussion	_____	_____
9. Withdraws from discussion	_____	_____
10. Makes tangential remarks	_____	_____
11. Manipulates for personal agenda	_____	_____
12. Resists consensus	_____	_____
13. Forms divisions within the team	_____	_____
14. Down-plays other's contributions	_____	_____
15. Sits apart	_____	_____
16. Arrives late	_____	_____
17. Leaves early	_____	_____
18. Is unwilling to clarify	_____	_____
19. Is defensive	_____	_____
20. Rejects feedback	_____	_____

Behaviors That Support Communication and Collaboration

SUPPORTING BEHAVIOR	SELF	OTHERS
1. Volunteers for roles	_____	_____
2. Encourages others	_____	_____
3. Speaks honestly	_____	_____
4. Asks for feedback	_____	_____
5. Supports the agenda	_____	_____
6. Brings team back to the agenda	_____	_____
7. Monitors time limits	_____	_____
8. Invites others to speak	_____	_____
9. Summarizes results	_____	_____
10. Acknowledges others	_____	_____

SUPPORTING BEHAVIOR	SELF	OTHERS
11. Is on time	_____	_____
12. Brings materials or refreshments	_____	_____
13. Mediates conflicts	_____	_____
14. Requests clarification	_____	_____
15. Is open to others ideas	_____	_____
16. Supports others in discussion	_____	_____
17. Suggests positive processes	_____	_____
18. Shares honest thoughts and feelings	_____	_____
19. Shares information	_____	_____
20. Encourages fun	_____	_____

We often find that people who engage in difficult behavior feel isolated, harassed, and alone. By including them, asking for their advice and support in making the relationship more successful, acknowledging their needs and interests while simultaneously refusing to accept their difficult behaviors, and suggesting constructive workable alternatives, it is possible to shift their attitudes and styles without rewarding their problem behaviors.

Classroom teachers know that "problem children" are often quite willing to give up their hostile or antagonistic attitudes toward other members of the class when they feel included and acknowledged or are assigned a role or job that is valued by others. As the poet Edwin Markham wrote,

> They drew a circle to shut me out,
> Heretic, rebel, a thing to flout.
> But Love and I had the wit to win,
> We drew a circle that took them in.

A team of teachers in an elementary school was trying to work together across grades and subjects but having tremendous difficulty including one of their team members. Fred, the only man on a team with four women, refused to take part in team meetings. He sat on the outside grading papers while the others tried unsuccessfully to draw him in. He routinely expressed his contempt for the team process, which he called "touchy-feely" and regarded as interfering with his right to teach however he wanted.

Toward the end of one team meeting, Fred announced he was leaving early because he had been called to the principal's office to meet with a complaining parent. The other team members stopped him as he got up and said that because they were a team, if there was any complaint from a parent it should be directed to the team as a whole and they would all go with him.

They adjourned the meeting and went together to the principal's office, and after listening to the parent's complaint about Fred's strictness, they spoke to the parent about Fred's outstanding teaching abilities and what they saw as his success in setting high standards for her child. They helped Fred see how he might be more effective in reaching parents and children who were not performing according to his standards. After that, Fred became an active, enthusiastic team member and an ardent supporter of the team process. They found a way of drawing a circle that took him in.

Feedback Versus Evaluation

As we have indicated, one way of discouraging difficult behaviors is for people who regularly work together to give each other frequent, open, honest, empathetic, and timely feedback about what is working in their relationship and communication, and what is not. Relationships are living, vulnerable, constantly changing, and highly sensitive to environmental influences. Yet they also seek stability and defend themselves against harmful changes. As a result, like all living things, they require ongoing effective feedback to grow, evolve, adapt—and simply to stay alive. When feedback dies, relationships start to wither and fall apart, generating apathy, cynicism, and chronic conflict.

Feedback is merely an honest, empathetic, nonjudgmental, subjective response to another person's communications or behaviors. Evaluation is a more objective, less personal intervention oriented to assessing the effectiveness of an action, strategy, event, or project. Unlike feedback, evaluation focuses on objective experiences, actions, and deeds, rather than on subjective perceptions, feelings, and behaviors. Both are useful in teams, as well as in conflict resolution, to assess what worked and what didn't, correct course, and reach closure on what happened.

When applied to people, personalities, or behaviors, evaluation usually implies judging, criticizing, grading, or exercising power or control over another person, usually to their detriment. When applied to actions, strategies, events, or projects, evaluation is an excellent way of identifying why one approach was successful and another was not, and correcting in midstream.

It is always best to begin a feedback or evaluation process by looking at yourself. In this way, you can model the level of honesty and nondefensiveness you expect from others and your ideas will be received more openly. After receiving feedback, whether it is disturbing or congratulatory, sincerely thank the person who gave it for helping you improve. Then consider how feedback did and did not support learning and collaboration, and identify ways of improving the next feedback session. Both feedback and evaluation are most effective when they are

- Begun with a request for permission to offer it
- Opened with a self-assessment by the person giving it
- Delivered as an "I" statement
- Reciprocally exchanged
- Given by one's peers
- Offered constructively
- Specific and detailed
- Balanced and fair
- Communicated in real time or shortly afterwards
- Presented without anger or judgment
- Supportive of learning, growth, and change
- Accepted with sincere thanks from the person receiving it
- Taken seriously
- Designed and intended to promote improvement
- Given reciprocally, collaboratively, and in tandem so no one is in a one-down position, immune from learning, or discouraged from doing better

In an electronics firm that produced equipment to support space exploration, Sam was a relatively new employee of about eight months, but a seasoned professional engineer and Ph.D. who had previously worked at another aeronautics firm. He had excellent skills and experience, and was hired as a nonmanager in a research area because of his outstanding qualifications.

Mike was Sam's manager, and had been a manager with the company for fifteen years. He joined the company as a nonmanager and been promoted through the ranks. He was an outstanding performer who was highly thought of both for his technical expertise and management skills. Mike had completed a bachelor's degree plus a master's while working full-time.

Mike liked Sam and was pleased to have someone on his team with such superior knowledge and experience. Sam, on the other hand, saw Mike as "beneath him" in education, skills, and experience. Mike could not figure out why Sam was behaving in a disrespectful manner, including interrupting him in front of his staff, correcting him with what he thought was the right answer (but not how the company did things), and repeatedly mentioning his Ph.D. and years of experience.

We met with Mike and Sam individually, then brought them together and asked them to give each other feedback and say what they needed from each other to build a more successful working relationship. Mike said he felt Sam was being overly competitive and uncooperative. Sam became silent, took a defensive posture, and began to sulk.

We probed a bit and Sam revealed that he felt lost in the new culture and was surprised and confused that his experience elsewhere and educational credentials did not seem to mean a "hell of a lot" to Mike. He asked Mike to tell him the truth—how did he view him as a fellow professional? He said he had no idea how Mike viewed him or if he valued his input; Sam added that he had a lot riding on this job.

Mike, in shock, told Sam in glowing terms how much he admired him, wanted him to be on the team, and desperately needed his expertise and wisdom to succeed with a new and very demanding customer. Sam sighed with relief and thanked Mike for the feedback and supportive response.

We then asked Sam to give Mike feedback, and he said how much he respected Mike's practical experience and leadership skills. In response, Mike asked him why he was so critical of him in front of staff and customers. Sam said he felt nervous because he was new to the culture and thought Mike didn't appreciate his expertise. Now that he knew how Mike felt and how he should behave, he would make sure he spoke more respectfully in public. As a result of this conversation, Sam's "difficult behaviors" melted away, and they continued to use supportive feedback in their ongoing interactions.

Responding to Difficult Behaviors in Meetings

Anyone who has worked in an organization has spent considerable time in meetings. In any collaborative group process such as team building, strategic planning, and organizational change, people end up meeting frequently with peers and coworkers. The number, variety, and pace of organizational meetings have increased steadily over the years, yet improving skills and effectiveness in conducting them seems to have lagged behind.

Difficult behaviors often blossom in meetings, leaving people frustrated and feeling powerless, or trapped and held hostage by behaviors that are difficult, embarrassing, or painful to experience. Nearly everyone feels there is little they can do in these meetings other than remain silent and wait for them to end. Our experience is different.

There are many ways we can respond to difficult behaviors in meetings that do not require advance agreement by participants and can be implemented unilaterally. In doing so, it is important to distinguish between those who disagree passionately with the direction a meeting is taking, or with a group policy or decision, but still want to make a contribution to the work—and those who are disruptive and engaging in difficult behaviors for other reasons, often emanating from unresolved conflicts in other areas of their life.

Successful meetings are those where learning takes place, there is active criticism and honest disagreement, and dissenting opinions are heard and openly discussed. Constructive conflicts make meetings interesting and valuable, and conscious efforts to acknowledge and satisfy the legitimate interests of anyone interested enough to disagree will make meetings more effective.

It is especially important not to be frightened because people feel passionately about an issue. Passion can be expressed or experienced as anger, an obstacle to open dialogue, a judgment of the other side's integrity, and a block to consensus. But passion and intense feelings can also represent a deep level of caring and be expressed and experienced constructively without triggering negative side effects.

If you are experiencing consistently difficult behaviors, consider one or more of the following approaches to improving your next meeting. These methods will help you call attention to difficult behaviors that are limiting the success of the meeting and identify ways of responding and transforming them.

- Before the meeting, request assistance from those who regularly engage in difficult behaviors in making the meeting more effective, or ask them to suggest ways of making the meeting more successful.
- Inform them that one of the topics on the agenda will be a discussion of what happened at the last meeting. Ask them to

say what they think could be done differently in the future so their meetings can be more satisfying for everyone.

- Interview them about what they think makes meetings effective and model empathetic and responsive listening.
- Be explicit about what you want to achieve. Listen to them during the meeting as you would like them to listen to others.
- Meet with other group members before the meeting. Ask them to include these people and acknowledge or validate their contributions. Ask them to calmly yet honestly confront behaviors they find difficult to accept, keep to the agenda, and refuse to engage in diversionary arguments.
- Negotiate ground rules for future meetings.
- Create listening teams to improve understanding, empathy, and acceptance of diverse positions. Ask everyone to pair up with someone with an opposing or different point of view and ask each person to present their partner's ideas and perspectives to the group.
- Create a "fishbowl" discussion of issues where pairs of opponents discuss the issues while other group members observe and give them feedback. Call time-outs and invite designated observers to offer feedback on the process.
- Draw out their motives and respond directly to what you imagine are their deepest, most positive, and constructive intentions, rather than responding to their critical statements or difficult behaviors, or perhaps even the content of their issues.
- Offer an honest, personal, and vulnerable response to their actions. Say, "I feel powerless to accomplish anything when you get so angry or talk so much during our meetings."
- Give them a special task or role in the meeting that is valued by the group, such as facilitating, recording, observing the process, or time keeping.
- Ask each person to summarize the other side's arguments. Ask the other side if the summary was accurate and correct it if it fell short.
- Suggest role reversal. Ask those who have been silent to do all the talking for five minutes and those who were talking to remain silent. Then debrief. Or, ask critics to argue in support and supporters to criticize, and again debrief the discussion.

- Create a moment of silence and ask everyone to think about what just happened in a difficult encounter, then encourage people to share their thoughts.
- Find some basis for agreeing with the person engaging in difficult behavior. Ask, "If everything else were acceptable, would that still be an issue for you?" and "If so, why?" Then discuss the issue and the person's problem with it.
- Support or agree with the interests being expressed and limit your disagreement to process or content.
- Reframe their statements to show how they might communicate more constructively. Ask, "Is this what you are saying?"
- Acknowledge their feelings and ideas, and ask if others share them. If not, move on.
- Ask clarifying questions first and open debate or discussion afterwards.
- Post issues neutrally on a flip chart without anyone's names, or refer to them as "proposal A and proposal B" to defuse ownership and "political" reasons for opposition.
- Post opposing points of view so everyone knows they've been heard and the point does not need to be repeated. When it is repeated, put a conspicuous check mark next to it.
- Take a straw vote on their idea to see if there is any support for continuing the discussion.
- Post significant contributions people make in the meeting to create a sense of group ownership.
- Consider recording the number of contributions, disruptions, or times each person spoke.
- At the end of the meeting, ask everyone to make one suggestion for how the next meeting might go better.
- Agree on ground rules for the next meeting and sanctions if they are repeatedly violated.
- Ask a professional to facilitate the meeting.
- Bring in a mediator to resolve conflicts before, during, or after the meeting.

A massive change process was under way in a large, well-known entertainment industry company, and meetings just increased their frustration and distrust. The group's vice president, Cathy, was a "nice person" who had few organizational skills. She meant well and was technically proficient, but seemed unable to create a clear agenda, delegate tasks, or answer important questions.

On the other hand, Ted, the organization's comptroller, loved to dominate meetings and used them to attack, criticize, cajole, and blame others for their failures. Everyone dreaded attending meetings with Ted and spent their time ducking his barbs or holding back their anger.

A group of employees felt strongly that Ted's behavior had to stop or "the organization will implode," and invited us to facilitate the next meeting. We began by asking each person to write down one suggestion for how they could make this meeting effective. Afterwards, we read their comments to the group. Many of the suggestions were for Ted to stop trying to control the meeting.

Ted was shocked, but immediately agreed to do so if the rest of the group would take more responsibility for making meetings more efficient. In the discussion that followed, we asked if everyone agreed with Ted that successful meetings were everyone's responsibility, and they did. The group then divided into small brainstorming teams and used a round-robin process to come up with creative ideas for improving their meetings. During the brainstorming process, Ted became just one participant among many and could not dominate the discussion.

The teams reported on their ideas and they easily reached consensus on changes they would implement. Volunteers drafted a set of procedures and ground rules for the next meeting, facilitated it, and everyone became more conscious of what was not working and agreed to stop it. They agreed to spend five minutes at the end of each meeting discussing how it went and offering ideas to improve the next session.

The meeting was a great success and everyone agreed that they would rotate facilitators and recorders at every meeting, review and reach consensus on ground rules for respectful communications and constructive behaviors, discuss issues more frequently in small teams, use a round-robin process for brainstorming, and evaluate each meeting at the end. As a result, Cathy was able to offer leadership in their meetings and they were able to control their comptroller.

Before moving too quickly to silence what you or your colleagues consider difficult behaviors, consider whether you may be engaging in some yourself, and whether the real reason for difficult behaviors might be the fact that no one is listening, or suggestions for improvement are not being heard, or people legitimately disagree, or there is a procedural flaw in the meeting. Walk in the other person's shoes for a while in your imagination and consider how you would feel before putting a stop to what may actually be a healthy response to an unhealthy or dysfunctional situation.

Imagining a World Without Difficult Behaviors

Every difficult behavior represents a lesson we can learn, a challenge we can address, and a skill we can develop. By rejecting people who engage in difficult behaviors, we may actually lose a unique opportunity to learn from them. This idea lies at the heart of the following story, related by Anthony De Mello:

> There was once a rabbi who was revered by the people as a man of God. Not a day went by when a crowd of people wasn't standing at his door seeking advice or healing or the holy man's blessing.... There was, however, in the audience a disagreeable fellow who never missed a chance to contradict the master. He would observe the rabbi's weaknesses and make fun of his defects to the dismay of the disciples, who began to look on him as the devil incarnate. Well, one day the "devil" took ill and died. Everyone heaved a sigh of relief. Outwardly, they looked appropriately solemn, but in their hearts they were glad.... So the people were surprised to see the master plunged in genuine grief at the funeral. When asked by a disciple later if he was mourning over the eternal fate of the dead man, he said, "No, no. Why should I mourn over our friend, who is now in heaven? It was for myself I was grieving. That man was the only friend I had. Here I am surrounded by people who revere me. He was the only one who challenged me. I fear that with him gone, I shall stop growing." And, as he said those words, the master burst into tears.

Carlos Castaneda, author of the Don Juan chronicles, has written about the value of having a difficult person or "petty tyrant" in one's life. Castaneda argues that only through a petty tyrant does one learn patience, endurance, and perseverance.

Who would we be without the difficult behaviors of others, without opponents, troublemakers, boat rockers, and gadflies? What one person finds difficult, another may find useful, or indicative of integrity or determination. Literature, drama, and popular culture would be uniformly bland, boring, and useless without the tension created by difficult behaviors. History would cease and social progress would certainly come to an end.

In some Native American cultures there were individuals who were highly regarded for doing everything exactly opposite to the way it was usually done by others. If everyone danced clockwise, they would dance counterclockwise. If everyone cried, they would laugh. They did so to preserve the harmony and balance of the universe, which is not one-sided but grounded more deeply in a unity of opposites. Just as there cannot be an up without a down, there cannot be easy behaviors without difficult ones. Difficulty can therefore be located not in what other people do, but in the *attitude* we bring to what they do.

Charles Swindoll has written powerfully about the importance of attitude in determining how we live our lives:

> Words can never adequately convey the incredible impact of our attitude toward life. The longer I live the more convinced I become that life is 10 percent what happens to us and 90 percent how we respond to it. I believe the single most significant decision I can make on a day-to-day basis is my choice of attitude. It is more important than my past, my education, my bankroll, my successes or failures, fame or pain, what other people think of me or say about me, my circumstances, or my position. Attitude keeps me going or cripples my progress. It alone fuels my fire or assaults my hope. When my attitudes are right, there's no barrier too high, no valley too deep, no dream too extreme, no challenge too great for me.

You can always choose not to have difficult people in your life and just go elsewhere when they appear. But if you choose to go elsewhere, make sure you do not give up too soon, let yourself off the hook and lose an opportunity for growth, resolution, and transformation. If you do not take time to understand and learn from behaviors that are difficult for you, and discover how you have contributed to them, wherever you go you will find yourself in the presence of someone who acts exactly like the person you left behind and be unprepared to respond effectively.

If you focus on trying to learn from those whose behaviors you find difficult, you will recognize that their behaviors are difficult for reasons only you can identify, learn from, and come to appreciate. You can use these behaviors to investigate and probe your discomfort; improve your skills in awareness, empathy, compassion and honesty; monitor and correct your behaviors; and improve your relationships by confronting and working through these difficulties rather than blaming them on others. You can search for creative and collaborative solutions, and create circles that draw others in.

STRATEGY 8

LEAD AND COACH FOR TRANSFORMATION

Where, after all, do universal human rights begin? In small places, close to home—so close and so small that they cannot be seen on any map of the world. Yet they are the world of the individual person: the neighborhood he lives in; the school or college he attends; the factory, farm or office where he works.... Unless these rights have meaning there, they have little meaning anywhere.

—Eleanor Roosevelt

It is in the small places in our conflicts that leadership begins and is most needed. Rather than lecturing or preaching to others about what they should do to resolve their disputes, we can lead by *being* a living example, as Eleanor Roosevelt was, of the things we believe in. We achieve this by "walking the talk"—seeking collaborative solutions and transforming our attitudes and approaches to conflicts through vision, coaching, and committed action.

Conflicts in the workplace call out for leaders who can envision and incite collaboration, even with their worst opponents; leaders who model conflict resolution skills and attitudes in the midst of intense disagreements, who teach and coach others in strategies for resolving their disputes, and are able to transform attitudes as well as organizations.

Transformational leaders recognize the value of diversity, dissent, and disagreement. They search conflicts for opportunities to resolve underlying issues, improve relationships, and reconcile differences. They surface hidden tensions in organizations, learn from their opponents, and collaboratively negotiate solutions. They invite feedback and evaluation, and help design systems, structures, processes, relationships, and cultures that support not only resolution but also prevention and transformational change.

Leaders as Committed Listeners

We observed a leader model what it means to be a committed listener in a workshop we led for teachers in a large urban school district, on the day he was hired as superintendent. We invited him to join our meeting with teacher leaders in the district and he came to the session, we assumed, to make a speech. Instead, he invited *them* to speak, found a seat in the audience, took out a pen and paper, and wrote detailed notes regarding their conflicts, issues, questions, and comments.

He repeatedly invited the teachers to tell him about the conflicts, problems, and difficult conditions in their schools, to specify exactly what they wanted from him, and to join and assist him in improving student learning. He asked open-ended questions and gave unguarded responses. He asked for advice and suggested partnerships to find solutions. He listened for feelings, meanings, intentions, and suggestions for improvement, and sent a clear message that he genuinely valued everyone's ideas, wanted their collaboration, and was a leader who could be an empathetic, responsive, and committed listener. As a result, his leadership debut was a huge success.

Effective leadership requires committed listening, not only to those who agree with us, but to those who criticize, distrust, and attack our ideas. The best leaders recognize that criticism, distrust, and personal attacks indicate that the person confronting them actually *cares* intensely about the problem, and is probably committed to creating successful outcomes.

These leaders regard criticism as an *invitation* to learning and achieving better results, so they listen as though their personal effectiveness depended not only on hearing what is said, but also on what is *meant* but not said, and letting others know they have been heard. Doing so changes the *form* of conflicts and thereby transforms them.

There is always a danger that leaders, managers, officials, and "higher-ups" in an organization will put on a show, pretend that everything is fine when it isn't, sweep conflicts under the rug, suppress dissent, reward "yes-men," and try to settle disputes through "more of the same" compromises rather than engaging in the difficult, time-consuming work of resolving and transforming them.

When leaders model avoidant, suppressive, and aggressive behaviors, others naturally follow, expecting to be rewarded for repeating what their boss or role model has demonstrated. Transformational leaders listen closely for signs of internal tension within their organizations, analyze their sources, and act in ways that encourage fundamentally different approaches to the conflict. They make their own disagreements explicit, respond to opponents directly, and proactively try to predict and prevent conflicts before they occur.

Tom was an example of just such a leader and, as one of the most powerful executives in the television industry, he was determined to surface conflicts quickly and resolve them immediately so they would not slow down the rapid pace of work in his company.

Tom was particularly interested in the success of William, one of the vice presidents in sales and marketing, who was the only African American at that level in the hierarchy. Tom was committed to making diversity work in the company, and wanted William to succeed in resolving any difficulties that came his way.

Tom began to get reports about conflicts on William's team, and knowing that these tensions could easily escalate, began looking into the source of the problem, which was several levels below his in the hierarchy. He found that William was facing unusual resistance and wondered if racial tensions were fueling the dispute below the surface of ordinary disagreements. He asked us to offer conflict coaching for William so that he could increase his skills and get the support he needed to successfully resolve disputes over his marketing plan and other team projects.

Sure enough, when we met with William and his team members and encouraged them to put their cards on the table, issues about his role as a manager emerged. One team member, in a painful but extremely honest confession, revealed that she had never worked for anyone from a different race before, did not trust him because he was different, and found herself resenting his success. She did not want to feel this way, and asked for coaching on how to tell William about her realization. Before she did, we coached William on how he might respond to her as her *leader*, rather than as her opponent.

In his private meeting with her, William handled her confession with great skill and empathy. He described his own journey as a leader and how difficult it was for him to lead people who did not really understand or trust him. He sent a message that these tensions had to be faced and worked through before they could escalate and block the team's success. He surfaced the issue himself in a team meeting without mentioning her, and led a remarkably open and honest discussion about race and leadership that shifted the team's attitudes and gained their trust.

When stress threatens organizational stability and creates an environment where disputes proliferate, transformational leaders help clarify the "big picture," identify possible strategies for intervention, and transform the context in which the conflict is taking place. When leaders listen empathetically and responsively to their opponents and publicly thank them for raising issues that lead to better solutions, they allow the pulse and promise of the organization to be felt by everyone and encourage collaborative efforts to intervene before conflicts become destructive.

Leaders only inspire trust if they consistently act with integrity and are congruent with their values. This means listening not only to those who agree with them, but to their opponents, critics, and those who engage in difficult behaviors. It means listening for deeper meanings and common interests, taking responsibility for what *they* contributed to the conflict, speaking honestly, and participating in open dialogues and collaborative negotiations over contentious issues.

Leaders as Transformational Change Agents

Leaders not only model collaborative, interest-based approaches to conflict resolution, they also assist in designing organizational systems, structures, processes, relationships, and cultures that promote heterarchical, innovative, and democratic solutions, rather than hierarchical, bureaucratic, and autocratic ones. They seek not just incremental changes but transformational improvements in the ways conflicts are handled.

When the leaders of a high-tech communications firm began to develop a conflict resolution system for their staff, they soon realized that their organizational culture was one of "public compliance and private defiance." Staff, managers, and executives commonly hid evidence of disagreements, disputes, and conflicts from those around them, and the message everyone got was that it was best to remain silent in the presence of conflicts, including sexual harassment, racial discrimination, bitter personal attacks, and bullying arguments.

Mark, the chief financial officer (CFO), reported to us that he needed a confidential consultation concerning a quandary he was facing. He reported that Elsa, a secretary to one of the managers who reported to him, had requested a private meeting. Since he had an open-door policy, he met with her and she reported, amid tears and great embarrassment, that Miguel, a manager who also reported to him but was not her boss, had been "bothering her, in that way."

Mark did not ask for details or respond, but asked for a few days to think about what she had told him and sent her back to her desk. He told us, "I guess in my reaction, I must have complied with our usual approach, which is to cover up any disagreeable news. I thought that if I showed any sympathy the problem might get worse. The truth is, I don't even know what it was Miguel did to her, and I guess I hoped she'd just forget about it so I could get back to my job. I need some help with this one."

We recommended that he first get clear about his own emotions, judgments, and assumptions regarding the matter Elsa had brought to him, and probe whatever feelings he had regarding Elsa and Miguel. We discussed the issue with human resources and the legal department, and it was decided that Mark would meet with Miguel to find out his side of the story. Miguel was shocked, admitted he had flirted a bit with Elsa, and said he wanted to meet with her to apologize.

It became clear that Elsa also wanted to reach an understanding with Miguel, whom she liked as a colleague, and had no intention of filing a lawsuit. In their meeting, Elsa and Miguel were able to move in and out of speaking Spanish and draw on their common Latino heritage and culture to communicate informally, which would have been far more difficult in the restrained and formal language and culture of the organization.

Elsa was able to tell Miguel that his "off-color" jokes near her desk and in the staff kitchen made her feel very uncomfortable and she felt he was singling her out. The week before, he had followed her to her car at the end of the day, asked questions about where she lived, whether she had a "guy" at home, and what she was doing that night, which made her feel *very* uncomfortable, especially as he was a manager and she was supposed to show him respect. She felt he stood too close to her when she got into her car and was afraid he was going to grab her or do something to her.

Mark asked Miguel if he understood what Elsa was saying and how she might be feeling. Miguel acknowledged that she was right in her description. He said he was feeling pretty lonely in his life outside of work, was recently divorced, and his twin sister, with whom he had been very close, had just died after a long and debilitating illness. He apologized to Elsa for intruding in her space and making her feel uncomfortable. He just felt he needed a friend and did not know how to ask her to be that person for him.

Elsa said she understood and was sorry about his sister, but did not have space in her life for a new friend. She hoped he would find someone who did and asked him to respect her as a coworker, which he agreed to do. Mark thanked them for their honesty and making their conflicting needs clear to each other. They ended their conversation by shaking hands and agreeing to say "buenos dias" to each other when their paths crossed in the mornings.

While Miguel and Elsa did not become friends, Mark helped them be more respectful by surfacing their conflict and working with them until they found a solution to which they could both commit. In the process, he enabled Elsa and Miguel to remain in the same organization, transformed his own complicity in their conflict culture, and became a leader by modeling a proactive approach to conflict communication.

A word of warning: sexual harassment claims are complex and can be very difficult to resolve. Be sure before trying to do so that you seek the advice and assistance of a professional mediator and work closely with human resources and legal departments to understand where your efforts might go awry.

Competencies of Leaders as Conflict Resolvers

Leaders who are willing to surface and resolve conflicts require a unique set of leadership competencies that enable them to learn what their conflicts have to teach, create paths to resolution, and reveal opportunities for personal and organizational transformation. The conflict resolution competencies for leaders that follow are based on Warren Bennis's seminal research on leadership. (See Warren Bennis and Joan Goldsmith, *Learning to Lead: A Workbook on Becoming a Leader*, Fourth Edition.) As you review each competency, ask yourself how you might incorporate it in your effort to become a leader in resolving conflicts at work.

Competency One: Master the Context

Conflicts take place not only between people but in social and organizational contexts that influence the way they play out and get resolved. Even conflicts over relatively minor issues can result from stresses and tensions that originate in the larger context of our work, including the structures, systems, and cultures that influence workplace environments; "big-picture" social, economic, and political issues that have an indirect impact on the organization of our work; and confusion or differences over the values and conceptual frameworks we use to understand or explain our conflicts.

Leaders are able to identify and address these larger contextual elements in conflict, whether they occur in organizations, communities, or the larger world, and use them to inform problem solving. They actively promote values that support resolution, but do not seek to impose them on others. They investigate contextual differences, disagreements, and diversity, but seek bridges and unifying elements that bring opposing sides together.

Competency Two: Know Yourself

Leaders who seek to resolve conflicts or mediate disputes between others need to know themselves, be aware of and sensitive to their personal conflict histories, understand their strengths and weaknesses in resolving their own disputes, and recognize the assumptions, expectations, biases, belief systems, and values they bring to each dispute. When in conflict with others, they are aware of their own deficiencies and invite others to fill any gaps they may have in understanding or skill.

Competency Three: Create a Vision for the Future

When leaders mediate and attempt to resolve conflicts, they are able to create and enlist collaboration and support for powerful unifying visions that excite people's imaginations, reveal what is possible for them to learn from each other, and encourage collaborative efforts at resolution and transformation. When they are insulted or confronted by their opponents, their vision allows them to maintain perspective and continue working to translate them into reality. Their vision reminds opponents of their larger purpose and encourages them to rise above petty grievances to create an inspiring future.

Competency Four: Communicate with Meaning

Communicating with meaning is an especially important leadership competency in conflict resolution. Leaders communicate in an effort to convey the deeper meaning of the conflict to those who are in it. They elicit frequent feedback to discover the meaning their communications have for others. For this reason, they avoid pronouncements, attacks, insults, judgments, and disrespectful statements, and use questions to reveal the underlying issues that are triggering the conflict.

Competency Five: Maintain Trust Through Integrity

Leaders in conflict maintain a clear sense of *unconditional* integrity and consistently demonstrate their values and vision by engaging in congruent and trustworthy behavior. They express their values and integrity in the smallest details and maintain them throughout the process. They seek, support, and value integrity and trustworthiness in those with whom they work. They understand that trust is essential to gain support for change and transformation, both in personal conflicts and in shifting the organization's conflict culture.

Competency Six: Realize Intention Through Action

Leaders are committed to demonstrating their intention of resolving conflicts and producing positive, concrete, lasting results through action. Whether as parties to a conflict or as mediators or coaches, leaders attempt to translate insights, decisions, and agreements into specific action steps that can be observed and measured. Leaders seek concrete changes in personal behaviors, as well as in organizational systems, structures, processes, relationships, and cultures.

As you review these leadership competencies, consider how you might gain greater insight into your own leadership skills and define areas of possible growth and development. Try completing the following leadership assessment instrument to help you discover how your conflicts might assist you in developing your leadership skills.

To complete the instrument, assess your current level in each leadership competency and indicate any actions you will take to improve your skills as a conflict resolver. Once you complete the assessment, you may want to discuss it with a colleague, supervisor, or someone who works for you to elicit feedback on each item.

WORKSHEET

Leadership Assessment Instrument

Please assess your leadership on the competencies below. Indicate a rating of 1 to 5:

1 = does not demonstrate this competency

5 = is highly successful in demonstrating this competency

On the right side of the page, indicate the actions you want to take to improve your leadership.

1. Master the Context

RATING	COMPETENCY	ACTIONS
	Is aware of issues in the larger context or environment and their impact on creating conflicts.	
	Listens to all sides in disputes and actively gathers input from all parties and from sources that may influence them.	

(continued)

Encourages diverse input and perspectives when seeking resolution in her own conflicts, or those brought to her for resolution.

Considers all possible outcomes, impacts, and alternatives when considering a proposal for resolution.

Takes calculated risks to improve conflict resolution resources in the organization as a whole.

2. Know Yourself

RATING	COMPETENCY	ACTIONS
	Focuses on self-learning and developing a learning environment for all staff to build conflict resolution skills and the capacity to learn from disagreements.	
	Cultivates relationships and alliances with teams and leaders and regards disputes as learning opportunities for herself and others.	
	Builds networks of colleagues to create professional learning communities to improve mediation skills.	
	Views conflicts, errors, and mistakes as learning opportunities for leadership development, both for herself and others. Is introspective and reflective.	
	Participates regularly in staff development sessions that are focused on mediation skills as a leader and a learner.	

3. Create a Vision for the Future

RATING	COMPETENCY	ACTIONS
	Is clear about her own vision for a conflict-free future and articulates it powerfully to increase consensus regarding conflict resolution in the future.	

Pursues opportunities for mediation and develops strategies for conflict resolution systems that are consistent with the articulated vision.

Helps individuals define personal visions and clarify roles and assists the organization in creating a vision for resolving disputes.

Revisits the organization's vision regularly to revise it, identify conflicts that flow from it, and align strategies to realize it.

Is able to let go of past practices and expectations that may be triggering conflicts and create a future in which there is greater unity and less friction within the organization.

4. Communicate with Meaning

RATING	COMPETENCY	ACTIONS
	Practices empathetic listening and honest dialogue with all staff and colleagues. Tells the truth.	
	Is willing to confront conflicts and pursue resolution of issues that are contentious.	
	Is clear about her own voice as a mediator and peacemaker and is able to make it heard.	
	Seeks feedback and changes behavior to prevent conflicts and to create greater unity through dialogue.	
	Constructively uses disagreements and conflicts to develop innovative, collaborative solutions.	

5. Maintain Trust Through Integrity

RATING	COMPETENCY	ACTIONS
	Has clear values regarding communication and respect for differences, and communicates them through behavior and commitments.	

(*continued*)

Provides others with opportunities to learn from mistakes and problems, and uses conflicts as signals that learning experiences are possible.

Values diversity and supports all viewpoints being heard and respected, and explores conflicts to reveal possible areas of agreement.

Returns people stuck in conflicts to trust and resolution by consistently upholding values, ethics, and standards. Integrity is made explicit by congruent behavior.

Provides opportunities for others to demonstrate and stretch their skills in resolving conflicts.

6. Realize Intentions Through Action

RATING	COMPETENCY	ACTIONS
	Gets results and adds value by transforming conflict resolution strategies into regular behaviors that produce results.	
	Assumes personal responsibility for decreasing time, energy, and focus devoted to conflicts and for improving achievement.	
	Eliminates bureaucratic roadblocks that prevent resolution of disputes and encourages creative action.	
	Evaluates systems and processes to improve conflict resolution processes.	
	Gives credit to others for their contributions to a resolution and creates prevention-oriented organizational systems and culture.	

Resolving Conflicts Through Social Networks

Research has shown that effective social and organizational change, educational reform, disease control, economic interventions, constructive responses to natural disasters, and conflict resolution all rely on the capacity of communities, organizations, families, and individuals to create supportive social networks.

Social scientists Nicholas Christakis and James Fowler analyzed data in a longitudinal study focused on the causes of heart disease. In their book, *Connected: The Surprising Power of Our Social Networks and How They Shape Our Lives*, they reported that people's positions in social networks have a deep effect on how they fare in their lives, and as a general rule, people with more friends and connections are happier, healthier, and have a greater sense of well-being.

Their research affirms an earlier study by Gale Berkowitz called *Friendship Among Women*, showing that social ties reduce the risk of disease by lowering blood pressure, heart rate, and cholesterol. When researchers looked at how well women functioned after the death of a spouse, they found that those who had a close friend or confidante were more likely to survive the experience without any new physical impairments or permanent loss of vitality. Those without friends were not so fortunate. Women who had no friends increased their risk of death over a six-month period following the death of a spouse, whereas those who had the most friends over a nine-year period cut their risk of death by more than 60 percent.

The decades-long Nurses' Health Study at Harvard Medical School found that the more friends women had the less likely they were to develop physical impairments as they aged and the more likely they were to be leading joyful lives. The results were so significant that researchers found that not having close friends or confidantes was as detrimental to health as smoking or carrying extra weight.

The greatest barrier to the creation of successful social networks, friendships, and communities are unresolved conflicts at home and at work. Many of these conflicts arise from chronic and consistent poor communication, difficult and disruptive behaviors, unrealistic and unmet expectations, lack of role clarity and uncertain responsibilities, perceptions of victimization when resources are scarce, fear or anxiety over changes in the environment or in one's status or role, contradictory self-interests, and unresolved fears and insecurities.

These sources of conflict are persistent and widespread in organizations where leaders do not seek to create environments that are life enhancing and that support positive social relationships. The challenge for leaders on every level is therefore to build skills in identifying and resolving conflicts and create networks and relationships that support people as well as organizations.

No leader can do this alone. Creating and leading organizations in which conflicts are openly and effectively addressed requires the active participation of employees who form the social networks that underpin all effective organizational systems and structures. Leadership in resolving conflicts is not limited to the top of the hierarchy or to publicly recognized officials, but includes everyone at work, even those on the lowest rungs of the organizational ladder. The ancient Chinese scholar Lao-tzu advised in his classic text, the *Tao Te Ching:*

> The best of all rulers is but a shadowy presence to his subjects.
> Next comes the ruler they love and praise;
> Next comes one they fear;
> Next comes one with whom they take liberties
> ... ...
> Hesitant, the best does not utter words lightly.
> When his task is accomplished and his work done
> The people all say, "it happened to us naturally."

The transformational power of leaders who enable people to resolve their conflicts and find viable solutions to shared problems requires not only the competencies we have explored, but the willingness to coach people to both sides of the conflict and assist them in learning to resolve their disputes so they can say "it happened to us naturally."

Leaders as Conflict Coaches

The increasing emergence of leaders and employees as "conflict coaches" and the escalating use of coaching to assist people in conflict reflect a growing need for personal advice, supportive networks, and strategic mentoring in responding to conflicts and problems. This trend is well described by Warren Bennis:

> I think it's generally a healthy sign that more and more people are engaging with leaders who are coaches, and it's becoming a more robust profession. That means that even leaders feel unembarrassed

> to ask for help. Once you become a leader, you are never fully prepared. I don't care how much experience you have, being a leader is like having your first child: it is always amateur night.

Most organizational leaders, managers, and employees have not been trained in conflict resolution techniques and feel like amateurs when facing complex disputes that can diminish their power and ability to succeed. The increasing need for *everyone* at work to learn, refine their skills, observe themselves, and improve their ability to respond to conflict requires that leaders on all levels both coach and be coached. There are few roles more powerful for leaders, more contributive to organizational success, or more satisfying than conflict coaching, especially when it is oriented to achieving transformational results.

Conflict coaching is a process by which professional or peer coaches work with individuals and teams to understand the sources of their disagreements, problems, and conflicts and identify better ways to constructively address and resolve them. Conflict coaches help people examine the sources of both interpersonal and organizational conflict, including

- Poor communication among staff
- Difficult behaviors that are disrupting systems, structures, processes, and relationships
- Problems in communications and relationships among the leadership team
- Unreal or unmet expectations
- Hierarchical, bureaucratic, and undemocratic structures that block participation
- Lack of clarity in roles and responsibilities among leaders and team members
- Scarce resources, especially those leading to layoffs and dismissals
- Fear or anxiety over changes, especially when dictated from above
- Externalization of internal conflicts projected onto others
- Contradictory self-interests pitting people against each other
- Jealousy over uneven rewards

- Failure to acknowledge contributions of those who are lower in the hierarchy
- Unintended slights and miscommunications, especially by managers to staff
- Perceptions of insults and disrespect, especially among team members

These challenges may seem overwhelming, but each creates conflicts that diminish organizational effectiveness. In most organizations, conflicts are a fact of life, which is why conflict coaches can be highly effective in advising people on better ways of solving these problems, constructively dealing with them, and learning new behaviors that can prevent their continuation and escalation.

A Coaching Questionnaire

Most conflict coaching relationships begin with a questionnaire, followed by an agreement or contract between the coach and the person being coached, who may want to respond more skillfully to a particular conflict, or develop skills in mediating conflicts in the organization, or improve his life in general.

To clarify their plans and intentions, guide their relationship, and provide both parties with a resource to remind them of their original intentions, a coaching questionnaire and coaching contract may be useful. Here is one version of a coaching questionnaire that you can adapt and modify to suit your circumstances:

WORKSHEET

Confidential Coaching Contract

1. My goals for the coaching process are

-
-
-

2. The conflicts I wish to address are

-
-
-

3. The results I want to produce are

-
-
-

4. The barriers or challenges I intend to address to more effectively respond to conflicts in the organization or in my life are

-
-
-

5. The talents and skills I feel I bring to resolving conflicts are

-
-
-

6.

People who might support me in resolving conflicts:	People who might block me in resolving conflicts:

(*continued*)

7. Time Line for Coaching:

DATES	ACTIONS	MILESTONES

Date: ____________

Signed: ____________________ ____________________

This agreement should not be a rigid yardstick but changeable, and a guide for both parties on what to expect and how to work together. They can revisit the coaching contract from time to time to adjust their agreements based on the progress they are making, to specify additional issues they want to work on, or to respond to questions or issues that emerge for anyone involved.

Questions for Leaders as Conflict Coaches

Most organizations that create successful conflict coaching programs provide training on a regular basis in conflict resolution and coaching skills. Some adopt peer coaching and offer support groups that allow leaders and coaches to report on what they experienced and learn more about conflicts and the coaching process. As a result, they gain insights into their own conflicts and develop advanced listening and communication skills.

In providing training, mentoring, and support for leaders who want to become conflict coaches, ask them to complete the following questions as a way of identifying and clarifying their histories and attitudes toward conflict. If you want to be more effective in leading, coaching, or responding to conflict, try answering the questions below and responding in detail:

- Have you experienced conflicts like the one you are being asked to address as a coach? When did you experience it and with whom?
- What does that past conflict have in common with this one? Why do you think it has happened to you again?
- What lessons did you learn about conflict in your family as a child? How did your family contribute to your later experiences with conflict?

- What part of your past seems to influence or control your present? How would your perception of conflict change if your past experiences were different?
- How much of your approach to conflict was chosen *by* you? How much was chosen *for* you or influenced by others? Who chose it, and why?
- What judgments do you have about what you do and who you become in conflict?
- How might your self-judgments and self-esteem affect your usefulness to the person you are coaching? How might you act differently if you felt better about yourself?
- By what standard are you measuring yourself? Who created this measure? Why? Who do you know who actually lives up to this standard of behavior? What price do they pay for doing so?
- List some of the things about conflict you *don't* know how to handle, such as bullying behaviors, or could not recommend, or do not do yourself, but think you should. What keeps you from doing them?
- List some of the things you *do* but think you shouldn't, such as respond to bullying by withdrawing or avoiding. What compels you to do them?
- What myths or assumptions about yourself as a leader or a coach shape your actions or influence your choices?
- Is there any difference between what you feel or think, and what you say or do in conflict or the coaching process? What were the different parts of you that feel, think, say, or do those things? Which part do you want guiding your actions?
- What judgments do you have about yourself that could influence your abilities as a conflict coach? How might these judgments affect your choices?
- What are some things you could do to view conflict in a more positive light? What might you gain or lose by doing so?
- What are the main reasons for not coaching someone regarding their conflict? What might either of you gain or lose by not doing anything?
- What do you think your life will be like in five years if you don't deal with your own conflicts in a more effective way? If you do?
- What are your conflicts asking you to learn, release, or resolve?

- What are the most important lessons you've learned from the conflicts in your life? How could you use those lessons to create better results for those you coach?
- What price have you or others paid for your conflicts? How long do you intend to continue paying that price?
- What benefits have you or others received from poor self-esteem? Can you get those benefits any other way?
- Can you imagine letting go of your tensions and problems regarding the conflicts in your life and releasing yourself forever? If you can't, why not? If you can, what would it take?
- What are the most important assets you bring to the conflict coaching process and how could you be a more successful leader in this role?

Obviously these questions require a great deal of insight and personal observation. As a leader you can use them to deepen your understanding of conflicts and capacity to address them. You can also use them in the coaching process, as probes to help others gain insight into their histories, attitudes, and behaviors regarding conflict.

Steps in the Conflict Coaching Process

In the example cited earlier, Mark was successful as a mediator and as a coach in the conflict between Elsa and Miguel. If Mark's intervention had ended with a compromise or settlement, he would not have had much influence on the culture of the organization. Because he also acted as a conflict coach, he was able to assist others in learning from the conflict and help make the organizational culture more effective in resolving similar disputes in the future.

When leaders act as conflict coaches, they observe the organization through the lens of conflict resolution, and become better at identifying incipient conflicts, responding more quickly to emerging disputes, and supporting others in acting strategically in their conflicts and promoting learning and collaboration. Conflict coaching typically begins with the following steps:

1. *Conduct a ruthless self-assessment as a coach*
   The object of the conflict coach's self-assessment is to become clear and conscious about personal goals in addressing conflict, and about the reasons for wanting to assist others to resolve

them. This cannot be done successfully unless the coach is willing to be ruthlessly honest with herself regarding her own motivations.

2. *Negotiate values-based, transformational coaching relationships*
The conflict coach negotiates a clear set of values-based goals and expectations for the coaching relationship with the person being coached. Successful coaching is built through small, subtle communications and collaboratively negotiated consensus-based agreements that enhance trust and partnership.

3. *Create a constructive coaching environment*
The conflict coach works with people to create an informal, constructive coaching environment that nurtures and supports honest communication and collaborative relationships. The leader as coach critically observes how existing environments and general conditions affect conflict, alters the environment based on input from others, and makes ongoing changes based on feedback.

4. *Design transformational strategies*
The real work of the conflict coach consists of developing strategies through insight, honest communication, and partnership. The focus is not merely on improving, but transforming the attitudes and behaviors of those involved in the conflict and helping them see it as an opportunity for improvement.

5. *Balance positive reinforcement with critical insight*
The conflict coach offers critical insights into problems and what may be sustaining the conflict, focuses on the strengths of the parties, and reminds each person of their positive qualities. Successful coaches reinforce positive aspects of the character, motivation, and performance of those being coached so they can integrate conflict resolution attitudes and techniques into their ongoing behaviors.

6. *Provide turnaround feedback*
Turnaround feedback is the most hazardous and consequential step in conflict coaching. When people are exacerbating the conflict, the coach needs to provide direct, honest, risky feedback to create a turnaround in their behavior. The coach is completely honest, yet empathetic and sensitive, inspiring a personal willingness to work through every issue until it has been understood, owned, and overcome.

7. *Plan and commit to strategic action*
   The coach helps develop a "personal strategic plan" that responds directly to the issues in conflict with steps to correct them, identifying specific actions that will be taken to increase effectiveness in resolving this and future conflicts, building better relationships, and improving long-term behaviors by designing systems that encourage conflict resolution throughout the organization. The coach makes sure there is commitment and follow-through.
8. *Move toward closure*
   The coach ends the process by building self-confidence, acknowledging successes, requesting feedback on the coaching process, and reinforcing personal and organizational learning.

Throughout these coaching processes, transformational conflict coaches assist others to become more skillful and successful in resolving their conflicts while encouraging them to *believe* in themselves and develop skills in communication and dispute resolution. Coaches help people achieve results that go beyond what they thought was possible, develop their untapped capacities, and cultivate awareness, authenticity, congruence, and commitment. They inspire others to succeed and see *themselves* as successful human beings who can resolve and transform conflicts more successfully.

Conflict coaching is an intimate, interactive, mutually supportive relationship between partners, both of whom are willing to improve their abilities to deal with difficult disputes. For the coaching relationship to be truly transformational, both have to feel free to choose to work together. If the one being coached resists or refuses to accept the coach's advice, the coach can simply turn resistance into an opportunity to discover new ways of communicating, overcoming defensiveness, and identifying more useful suggestions.

A dispute, disagreement, or seeming impasse in the coaching relationship may also reveal a deeper cause of the conflict, which is mirrored in dysfunctional behaviors within the coaching relationship. Or the coach can view resistance as feedback regarding her own coaching clarity, intention, powers of observation, or personal skills, and use it to improve the coaching relationship and her own effectiveness.

Ultimately, transformational conflict coaching relies not on coercion, but on a voluntary commitment by those being coached to significantly alter their responses to conflict. Coaches cannot make a difference unless those being coached agree to listen and act on the advice being given.

Leaders and conflict coaches offer the following skills, supports, and resources to those who are interested in developing strategies for resolving their disputes more effectively. For example, a conflict coach may

- Be a sounding board or advisor regarding reflections on life, conflicts, relationships, and work, recognizing and encouraging talents and passions.
- Support creating a vision for life, health, work or career, family, and finances.
- Express a philosophy, artistic vision, or social values and explain how these can provide a context for experiencing conflicts as learning opportunities.
- Enable the discovery of turning points, new orientations, and meditative practices that can improve relationships and resolve disputes.
- Be available for regular and ad hoc coaching sessions by Internet, telephone, and in person to discuss, analyze, and plan key actions that can be taken to resolve disputes, develop a more powerful and successful attitude toward conflict, and maximize skills in realizing one's vision for life and work free of the conflicts that restrict them.
- Provide readings, resources, and ways of building supportive social networks to take advantage of organizational and community expertise.
- Partner in developing satisfying new skills and ideas regarding conflict resolution, and building better relationships both at work and in life.

Elements in the Coaching Process

The best leaders and conflict coaches are flexible and take into consideration changing demands, shifting goals, and evolving opportunities for success. There are no cut-and-dried steps in this fluid, life-developing process, yet there are common elements in the process with bases to touch, points to cover, and difficult issues to address as it unfolds.

Once an agreement has been reached to create a conflict coaching relationship, the coach may ask the person being coached to join in defining the following elements in the coaching relationship. Each element can assist in gaining new insights, modifying dysfunctional behaviors, and expanding conflict resolution skills:

- *Initiate the relationship.* Both parties to the coaching relationship clarify their assumptions, needs, and expectations; surface any doubts they may have; and agree on the ground rules they want to follow throughout the process, including how they will resolve any disputes that arise between them.
- *Negotiate the contract.* Clarify what each person wants from the process and what each can provide. Come to agreement on the roles and responsibilities of each person through a coaching questionnaire like the one provided earlier in this chapter. The answers will create a foundation for agreement on a coaching contract.
- *Make your needs explicit.* Each person has needs and expectations that should be made explicit. Communicate and discuss what is needed from both sides to make the relationship work.
- *Understand the problem or conflict.* The coach should not immediately provide answers or jump in and try to solve the problem, but fully explore the conflict, ask questions, investigate the problem, and analyze it so that both can learn as much about the deeper issues as possible. The coach should also explore outside, unusual, and alternative perspectives on the conflict.
- *Focus on vulnerabilities and fears.* The coach should ask the coaching partner to express any emotions, including fears, desires, vulnerabilities, frustrations, and worst-case scenarios. Together they can then look at what has been done in the past, and how to successfully overcome these fears and vulnerabilities, improve on what others have done, and decide what to do differently.
- *Go deeper into the problem.* The coach asks for more information and deeper insights to uncover the hidden or underlying issues that are not being discussed or considered in trying to solve the problem, asking risky yet empathetic questions and giving honest responses.

- *Offer ideas, suggestions, or recommendations.* When the circumstances are right, the coach shares observations and recommends options or actions. These suggestions should be offered with humility, recognizing that the only one who can decide what to do to resolve the conflict or prevent it from occurring in the future is the one being coached.
- *Ask for feedback on the coaching process.* The coach should request detailed feedback on the coaching process, especially regarding successful or failed interventions, and continue improving coaching skills. If both parties provide honest feedback to each other they will also improve their ability to use the feedback process to increase learning.
- *Acknowledge successes.* Both parties to the coaching contract should periodically identify what was done well. They should use compliments to reinforce self-confidence and identify what they each did that enabled them to be successful in resolving the conflict, without minimizing or remaining silent about what they did that failed.
- *Determine next steps.* Both parties should then plan next steps. They may require fresh roles and responsibilities or new agreements regarding anticipated next steps, and may consider how to change the organizational culture so that conflicts can be more effectively resolved. Finally, they should thank each other, celebrate what they did, and wish each other well.

These elements in the coaching process need not be followed rigidly and can be introduced at any time in the relationship, whenever they seem appropriate. You can always return to these elements when the coaching gets risky or you encounter resistance.

Risky Transformational Coaching

There are times when coaching becomes arduous; for example, the coach may observe difficult behaviors on the part of the person they are coaching, or there may be issues that require risky feedback from the coach. These situations permit the use of a transformational coaching process that can go right to the heart of a conflict and produce significant shifts in behavior by confronting the problem in a supportive, yet risky and transformational way.

We have used the following risky comments and interventions on occasion with the people we have coached. They should be modified to fit particular circumstances and offered as gently, empathetically, and nonjudgmentally as possible:

- **It's not about them or what they do, but about how you handle it.** It's easy to slip into criticizing what others do, but that lets you off the hook and fails to recognize that you can always improve the way you handle them. Ignore other peoples' behaviors and focus only on the success or failure of your own responses.
- **Don't say, "I tried that and it didn't work." Say, "How can I do it so it will work?"** The fact that earlier efforts failed means *nothing*, perhaps because the timing or mood wasn't right, or the intention behind it was untrusting or suspicious, or there wasn't a 100 percent commitment to make it work, or the underlying problems hadn't been surfaced, or the process was flawed, and so forth. Don't ask if it is right or true, but what is right or true *about* it; not what went wrong, but what you can learn from what happened.
- **It doesn't matter what you meant. What matters is what they *get*, and they didn't get it.** If they don't *feel* they have been heard, it's not their fault. It means you haven't been listening well enough. The next time you hear a criticism do *not* respond, except with a clarifying question like: "What did I do that caused you to feel that way?" or "Please tell me more," or "What can I do to solve that problem?"
- **It's not about them, it's about the problem.** You are not the problem, and neither are they. The problem is an "it," not a "you" or a "them." When you personalize the problem, it becomes emotional and about rejection and loyalty. When you depersonalize it, the problem turns into an obstacle that is vulnerable to a good strategy.
- **You don't own the solution. It's not up to you to make it happen.** If you own the solution, by definition you also own the problem. If what you want is collaboration, you have to *not* fix it by yourself. If every time a child is asked to do the dishes a parent steps in and does them instead, the child never learns how to take responsibility for problems. And yes, in the beginning the dishes may get broken or not be as clean.
- **Ignore the content, watch the process.** It is easy to get hypnotized by the problem so that you can't see the solution.

Ignore the problem and focus on creating a problem-solving process that has the capacity to improve the way you respond, and how others respond to you.

- **Invite criticism.** Go out of your way to seek out those with whom you disagree and ask *them* what you can do to improve your skills. After every conversation, ask for feedback about how you did or what you might do better. Take notes and work on it.
- **It's all relationships.** *Everything* is interactions, transactions, and relationships. This is what transforms a group into a team, or a house into a home. If you push too hard for what you want you may get it and lose what really matters. If you focus on building relationships you will also eventually get what you want.
- **Drop the victim role. Play the hero.** Don't slip into feeling sorry for yourself. If you buy it, others will too and you will lose the power of *selfless* action. Do not talk about what anyone else has done to you. Talk only about what you plan to do. Drop the past completely and speak only of the present and the future.
- **It's not about fault, it's about improvement.** Begin with the assumption that you did it to yourself, that you chose every one of the results you produced. Then let it all go, because blaming doesn't help—unless you want to get stuck. Leadership is not about fault, or even about taking responsibility, but about creating a sense of *collective* responsibility that is greater than and beyond fault.

You may decide not to offer these specific items as feedback during your conflict coaching relationship because they are too risky or inaccurate or you have not yet built the empathy required for such honesty. Still, they may stimulate some ideas regarding the kind of feedback you decide to offer as you work your way through the coaching process.

Leading Through Committed Action

Being a conflict coach offers unique learning opportunities and gives leaders a chance to see their visions reflected back in the behaviors of others. It gives them greater access to intuition and introspective sources of leadership, and a great deal of information regarding their own conflicts and those in the organization by turning insights into actions.

The last act of every leader and conflict coach is to create a clear, unambiguous choice: we can commit to act on our agreements and change the way we behave, or we can say all the right words and waffle, passing on to someone else the responsibility for resolving our disputes and behaving differently.

If you are committed to deepening your understanding, improving your relationships, learning from your problems, resolving your conflicts, and transforming yourself, your opponent, and your organization, you will ultimately be required to make a commitment to action and work through the issues with your opponent until they have been resolved. The last step in coaching, leadership, creative problem solving, strategic planning, collaborative negotiation, and conflict resolution is therefore to implement solutions and engage in clear and committed action to change the way we communicate and relate to each other in the midst of our conflicts.

Committed action is different from going through the motions, taking a stab, or giving it a try. It means taking risks, making a stand, and acting before the real outcome can be known with certainty. It is not only the last step in the conflict resolution process, but the ultimate, final, and pragmatic meaning of integrity, values, ethics, collaboration, and leadership.

Without committed action, even the best solutions become worthless and the most effective processes and techniques dissolve into dust. Those who are contemplating committed action can take heart from the reflections of W. H. Murray in his book, *The Scottish Himalayan Expedition:*

> Until one is committed there is hesitancy, the chance to draw back, always ineffectiveness. Concerning all acts of initiative (and creation), there is one elementary truth, the ignorance of which kills countless ideas and splendid plans: that the moment one definitely commits oneself, then Providence moves too. All sorts of things occur to help one that would never otherwise have occurred. A whole stream of events issues from the decision, raising in one's favor all manner of unforeseen incidents and meetings and material assistance, which no man could have dreamt would have come his way. I have learned a deep respect for one of Goethe's couplets:
>
> > "Whatever you can do, or dream you can, begin it.
> > Boldness has genius, power, and magic in it."

Committed action finally means being willing to *actually* end our conflicts, allow our past to die, and accept an unpredictable future. It means negotiating collaboratively with our opponents, standing by our agreements, releasing ourselves from past grievance, giving up being right, and acting in ways that invite a qualitatively different future.

Until problem solving turns into commitment and commitment into action, we can easily delude ourselves into thinking we are resolving our conflicts when we are only playing it safe. By acting on your commitment and risking significant change, it will immediately be apparent how far you have traveled and how far you still have to go.

Commitment is a reflection of how close we feel to the problem. The more removed we feel, the less committed we are to solving it or acting in a committed way to change it. Commitment also measures the degree of our authenticity and integrity. It signifies ownership, not only of outcomes but processes, relationships, ethics, and values.

Every action is therefore a choice, and our choices belong to us, including the choice of not choosing. Committed action means taking responsibility for our choices and the effects they have on others. Initially, it does not matter whether our choices are conscious or unconscious, well-intended or hostile, accidental or on purpose, petty or grand. What matters is that we accept responsibility for them and do not try to diminish or deny their consequences.

Committed action therefore requires and reinforces integrity. It models for our opponents how to be responsible and true to what we believe in. It encourages closure by allowing us to feel complete about what we have done and helps us discover who we are without actually intending it.

Taking Responsibility for Actions and Inactions

It does not matter how creatively we rationalize or evade responsibility for our conflicts. None of these troubling situations or upsetting disputes could take place or endure for long without our active complicity or passive acceptance. We can obscure but not eliminate the truth: the responsibility for every conflict extends not only to those who spoke or acted and *should not* have, but to those who did *not* speak or act and should have.

After the Nuremberg trials, it was widely acknowledged that legal responsibility for war crimes extends not only to those who committed the crimes, but also to those who proposed, profited from, supported, defended, rationalized, and covered them up. Morally, responsibility extends even further to those who knew about them and did nothing to stop them, to those who engaged in conspiracies of silence, and to those who ought to have known but chose to remain silent or ignore them—in other words, to everyone who was conscious and within reach.

The same can be said of other conflicts. One reason for using empathy and honesty in conflict resolution is that doing so makes each of us responsible for how we act toward our opponents. We can act responsibly *just* by asking profound questions, treating our opponents with respect and empathy, being honest and speaking the unspeakable, inviting dialogue and mutual understanding, collaboratively negotiating and solving problems, being honest with ourselves, and embracing responsibility for our actions and inactions in the conflicts in our lives.

Taking responsibility for what we say and do in conflict, and for what we don't say and do, allows us to be honest with ourselves and others. It encourages us to feel we are in control of our lives and can appreciate, learn from, and live with our conflict choices. Taking responsibility for our conflicts extends not only to what we think, say, and do, but inevitably to who we *are,* to our attitudes and the values we silently stand for.

Taking responsibility for your conflicts starts by acknowledging what you have contributed to them, and the pain you have caused your opponent. Here are several steps you can take to accept greater responsibility for your conflicts:

- Start by giving yourself an honest appraisal and identifying what you contributed to the conflict.
- Unhook yourself from judgments about other people's personalities and motives, and try to describe their behavior in nonjudgmental terms.
- Do not dismiss other people's critical comments or take them personally, but search for what is true about them.
- Listen to others empathetically and acknowledge their honest responses.
- Tell the truth yourself. Speak the unspeakable, but in ways that others can hear.
- Express a willingness to reassess your own statements, actions, and positions.

- Surface and discuss covert behavior, including any you may have fostered, accepted, rewarded, or supported.
- Be unwilling to engage in covert behaviors yourself.
- Search for alternative ways of achieving what you both want or desire.
- Find honest forms of expression that allow others to listen and save face.
- Help others take baby steps toward honest, empathetic dialogue. Start by asking questions, responding, and acknowledging their contributions.
- Look for ways of forgiving, reconnecting, and reintegrating with your opponent.

By accepting not just 50, but *100 percent* responsibility for your conflict choices, you will close the door on the possibility of blaming others. Clearly, no one is ever 100 percent responsible for their conflicts, but making the assumption that you are will magnify what you are able to learn as a result. It will open the door to discovering hidden opportunities, correcting mistakes, becoming more skillful in resolving future conflicts, and freeing yourself from feelings and behaviors that led only to impasse and disappointing results. Doing so will increase your ability to lead and coach, and invite transformational results.

STRATEGY 9

EXPLORE RESISTANCE AND NEGOTIATE COLLABORATIVELY

Conflict develops when one feels [oneself] to be in the right and runs into opposition. If one is not convinced of being in the right, opposition leads to craftiness or high-handed encroachment but not to open conflict. If a man is entangled in a conflict, his only solution lies in being so clear-headed and inwardly strong that he is always ready to come to terms by meeting the opponent halfway. To carry on the conflict to the bitter end has evil effects even when one is in the right because the enmity is then perpetuated.

—I Ching

Some conflicts will always be beyond our skill or capacity to handle, even after trying all the techniques and suggestions outlined in preceding chapters. Sometimes we are simply too close to the problem to respond creatively, the issues are too complex to resolve on our own, or our skills are not adequate to the challenge. Sometimes emotions or positions have become too entrenched, the organizational culture is too avoidant or discouraging of resolution, or our opponent is too committed to keeping the conflict going for psychological reasons we are unable to approach, assuage, or abolish. What do we do then?

The penultimate strategy in conflict resolution is to explore the resistance that inevitably emerges whenever the resolution of an important, intense, or long-lasting conflict becomes possible. We need to negotiate collaboratively when no solutions are in sight and agree to disagree when there are stark, fundamental, and overwhelming differences between implacable opponents. Each of these strategies requires persistence, skill, and tireless efforts to do what is right in the face of conflict.

Success and Failure in Conflict Resolution

Before proceeding, it is important not to feel you failed in your efforts, even though you are at impasse and have been unable thus far to reach a resolution. You may want to stop for a moment and acknowledge that statements regarding success and failure are often deceptive and inaccurate. Success and failure in conflict resolution depend sensitively on what you *and* your opponent do or say, and do or say in response. They depend equally on the level of awareness, self-confidence, and integrity on both sides, on each person's readiness to learn and change, and on the actual nature and underlying meaning of the conflict to each of you.

Sometimes what appears to be a success turns out to be a failure in disguise, and vice versa. For example, you may succeed in coercing your opponent to accept your proposal and undermine your long-term relationship. On the other hand, you may settle a superficial issue and provoke a deeper conflict that leads to more pain and stress. Or you may fail to resolve a conflict at all and later discover a better solution, rebuild trust, and learn an important lesson as a result.

Moreover, the likely outcome of success is generally that you will repeat what you did successfully and as a result be less likely to grow, learn, or change in future conflicts. But the likely outcome of failure is that you will critique what you did, experiment, take risks, and be more creative. As a result, you are more likely to grow, learn, and change the way you respond to future conflicts. So which is the success and which the failure?

If your goal is to learn from your conflicts, labeling your efforts successes or failures will not be helpful. The real questions are: Did you make any fresh discoveries? Did you increase your skills? Are there changes you could make to improve your approach to conflict? Were you seduced by your desire for success? Were you willing to experiment and take risks without fear of failure? Thus, failure often consists of trying too hard to succeed, whereas success consists of risking the possibility of failure.

Winston Churchill, in the midst of war, famously defined success as "proceeding from failure to failure with undiminished enthusiasm." We apply a similar definition to conflict resolution, which always begins at impasse and remains there until, often for no discernable reason, an opening appears and resolution occurs.

The implications of reversing our attitude toward success and failure are far-reaching. They encourage us to adopt a learning orientation to problem solving, explore the reasons for resistance, and use negotiation mediation to overcome impasse. They discourage conflict suppression and avoidance while encouraging prevention and deeper levels of resolution. They *automatically* make us more successful by inspiring us to develop better skills in listening, emotional intelligence, honest dialogue, collaborative negotiation, and creative problem solving.

Some Reasons for Resistance

There are many reasons why we resist resolution, get stuck in conflict, and end up in impasse. In fact, we are *always* resisting resolution and at impasse in every conflict until the moment arrives when we find a solution that works for both sides. Resistance and impasse simply mean that whatever we have been doing until now has not worked and we need to try something different.

People who resist resolution do so for a reason. Instead of regarding their refusal as irrational, crazy, or an example of difficult behavior, start with the assumption that *all resistance reflects an unmet need.* Try to find out what that need is and search for what we could do to meet or satisfy it.

Sometimes resistance is an indirect request to be listened to more respectfully, or an indication that our deeper fears and anxieties have not been resolved. As a result, it is important to find out what deeper fears may be causing the stalemate and invite our opponent to join us in searching for solutions that might move our communications and negotiations toward resolution.

We were asked to mediate a dispute in which an employee, Sam, had applied for a position as team leader, a job he felt he should be his because he had been a team coordinator for six months on a successful project. His manager, Betty, disagreed and favored a more traditionally qualified candidate because Sam had not had any leadership training.

When Betty told Sam he did not get the job, she felt bad about the decision because she liked Sam, and covered over her feelings by being abrupt and insensitive. Her rejection surprised Sam because he thought she liked his work and that the job was his. He tried to convince her he was qualified but she refused to listen and brushed him off, adding insult to injury.

Sam then went to the organizational ombudsman in charge of conflict resolution to request a hearing and to human resources to file an internal grievance. He complained bitterly to his colleagues and "bad-mouthed" Betty, who became more and more angry—to the point that she retaliated when she heard about his insulting comments, telling him that if it were up to her he would never get the job. Various proposals for settlement were offered but Sam was resistant to all of them.

In mediation, we asked Betty to listen empathetically to Sam as he presented his case. She did so in a genuine and honest way and Sam felt respected, acknowledged, and heard for the first time. As a result, Sam thanked her, and Betty was able to apologize for not having listened earlier, failing to acknowledge the excellent work he had done, and making vengeful, retaliatory comments. She admitted that he was highly qualified for the job but lacked leadership training that was required to build the strong team they needed.

In response, Sam apologized for his comments and efforts to undermine Betty, and agreed to withdraw his complaint and grievance. Together they agreed that Sam would have an opportunity to participate in the next leadership training program to earn the credentials he needed for the position, the team would be consulted first on future hires, and Betty would request feedback from the team and coaching from human resources on how to improve her communication skills.

The proposal Betty made in mediation that Sam finally accepted was identical to the one offered earlier by the ombudsman that Sam had resisted—not because the proposal was inadequate, but because Betty had not listened to him, apologized, acknowledged his skills, or directly offered it to him herself.

The reasons for resistance in conflict are often subtle and unstated. Consider whether you are experiencing any of the following reasons for resistance in your conflict:

- There may be a perception that the process used to resolve the dispute is unfair or one-sided.
- One person may not have agreed to use the process, may feel it is being used improperly, or may not be committed to following through.
- There may not be adequate ground rules to keep the conversation on track, or the ground rules have been disregarded and previous violations have been ignored or condoned.
- The process for reaching resolution may be too structured and formal—or, conversely, too unstructured and informal.
- The process may not allow for a real exchange of views or permit the real content of the dispute to emerge.
- People may feel they have not been listened to deeply or sincerely, or that the other person has not been honest or empathetic, or has tried to manipulate the process.
- There may be unresolved issues in the relationship, or one person may have adopted an adversarial style or a control orientation that is creating a perception of disrespect or prejudgment.
- One person may be trying to fix blame or humiliate the other, or have false expectations that have not been addressed.
- One person may need an apology or acknowledgment, or feel that these have not been offered explicitly, authentically, or generously.

We were invited to a large urban high school that was being torn apart by conflict. We found that parents had accused the administration of institutional racism, citing remarks made by teachers in their classrooms and the collection and posting of data on students' achievement tests based on their race and national origin. The administration was willing to mediate but the parents and teachers refused to meet. There was great distrust and resistance as the parents felt they had been treated unfairly in the past, the teachers felt they had been personally attacked by the parents, and the administration felt they had been blamed by everyone.

All this resistance started to diminish when a newly appointed district administrator addressed the parents' group and apologized sincerely for all the mistakes the administration had made. He acknowledged that institutional racism *had* existed in the school and in the district as a whole, and stated clearly that it was his priority to end it. He indicated his commitment to work with them over the next year to eliminate disparate treatment and to make sure all students were treated equally and fairly.

At the same time, he reached out to the teachers and administrators by stating that institutional racism was not anyone's personal fault and offered resources and support to improve student achievement. His sincere apology, acknowledgment of the problem, willingness to speak directly to all groups, and his commitment to deliver needed resources reduced resistance and allowed everyone to create an improved educational environment for the students.

Resistance and Change

Personal and organizational change is constant, and as we search for the sources of resistance, we may find that many are merely disguised forms of issues regarding change, or result from failures of leadership, or are the consequence of unwillingness to involve others from the beginning in establishing goals and expectations or defining the process or content of changes that affect their lives.

Resistance to change comes in many different guises. For example, a cynical corporate vice president at a telephone company overwhelmed a creative, innovative, and enthusiastic director who reported to her by making demands for meaningless paperwork as a way of resisting the director's efforts to restructure her department into self-managing teams. An entire staff in a public school sabotaged a school reform effort because their ideas, suggestions, and contributions had not been solicited or respected by the principal. The department manager of a large government agency undermined the efforts of his social work staff to provide more responsive customer service by refusing to meet with a planning delegation and demonstrating complete disinterest in what they had to say by opening his mail as they presented their plans.

Resistance is often based on a fear that change will lead not to improvement, but loss. The result is conflict, because *every* change involves loss, insecurity, and fear, and these emotions easily translate into resisting behaviors. Nonetheless, organizational change can be designed to reduce resistance and difficult behaviors. For example, it is clear that change takes place more smoothly when

- Everyone is involved in planning the change.
- People know where the change is headed and what it will achieve.
- There is effective leadership on all levels in carrying it out.
- Goals and outcomes are clearly and collaboratively identified.
- Small changes are tested first.
- False expectations are exposed and corrected.
- People who resist change are won over or moved to neutrality by having their objections answered and their interests met.
- Conflicts are addressed openly and resolved fully.
- Feedback, evaluation, and self-correction are built into the process.

Resistance encountered during change may express people's disagreement with the substance of the change, their anxiety that they do not have the skills to succeed under the new system, their worry that something valuable may get thrown out by mistake, or their lack of opportunity to grieve over the loss of the old relationships and ways of working that are about to be dismantled.

If you can welcome those who resist and affirm, and even celebrate their gift of a different perspective, you will regard their resistance as an opportunity to improve the substance or process of change, encourage their criticism, and value their dissent as a contribution to understanding and improvement. Your opponents may become allies, allowing you to jointly transform what made you opponents in the first place.

Techniques for Reducing Resistance and Overcoming Impasse

Though helpful, listening, apologies, and acknowledgments may not be enough to resolve the conflict. If you feel stuck in resistance and unable to move beyond impasse, here are some methods drawn from mediation that may help you discover or create a breakthrough. As you read through them, consider how you might adapt, reconfigure, and apply them in your conflicts.

- Examine each issue separately. Subdivide larger issues and break them down into smaller parts, addressing them one by one and saving the most difficult for last. Identify the easiest, most manageable elements that might be solved first, then move on to more complex issues. Develop an algorithm, template, or set of instructions for deciding future issues. For example, we mediated a dispute involving over $500,000 by first reaching sixteen points of agreement on how the parties would talk to each other on the telephone, after which all the other issues were easy.
- If the other side rejects your proposal, ask why it is unacceptable and look for narrow solutions that are tailored to the reasons they offer. If someone rejects your solution because they do not believe it will work, suggest trying it for a month to see. For example, we resolved a sexual harassment dispute by asking the accuser why she refused a generous offer of settlement. It turned out that she did not really want the money as much as she wanted the company to train her so she could move to a higher-level job she preferred. The company agreed, allowing her to work part-time in the new job until she showed she could master it; both sides were satisfied.
- Take a break, and perhaps ask each person to come up with three to five ways to improve the conversation or negotiation. When people take time out and step away from their conflicts, they become a bit more reasonable and realistic about what they need, and the cycle of escalation stops. For example, we sometimes suggest that both sides think about the problem overnight and return with three proposals for resolution that they think would be acceptable to the other side.
- Review the other side's priorities and reveal any interests or values you may have in common. Go over your priorities together and create a merged list. Identify your interests or goals to see whether they match. We mediated between two teachers in a bitter conflict who agreed that their top priority was helping the children. Their shared interests in school safety and improving the language arts curriculum allowed them to create a partnership and overcome their differences.

- Explore hidden agendas and ask if there are any areas where they might be willing to compromise. Hidden agendas can often be detected by the effects they produce, for example, in distorted communications, false priorities, and minor issues that keep people from reaching agreement. If you surface and explore these agendas you may invite a compromise—or see why the one you suggested is impossible. In mediation we discovered the hidden agenda of a manager, which was to appear managerial to his boss and enhance his chances of promotion by appearing decisive and solving problems quickly. When the employee with whom he was in conflict understood his agenda they were able to negotiate a collaborative solution that made the manager look good to his boss.
- Split the difference. Simply dividing a sum in half and splitting the difference is an easy way of settling a dispute without resolving it. For example, we mediated a conflict in which the parties agreed to settle $400,000 worth of claims, and the entire mediation nearly fell apart over $35. We suggested they split the difference and each side quickly agreed.
- Try to reach agreement on original expectations. Going back to initial conversations and expectations before the dispute began can encourage both sides to stand by their original agreements. In a dispute we mediated between two business partners who had worked together for several years, there was a heated conflict over how to resolve an unfair division of labor and they were considering dissolution. In mediation, they recalled their original agreement, which was to share the work equally, and were then able to identify all their tasks, break them into two equal groups, and flip a coin to decide who would take which ones.
- Look for possible trade-offs or exchanges of services. You may find solutions to your conflicts by discovering collateral needs that can be satisfied, bartered, or traded against each other to resolve the dispute. For example, we mediated a conflict between a model and a photographer over fees for a set of prints he had taken of her. She thought his photographs were unflattering and refused to pay for them. He claimed she had not looked very good when he took the shots and refused to take his advice when he suggested how she might look better. She wanted a flattering set of prints and he wanted to be paid to do his job without interference. They traded, accepted each

other's conditions, and reached an agreement that he would take new photos and she would accept his suggestions and pay him for his work, including film costs for the earlier shoot.

- Recognize, acknowledge, and accept other people's feelings and points of view, and encourage them to recognize, acknowledge, and accept yours. One reason for impasse in your conflict may be inadequate recognition, acknowledgment, or acceptance of feelings and experiences, either by you or your opponent. It is extremely difficult to *over*-acknowledge someone in a way that is sincere. If your opponent says, "You don't think I'm a very good person," switch gears and praise actual specific things he or she does well, then offer honest feedback. If you are unable to think of *anything* positive to say, your emotions have probably obscured your vision. We once resolved a dispute between a male manager and female employee after she told her coworkers he was incompetent. The manager complained that she was always resisting his ideas and had a "bad attitude." We asked them to describe three things they respected or liked about each other and acknowledge each other for something they had done well. It turned out the entire dispute was based on both parties thinking the other did not like them and acting defensively. After they praised and acknowledged each other, their resistance began to disappear.
- Say you are stuck and ask the other person for help. Sometimes telling people you need their help encourages them to come forward with creative ideas or let go of their resistance to seeing your point of view. We resolved a dispute in an elementary school in which most teachers requested that the principal be removed. We convened a faculty meeting in which the principal admitted she was stuck and asked for their help. In small groups, the faculty came up with a list of things she was doing that were causing problems, a list of things the teachers were doing that were not helping, and a list of creative ideas for how they could work together in the future.
- Ask the other person to indicate what would change or happen if a solution were reached. One reason for impasse is a perception that if you reach agreement the result will be unpleasant. We mediated a dispute in which an employee was taking a long time to sign a separation agreement, insisting that

commas be changed into semi-colons then back into commas again. We asked him what he thought would happen if he actually signed the agreement. He dodged the question three times. We asked him if he was dodging the question and he finally admitted he was afraid he would never find a better job. We assisted him in accepting the inevitable and helped him strategize about how he could find a more satisfying job, which allowed him to let go of the past and move on with his life.

- Stop the process and consider whether it is actually helping you get where you want to go. If the process is not working, or is preventing open, honest, and empathetic communication, stop it and try to improve the way you are communicating. We mediated a dispute in a U.S. government agency where the director encountered employee resistance to a number of changes she wanted to implement. She ran staff meetings with an iron hand, rarely asking employees what they thought. She did not even give them an opportunity to speak before telling them what they were going to do. We stopped a meeting midstream and asked her publicly if she *wanted* to hear what the employees thought about her plan. When she said she did, we changed the process by dividing into small teams of four or five employees, asking them to identify three to five useful elements in her plan and three to five ways it could be improved. Their creative and constructive ideas shocked her and she realized that her employees were well meaning and knew how to make her plan work better than she imagined.
- Compliment others on reaching earlier points of agreement and encourage them to reach a complete agreement, put the dispute behind them, and move on with their lives. Every conflict resolution process creates a momentum toward resolution and is increased by periodically recognizing gains and acknowledging successes. We met with a team in the information systems department of a large corporation that was blocked from delivering on its commitments to clients because they had reached impasse over a strategy for developing new software. We convened the team and asked each person to identify one point on which they were in agreement regarding the strategy and one issue that needed improvement. It turned out they actually agreed on twelve points and only disagreed about two. They identified the problems that were preventing them from

reaching agreement over the last two and they were able to come to complete agreement in three hours.

- Remind the other side what will happen and what you each stand to lose if you do not agree, or ask what it will cost to continue the conflict. We mediated a dispute between two competing managers and asked them what they each stood to lose by not resolving their dispute. They both answered that they would lose their jobs and chances for promotion. We asked if this was what they wanted and they both said no. Once they saw what was at stake, they were able to reprioritize, put their less important personal animosities aside, and negotiate a working relationship that made them both look good.
- Ask each person to take a minute of silence to think about their priorities, how they got stuck, and what to do about the problem. In conflict, it is easy to get caught up in emotional dynamics and lose sight of the forest for the trees. Silence allows you to stop what is not working, encourage people to reassess their positions, center themselves, and return to what is really important. For example, we mediated a dispute between former spouses who were business partners, in which the ex-husband made a very generous offer to purchase the business from his former wife. We asked her what she thought of the offer and she said, "I don't know." We asked what she needed to know in order to respond, and she said, "I don't know that either." We asked them to take a minute of silence to think about it, and before a minute passed she said, "I'm afraid if I say yes and agree to his offer our relationship will be over." We now understood the real source of her resistance and began working with her on letting go of their old relationship. She told her ex-husband that what she really wanted was to have a friendship with him, and they were able to negotiate a nonbusiness friendship that would not be emotionally or financially confusing, after which she gratefully accepted his offer.
- Ask more questions—not only about problems, but about feelings, priorities, creative solutions, flexibilities, hidden agendas, compromises, and unresolved issues—then return to problem solving. If you are completely stuck, double back to the beginning and ask questions as though you were just starting to resolve the dispute. We mediated a conflict over a negative performance evaluation in which both sides had hired attorneys.

We quickly reached impasse because the original reasons for their dispute had been forgotten in a flurry of legal issues and aggressive advocacy. We asked the parties to meet with each other privately without their lawyers; we then asked questions that returned them to their original goals. This allowed them to agree on changes that would improve the performance evaluation process and they were able to get their relationship back on track.

- Generate options by asking the other person to join you in brainstorming ideas. Ask your opponent if he has any suggestions for how to resolve the dispute, then piggyback and add your own. Don't critique or evaluate until all the ideas have been expressed; use a flip chart if the conflict is especially hot. In a dispute between family members who were operating a business, two brothers were competing to see who would run it. We brainstormed options and discovered that *neither* of them really wanted to run it, they just didn't want the other one to win or look better or be more successful financially. They agreed that their general manager was far more capable, qualified, and motivated than either of them and actually wanted the job. They agreed to hire him and split the net profits equally.
- Ask an expert or third party to identify which alternative is more appropriate or fair, and why. Going to an expert or someone who has a reputation for fairness to request advice can often resolve an impasse, as can jointly researching options and dispassionately discussing the merits of each proposal. For example, we helped settle a collective-bargaining dispute concerning the salaries of a large group of employees. Both sides agreed to consult an expert who was able to put a value on the pensions and benefits offered by each side and compared these packages with what employees were receiving in similar organizations. They were able to reach a contract that both sides felt was fair.
- Ask your opponent if he or she is willing to mediate the dispute and, if not, ask to take the dispute to arbitration rather than starting litigation. If all else fails, bring in a third party to mediate or arbitrate. A mediator may have the skills to create the communications needed to resolve the dispute and may succeed merely because he is outside the conflict and perceived as unbiased or impartial. If mediation is unsuccessful or unacceptable to either

side, consider using final and binding arbitration, which is quicker and less expensive than going to court.

Collaborative Negotiation

Negotiation skills are a critical part of solving problems and resolving conflicts. To end any problem or dispute, it is first necessary to negotiate a common definition of what needs to be solved, a process for solving it, a solution everyone agrees on, and a commitment to implement it.

If, after applying the techniques in earlier chapters, you are still unable to arrive at a mutually acceptable solution to your problem, you can try to negotiate the issues, allowing you to identify a better process or approach, reach a compromise, or agree to disagree in respectful ways that do not interfere with your ongoing communications, relationship, and ability to work together.

In any conflict, it is possible to negotiate in two fundamentally different ways: either aggressively, based on positions in search of win-lose outcomes; or collaboratively, based on interests in search of win-win options. Most people who are stuck in conflict or in the grip of negative emotions negotiate aggressively, asserting and debating their positions and trying to win, or at least cause their opponent to lose.

In *collaborative* negotiation, people seek to satisfy *both* sides' interests, reject the use of negative and destructive tactics, and look for "mutual gain" outcomes. Sometimes collaborative negotiation results in mutually acceptable lose-lose compromises in which each side receives only part of what it wants or needs. Sometimes it results in temporary cease-fires that leave the fundamental dispute unresolved. More often, however, collaborative negotiation is a key element in resolving conflicts at a deeper level, encouraging positive and constructive communications, and building and sustaining successful relationships.

In successful organizational cultures, conflict and collaboration are inextricably linked. Collaboration without conflict results in formality, conformity, inauthenticity, politeness, and a lack of creative solutions, whereas conflict without collaboration results in aggression, alienation, disrespect, and impasse without solutions. In successful organizations, people are less focused on being polite than on openly expressing their differences, communicating honestly and empathetically, and negotiating collaboratively to invent solutions that creatively combine diversity, unity, and interdependence.

Collaborative, interest-based negotiation techniques encourage people *not* to suppress their disagreements and differences, which only results in their effective disenfranchisement, but to speak up and become organizational citizens. The collaborative approach to negotiation acknowledges that everyone needs to discuss, probe, challenge, criticize, debate, and participate in making decisions regarding issues that are important to them, and to do so in ways that leave them stronger, more successful, and more united.

In collaborative negotiations, everyone openly and honestly discusses the issues that divide them, analyzes their disagreements in the context of their larger agreements, goals, vision, and shared values, and searches together for solutions that satisfy both sides' interests.

Collaborative negotiation is therefore as important a strategy and skill in resolving conflicts as listening, acknowledging emotions, separating what matters from what gets in the way, learning from difficult behaviors, creative problem solving, and leading or coaching for transformation. To do so, it is important to determine, as with problem solving, not only *what* needs to be negotiated, but *why* and *how* you will negotiate it. This means surfacing both sides' subconscious expectations and assumptions and subtly shifting their relationship by altering the ways they interact throughout the negotiation process.

Aggressive Versus Collaborative Negotiating Styles

Everyone negotiates all the time. Most often, we negotiate to secure *quantities,* such as money, time, or space. Yet, while doing so, we are also indirectly negotiating *qualities*, which are less visible and rarely discussed. For example, while we are negotiating the size of our office, we are also negotiating our status at work; and while we are negotiating our salaries, we are also indirectly negotiating recognition for our work and respect for ourselves as employees.

The qualities we seek are nearly always far more important than the quantities we are requesting. Unfortunately, we often lose sight of the qualities that are important to us and pay a high price in trust for small victories in dollars. In conflict resolution, the best strategy for encouraging personal and organizational transformation is to collaboratively negotiate both elements throughout the process.

If we care about the people on the other side of our conflict or are in an ongoing relationship with them, we cannot afford to negotiate only for quantities. Simply by negotiating only for quantities, we imply that qualities don't matter, that it is acceptable for our future relationship and communication to be formal, cold, and distrusting. We negotiate qualities as much by our style, or *how* we negotiate, as by our concern for substance, or *what* we negotiate.

In any negotiation for quantities or qualities there are two fundamental styles from which to choose. *Aggressive* negotiators generally move *against* their opponents in a competitive struggle for power and unilateral victories. It is acceptable in aggressive negotiations to reduce or destroy trust by being inflexible, intimidating, demoralizing, withholding, or threatening; and to browbeat one's opponents, conceal facts and motivations, refuse to listen or compromise, attribute blame, define problems as caused solely by one's opponents, and manipulate the process to get what they want.

Aggressive negotiators make exaggerated demands and offer few concessions. If concessions have to be made, they do so grudgingly and make small ones. They create "false issues" to trade off in order to gain advantages elsewhere. The aggressive approach to negotiation is a key element in maintaining hierarchical, bureaucratic, and autocratic organizational cultures, and fuels a control orientation to problem solving.

Collaborative negotiators, on the other hand, move *toward* their opponents in a mutual effort to satisfy interests and achieve win-win outcomes. They listen respectfully, establish common ground rules, emphasize shared values, discuss issues openly and honestly, and take responsibility for having created problems, as well as for implementing solutions. They unconditionally act in a trustworthy, fair, objective, and reasonable way. They refuse to manipulate the process and consistently work for what *both* sides want or need.

Collaborative negotiators establish credibility and good faith by making significant concessions, sometimes unilaterally. They are clear about their priority issues, seek the highest joint outcome so both sides can feel they won, and minimize the importance of false issues. The collaborative approach is an integral component of heterarchical, participatory, and democratic organizational cultures, and fuels a learning orientation to problem solving.

In most organizations, the aggressive approach generates greater distrust and misunderstanding; agreements take longer to reach, and conflicts consume greater resources. When aggression takes over, not only are there more failures and a greater likelihood of retaliation even when the aggressive approach "wins," but the resulting culture also can permit vitriolic personal attacks and, in some terrible circumstances, even more extreme forms of retaliation.

In any ongoing relationship, when you are likely to negotiate repeatedly over persistent problems, and when you are seeking to maximize relationships, improve communications, or increase personal satisfaction, aggressive negotiations have been shown to result in smaller gains over the long run than collaborative ones.

Preparing for Collaborative Negotiation

One reason collaborative negotiations are more successful in resolving conflicts is that their elements and techniques dovetail nicely with those used in other interest-based methods and collaborative work processes, making the preparation consistent with organizational goals that are based on unity and teamwork.

In preparing to engage in collaborative negotiations, mediations, or other relationship-building processes, it is important for you and your opponent to understand the principal elements in the process. Most of the elements we list below are drawn from Roger Fisher and William Ury's classic book, *Getting to Yes,* which we highly recommend. We include several questions for you to consider in preparing for your own collaborative negotiation.

- *Goals:* What are your goals for your relationship and communication? For the negotiation? What do you want? What does the other side want? How do these goals intersect or conflict?
- *Issues:* What issues does each side want to see addressed? In what order? What are the real priorities on each side? What are the false priorities and distractions?
- *Interests:* Why do you want the things you want? Why is the other side asking for what it wants? Which of these interests could be mutually satisfied?
- *Allies:* Who are your allies and how can they help you get what you want? Do you have any allies who are on the same level in the hierarchy as your opponent? Can you enlist their support?
- *Environment:* What setting will be most comfortable for you and your opponent when you meet to negotiate? What kind of environment will send a message of collaboration, informality, and comfort?

- *Respect:* What can you do or say to communicate to the other side that you respect and value them and your relationship? How can you send a message of commitment to collaboration before the negotiation?
- *BATNA:* What is each side's "best alternative to a negotiated agreement"? What is the best that could happen if no agreement is reached? What would you do if that happens?
- *WATNA:* What is each side's "worst alternative to a negotiated agreement"? What is the worst that could happen if no agreement is reached? What would you do if that happens?
- *Options:* What creative solutions can you identify that could satisfy both of your interests? Can you think of any others?
- *Relationships and communication:* What impact will either side's proposed solutions have on your ongoing relationship and communication?
- *Criteria:* Are there criteria or standards that could help you agree on what is fair?
- *Reality testing:* Are the ideas that either side is proposing realistic? Will they work for *both* sides? What could go wrong in implementing them?
- *Satisfaction:* What do both of you need in terms of content, process, and relationship to feel satisfied or pleased with the outcome?
- *Commitment:* What are both sides willing to commit to doing to make the proposed solution work? Is there genuine commitment? If not, what is needed to create it?
- *Improvement:* What can you do in these negotiations to improve trust and make the next round of negotiations more successful?
- *Completion:* What can you do to complete the process so neither side has any lingering anger, distrust, or doubt? What can you do to complete the process and reach closure with the other side so neither of you has remaining unresolved negative feelings?

The best way to prepare for collaborative negotiation is to spend a great deal of time listening to your opponents and trying to understand their interests, as Abraham Lincoln advised: "When I'm getting ready to reason with a man, I spend one third of the time thinking about myself—what I'm going to say—and two thirds thinking about him and what he is going to say."

Participating in Collaborative Negotiations

Participating in collaborative negotiations is not simply a matter of preparing and having the right intention. It is also a matter of using the right process at the right time for the right reasons throughout the negotiation, and of consistently encouraging mutual satisfaction, creativity, and successful outcomes.

Many of the steps outlined below address organizational negotiations and collective bargaining that are commonly conducted by teams of three to five or more on each side. In many organizations, negotiations also take place in departments, divisions, or teams, where staff and executives may serve as observers, coaches, or advisors who provide input to the process. If you are engaged in one-on-one negotiations with a colleague at work, consider how to extrapolate the steps below and adapt the process to work with a single person.

Before the Negotiation Session Begins

AGREE ON GROUND RULES FOR THE PROCESS. Establish a timetable for discussions and agree on a set of ground rules, possibly including an agreement to keep communications confidential so as to increase trust. Ground rules may include fail-safe devices, reset buttons, and escape hatches in the event collaboration fails. They may also include a preamble or joint statement of the reasons each side is committed to a collaborative bargaining process and an affirmation of both sides' intentions to work together to reach a full resolution. See page 158 for a set of sample ground rules.

FORM A JOINT PROCESS IMPROVEMENT TEAM. Form a team to monitor the negotiation process, improve it, and keep it on track. The team may encourage the parties to operate by consensus, create mutually agreed-upon agendas, suggest and remind people of ground rules, stop the process when it is not working, offer feedback on process, and make certain the negotiation is running smoothly. By drawing up and agreeing on an agenda, the team can focus on issues that are of primary concern to everyone. The experience of coming to consensus on process improvement proposals on the team can give both sides a sense that their goals are achievable, especially if collaborative negotiation is new for them.

AGREE ON COMMON GOALS FOR YOUR RELATIONSHIP. Meet together and agree on four or five goals each side has for their relationship. Alternatively, caucus and develop lists of relational goals separately, then come together and share them, noting those you have in common or those on which you can easily agree. Next, identify problems or barriers that stand in the way of achieving common goals. Share results and again recognize those you have in common or those you can easily modify and accept. Next, jointly brainstorm strategies for overcoming the barriers and achieving your common goals. Reach consensus on goals, barriers, and strategies, and postpone discussing those you can't easily modify and accept.

IDENTIFY ISSUES AND INTERESTS. Call a joint meeting of both negotiation teams and ask each person to sit next to someone from the opposite team around a circle rather than on opposite sides of a table. With a facilitator, joint process observers, a flip chart, and someone to record ideas, start a round-robin process in which everyone states an issue or problem for negotiation, says what they feel is important about it, why it matters to them and one suggestion for how it might be solved. Keep going around the circle until no one has any more issues or problems. Next, group similar issues together into a single manageable list. Either as a large group or in teams, analyze, categorize, and prioritize the issues under each topic and identify the principles or values you share with respect to each issue and ways it could be resolved.

USE INFORMAL PROBLEM SOLVING. Meet informally to see if you can solve the problem simply. Follow the problem-solving procedures in Chapter Six and brainstorm ideas, suggestions, and recommendations for solving each problem. Distribute the list of recommended solutions for everyone to revise and adapt as ideas change. Afterward, ask process observers to report on what they saw, and then discuss ways of improving future problem solving.

DEVELOP SHARED VISION OR VALUES. As an alternative to the first two steps, meet together to create an inspiring vision for the future of the organization. Next, analyze the barriers or hurdles that stand in the way of getting there, and agree on goals, strategies, and small actions to overcome them. Another alternative is to agree on a set of shared values. List the behaviors either of you are engaging in that support or undermine those values and agree to encourage supporting behaviors and discourage undermining ones. Give each other feedback on what each side has done that demonstrates or reinforces each set of behaviors.

DISCUSS PAST NEGOTIATION EXPERIENCES. Meet informally to discuss in detail what happened during the last round of negotiations. Ask participants to switch sides and role-play their best and worst negotiation experiences. After the role play and discussion, brainstorm ideas on how to improve the next negotiation and recommend improvements. Alternately, ask each side to meet separately and identify the behaviors *their* side engaged in during the last round of negotiations that did not work for them or for the other side, share them, request feedback from the other side, and agree not to repeat them.

DEVELOP BATNAs, WATNAs, OPTIONS, AND POSITIONS. Meet separately to identify your best and worst alternatives to a negotiated agreement for each interest, then imagine them for the other side. Next, brainstorm alternate ways of achieving those interests and develop initial, fallback, and bottom-line positions. Imagine what the other side's positions will be and prepare to respond. Share your findings confidentially with someone you trust on the other side or discuss them openly in the group.

MEET INFORMALLY. Develop more trusting relationships by frequent socializing, storytelling, informal gatherings, and personal sharing. Consider holding a retreat or having a potluck dinner, barbecue, seminar, sports event, family party, or social event to give everyone an opportunity to get to know each other on a personal level.

RECEIVE JOINT TRAINING IN COLLABORATIVE NEGOTIATION. Agree to participate in joint training sessions on techniques for collaborative negotiation, effective communication, relationship building, and conflict resolution. Use courses, workshops, and outside consultants to raise issues and improve your skills throughout your relationship. Use the training to add an element of openness to the negotiation process and allow both sides to share a learning experience that reinforces collaboration by encouraging them to use the same language and techniques.

USE AN OUTSIDE FACILITATOR OR MEDIATOR. Jointly interview and hire an outside facilitator or mediator to assist both sides in being more collaborative during the negotiating process. An experienced outsider can bring a fresh perspective, give both sides honest feedback and personal coaching, and help resolve disputes before, as, and after they occur.

SEEK ADVICE FROM ALLIED THIRD PARTIES. Form a joint advisory committee or board consisting of representatives from concerned outside groups, customers, clients, or third parties who may be affected by the success or failure of your negotiations. Report to them periodically on your successes and failures and seek their advice or intervention when you get stuck. Be cautious about the positions of any third parties you involve and make sure they support and do not sabotage the collaborative process.

HOLD A FACILITATED PUBLIC FORUM. Consider holding an open, participatory, facilitated public forum where representatives of all interested groups can openly discuss the issues being negotiated. This public venting process can be helpful in putting an end to rumors, gossip, and negative publicity. It can be an opportunity for people to hear and develop fresh ideas before problem solving or after an impasse has been reached. After the group has analyzed the issues, ask them to suggest alternatives and recommendations and take time to consider each other's contributions.

JOINTLY RESEARCH ALTERNATIVE METHODS OF NEGOTIATING. Research efforts might include jointly examining and summarizing alternative negotiation literature, experiments, and methods. Both sides might agree to visit individuals and organizations that have used collaborative negotiation techniques or to interview participants and consultants to learn what worked for them, what did not, and how to improve the process.

CHOOSE NEGOTIATING TEAM MEMBERS JOINTLY. Select people to negotiate who have good interpersonal skills and are respected or seen as credible by the other side. Consider allowing the other side to veto anyone they do not trust, or even select one or more members of the other side's bargaining team.

KEEP LINES OF COMMUNICATION OPEN. Allow sufficient time to communicate fully with each other and plan to meet on a regular basis with added sessions when needed. Make sure formal and informal lines of communication are left open and ask to meet with the other side in an informal setting away from the table if either side gets stuck or runs into problems.

During the Negotiation Process

MEET IN COMFORTABLE, INFORMAL SURROUNDINGS. If possible, meet in a neutral setting and avoid an "our side against your side," across-the-table setting. Sit in an alternating pattern rather than on opposite sides and hold some meetings without a table. Use a round-robin speaking order or toss a coin to determine who goes first. Dress informally, bring food and beverages, welcome the other side, and allow time for informal personal conversation. Help every person feel part of a collaborative effort.

USE EXPERTS. Agree to bring in advisors who have subject matter expertise on a given issue, a strong interest in a particular area of the negotiation, or an ability to solve problems. Ask them to meet with both sides to agree on information protocols and procedures and make joint recommendations.

CREATE A SINGLE VERSION OF THE FACTS. Select representatives from both sides to agree on a single set of facts that can be used to define and solve the problem, especially when chronology, essential characteristics, and economic or financial information are critical to reaching an agreement. Agreement on the facts will prevent disagreements over questions that should have only one right answer and ease tension over potentially hot issues.

ELIMINATE SURPRISES. Ask the other side to reveal their bargaining agenda in advance and agree that both sides will avoid making surprise demands at the last minute. Joint agenda and process improvement suggestions can be used to limit or prioritize topics for discussion. When each side is clear about the maximums they are willing to concede and the minimums they are willing to accept, they will be prepared for trade-offs and compromises and better able to alter their expectations and improve their relationship.

ALLOW EACH SIDE TO SAVE FACE. Search for opportunities to support each side in looking like a committed participant in the process, appearing to negotiate effectively, and not losing face with their constituencies or supporters. The need to save face can drive negotiators to dig in their heels, agree on unclear language, claim victory over the other side, cause them to feel they suffered a defeat, and create problems for future negotiations.

RECORD EVERYTHING. Pick a mutually acceptable recorder to note the issues, discussions, recommendations, ideas, actions, and issues for future discussion. Minutes of meetings should be available to both sides. At the end of every session, ask each person to give a brief plus-and-minus evaluation of the process used during the session and suggest what could be done to improve the next session. Make sure these ideas are included in the minutes and that changes are implemented at future meetings.

NEGOTIATE IN A SPIRIT OF PROBLEM SOLVING. Agree that anything that is a problem for one side is a problem for both sides. Refocus on the future, recognizing that everyone is in the same boat and likely to remain there. Establish that it ultimately does not matter whose end of the boat is leaking because everyone will end up going down together. Therefore, do not adopt strategies that run the risk of jeopardizing long-term relationships. Make a good-faith effort to resolve all issues through a collaborative process, and approach your problems with the idea that it is "us versus it" rather than "us versus them" or "me versus you."

WHEN YOU GET STUCK, CHANGE THE PROCESS. If the process is not working, change it. You can *always* stop cold and start all over again. Both sides can agree to appoint a facilitator, recorder, timekeeper, or process observer, or to bring in an outside mediator or facilitator to offer advice on how to make the process work. You can also encourage process interventions, acknowledge criticisms, hold regular discussions of process issues, and elicit ideas from dissenters for continued improvement of the negotiation.

WHEN YOU GET STUCK, OPEN UP THE NEGOTIATIONS. If you get stuck, allow concerned individuals to observe the negotiations and provide feedback. Customers, coworkers, colleagues, community members, and partners can express their sentiments, make suggestions on how to resolve difficult issues, or break impasses by suggesting new strategies. Alternatively, you can videotape the session, play it back, ask people to comment on what they saw, and make changes. You will need to decide whether to keep the recording confidential or use it to train future negotiators, but retain control over it so it is not misused.

WHEN YOU GET STUCK, GENERATE OPTIONS. Jointly brainstorm options based on the interests each side has expressed. Choose the best alternative, then fine-tune or improve it by incorporating the other side's ideas. You can also identify the barriers to achieving each objective and create specific solutions that are tailored to overcoming these barriers. Consider asking each side, "What would it take for you to give that up?" When you hear their answers, look for options that might satisfy their deeper interests. Alternatively, ask each side to identify what they would want or need to have in exchange for agreeing to what the other side has requested, then expand the scope of the negotiation to include these requests.

IDENTIFY THE REASONS FOR IMPASSE. Specifically identify the issues that are at impasse or blocking agreement. Reach consensus on a definition of the reasons for impasse and the reasons for overcoming it. Have each side state the reasons they find the other side's proposal unacceptable and identify specific ways in which it could be improved. Delegate small, bilateral subteams to discuss a problem, prioritize options, and report back on their top choices, or make consensus recommendations to both sides.

EXTEND THE NEGOTIATIONS. Create year-round negotiations, and build small negotiations into everyday life. Do not wait for the agreement to end or problems to develop or conflicts to occur before discussing how you will act to resolve important issues with each other in the future.

After Negotiation Ends

IMPROVE THE PROCESS. At the end of the negotiation, ask everyone on each side to summarize their experience and thank each other specifically for what they did that helped the group negotiate more collaboratively. Ask each person to indicate what worked and what did not in the negotiation, and one thing that could be done to improve the process next time.

PUBLICIZE YOUR ACCOMPLISHMENTS. Generate support among nonparticipants for the collaborative negotiation process. Focus on what you achieved and be completely open and honest about what you did not. Periodically remind yourself and others how much worse it would have been if you had used an adversarial approach.

SUPPORT THE OTHER SIDE IN THE EYES OF ITS CONSTITUENCY. Acknowledge the legitimacy and cooperation of the other side, not only to the participants personally, but to their constituencies as well. In conflicts between groups, be cautious of praising the other side's negotiators too highly. Recognize that some people are afraid of collaboration and need to feel their particular self-interests have been advocated. Negotiators always need to strike a balance between cooperating and pressing for the satisfaction of their constituency's needs. Because they are expected to be strong advocates for opposite sides, professional negotiators cannot appear to become too closely aligned with the other side. When a settlement proposal is presented, both sides should take steps to alleviate the concerns of those who feel they may be sacrificing something because agreement was not reached through an adversarial process.

REMEMBER THE PROBLEMS. Make sure both sides recall the problems and issues that were encountered during the negotiation process; return to topics that were postponed or not fully resolved, and discuss any glitches you encounter in administering the agreement afterward. Keep everyone informed and try to solve recurring problems informally before taking them to the negotiation table. Encourage those who were not happy with the process to air their feelings. Hear them out, and treat their comments not as criticisms, but as suggestions that can help you identify what did not work for them and elicit ideas about what might be done better in the future.

HONOR YOUR AGREEMENTS. Be committed to fully honoring the agreements you reach. Nothing undermines collaborative negotiation more than the failure to follow up, live up to, and implement agreements. Create a joint evaluation team to make sure that all the agreements are being honored and fine-tune any that may require adjustment.

CONTINUE SOLVING PROBLEMS. Keep track of unresolved issues or problems and return to them in the future to continue searching for solutions. Keep a record of objections or complaints about the process or the agreement. If necessary, stop and reopen negotiations to discuss these issues. Establish a joint team to identify problems that arise following negotiations. Put a process in place for defining how these issues will be handled, making sure that channels are available for resolving them outside negotiations and that everyone is aware of their existence. The primary purpose of collaborative negotiation is to reach agreements as well as create mechanisms for solving future problems *without* negotiations, improving relationships, and institutionalizing the ability to satisfy both sides' long- and short-term interests.

CONTINUE NEGOTIATING. Do not allow unresolved issues to accumulate. Instead, negotiate solutions before, during, and as soon after they occur as possible. Identify ongoing issues and create a permanent way of searching for solutions. Schedule regular problem-solving meetings to deal with troublesome issues before they are blown out of proportion. Meet regularly, even if there are no items on the agenda, to continue communicating, solving problems, and building trust.

CONTINUE COMMUNICATING ABOUT THE SUCCESS OF COLLABORATION. New people who enter the process or join the organization should receive an orientation to collaborative negotiation and be trained in its methods. Collaborative negotiation is based on common sense and a team approach to problem solving, but it should not be taken for granted or assumed that everyone will understand it. Make efforts to rotate leadership and include different people in the process to broaden the range of support. Offer year-round opportunities for negotiators to continue improving their skills.

EVALUATE YOUR PERSONAL PARTICIPATION. Honestly assess what you did or did not do during the negotiations, and what you might have done instead to feel more successful and satisfied. Consider what you actually accomplished, at what cost, and what is left to accomplish. Communicate your self-assessment to others.

CELEBRATE YOUR SUCCESSES. Take time out to jointly acknowledge and celebrate what you have accomplished. Hold a party, celebratory meeting, or open house. Congratulate yourself and the other side generously on what you have done.

If you are unable to reach agreement using collaborative negotiation skills, you can always "agree to disagree." But it is possible to take the process one step further and agree *specifically* and exactly on *how* you will disagree. For example, you may agree not to yell or scream at each other, not to use insults or act disrespectfully, to speak openly and honestly about your differences, and to continue searching for solutions no matter what obstacles are in your way. These agreements on how you will disagree can help rebuild trust, making it possible for future negotiations to succeed.

Above all, remember that most of our lives and work experiences consist of negotiating solutions to an endless round of profound and trivial problems. Therefore, improving your skills in collaborative negotiation should be considered a lifetime effort whose principal outcomes are improvements in communications, processes, and relationships.

STRATEGY 10

MEDIATE AND DESIGN SYSTEMS FOR PREVENTION

By the very fact of his being human, man is asked a question by life: how to overcome the split between himself and the world outside of him in order to arrive at the experience of unity and oneness with his fellow man and with nature. Man has to answer this question every minute of his life. Not only—or even primarily—with thoughts and words, but by his mode of being and acting.

—Erich Fromm

Mediation is the unifying element and final recourse for every conflict resolution strategy we have mentioned. If your efforts to solve problems and negotiate solutions have not resulted in resolving your disputes, the next step may be for an unbiased third-party mediator to assist you in communicating your ideas and feelings to each other, discussing the most difficult, sensitive, and emotional issues, and searching for solutions.

Mediation has its roots in the ancient indigenous conflict resolution practices of preindustrial cultures. Yet it is also a modern, intricate, sophisticated set of techniques for depolarizing, depersonalizing, and deconstructing conflict. Many of these techniques have been mentioned in earlier chapters, but their effectiveness can be enormously enhanced in the hands of a skilled practitioner.

In essence, mediation is an informal problem-solving conversation facilitated by an experienced third party who is outside the problem. It is a voluntary, consensus-based approach that uses facilitated communication, emotional processing, creative problem solving, collaborative negotiation, brainstorming, impasse resolution, heart-to-heart communications, and similar techniques to bring conflicting parties into constructive and creative dialogue.

Mediation differs from litigation and arbitration because the mediator is not a judge or arbitrator who decides the issues for the parties. Instead, the mediator invites the parties to work together in defining the issues, identifying creative solutions, and collaboratively implementing solutions. Mediation is future-oriented and less concerned with deciding who is right or wrong than with solving problems so they do not occur again.

Mediators are not so much neutral as "omni-partial," and on both parties' sides at the same time. Mediators often work in co-mediation teams that combine diverse racial, gender, ethnic, and cultural experiences, along with contrasting areas of professional expertise and personal styles. Mediation sessions are generally informal and confidential to encourage direct dialogue.

Mediation has proven highly successful in resolving a wide range of conflicts, including interpersonal, workplace, discrimination, public policy, environmental, and organizational disputes, as well as divorce, family, marital, neighborhood, criminal, and community disputes.

Mediation is often able to reach solutions quickly, saving time, costs, and attorney fees, and preserving privacy.

Mediation can help people at work learn more effective communication skills and avoid bitterness and hostility. On average, experienced mediators resolve 80 to 95 percent of the disputes they address. Success depends on the insight, competency, training, and experience of the mediator, as well as on the timing of the intervention, the complexity and emotionality of the dispute, the mediator's ability to personally connect with the parties, and their readiness to participate in the process.

Agreements are often reached in a single session, and in the workplace it is common for sessions to last one to three hours. These sessions may take place on the assembly line, in the manager's office, in a neutral conference room, or at a location outside the workplace. The process is informal, can be done by peer mediators selected from the workplace, and may or may not include attorneys or union representatives. Agreements are reached in a voluntary process through consensus, which encourages responsibility for implementation.

There are many ways of motivating people to try mediation. But even if you are certain the other side will not accept mediation, we recommend you ask a mediator to try anyway, because mediators can often convince people to try the process even after they have refused their opponent's request to do so.

You can find a professional mediator by contacting a local or national mediation organization, or the Association for Conflict Resolution in Washington, DC, or by going to www.mediate.com, asking a personal friend, union or management representative, therapist, lawyer, church, or community agency, and they will help you try to locate someone in your area.

Why Mediation Works

Having conducted thousands of mediations over the past thirty years, certified hundreds of mediators, and conducted workshops for tens of thousands of people in mediation and conflict resolution techniques, we have grown to appreciate the extraordinary value of mediation and increased our understanding of how and why it works, often miraculously and against all odds.

Mediation works on many levels. It stops people from fighting, de-escalates their aggressive behaviors, initiates deep listening and dialogue, acknowledges and affirms negative emotions, facilitates informal problem solving and collaborative negotiation, settles issues in dispute, resolves underlying issues that gave rise to the dispute, promotes forgiveness, encourages reconciliation, and helps design preventative conflict resolution systems.

As mediators work through successive levels of conflict, the skill and experience required to overcome obstacles and move to the next higher level increases exponentially. Each new level also requires greater willingness and commitment on the part of the participants, and greater subtlety and artistry on the part of the mediator. But what exactly is it that makes mediation successful? We believe it is because mediation

- Invites adversaries to become human and real with each other
- Allows dialogue to take place in the language of metaphor
- Acknowledges the emotional needs of the parties and encourages both sides to tell their inner subjective truths, as well as their outer objective points of view
- Brings people together through empathy, curiosity, and listening, rather than dividing them in anticipation of revenge or unilateral victory
- Draws on their compassion, affection, and love for one another, rather than their hatred, distrust, or detached neutrality
- Asks each side to listen for deeper meaning and encourages them to participate in small collaborations without triggering distrust and defensiveness
- Helps opponents reestablish their lost connections and emphasizes the wholeness of human experience, as opposed to demonizing it or rendering it unintelligible
- Allows opponents to surrender, let go, and move on with their lives
- Lays open the secret sources of their motivation
- Recognizes every human interest as valid and important
- Empowers everyone equally and democratizes their conflict
- Looks to the future rather than the past
- Offers constructive feedback
- Aids people in creating solutions for themselves and accepting them, rather than having them imposed from the outside

- Acknowledges that no one enjoys being the object of another person's wrath or being trapped inside their own, releasing them from their own and others' rage and fear
- Creates an expectation of resolution, encourages hope, gradually reestablishes trust, and allows people to imagine living in and being at peace
- Encourages people to move beyond rigid positions and understand each other's underlying interests
- Promotes authenticity and unconditional respect, minimizes difficult behaviors, discourages aggressiveness, reduces stress, and elicits mutual compromises
- Makes the positive motivation of each person the center and object of the process, respects people and accepts them as they are, while simultaneously encouraging them to improve
- Does not judge actions or intentions but helps each person do what is right
- Reinforces and encourages empathy, hospitality, honesty, friendship, partnership, and respect, while acknowledging disagreement, anger, disappointment, rejection, denial, aggression, and revenge
- Supports everyone in getting what they want and need and allows them both to win
- Seeks to unite reason and intuition, love and self-interest, freedom and order, law and justice
- Is unique in every case yet fundamentally the same in every culture
- Gives everyone an opportunity to recognize their enemy as a reflection of themselves and to see themselves as no greater than the least nor worse than the best among them
- Reveals the possibility of resolution that already exists inside each of us, waiting to emerge
- Invites each side to speak from the heart and let their spirit, authenticity, and integrity shine forth
- Encourages people to reach out to their opponents and trust their intuition

Mediation is not easy, but if it can do even a few of these things in your conflict, you will be successful.

Designing Conflict Resolution Systems

Every conflict takes place between individuals, within them, and one at a time. But resolving single conflicts will not change organizational systems, allow us to act preventatively, or permit us to design systems that avert potential conflicts before they occur. Resolving isolated individual conflicts will not enable those who did not experience or participate in them to learn, or develop skills in conflict resolution, or permit everyone in the organization to learn from the suffering of others.

In the early 1960s, Douglas McGregor, a social scientist at Massachusetts Institute of Technology, realized that the properties and dynamics of organizational systems had to be considered as a whole, rather than as a collection of parts. He wrote:

> We study characteristics of cells, of organs, of the nervous system as a whole, of the human being as an organism, of groups, and of larger aggregations of human beings. Certain characteristics are common to all these "systems"; others are unique at each level. ... Management's insistence that the individual is the unit of organization is as limiting as an engineer's insistence that the atom is the unit of physical systems.... A molecule is an assembly of atoms, to be sure, but certain *relationships* among the atoms result in molecules with given properties, whereas other relationships result in entirely different properties. These properties of molecules cannot be predicted solely on the basis of knowledge of the properties of atoms.

In a similar way, conflicts in general cannot be reduced to any particular conflict. In most organizations, conflicts are addressed only partially and in a piecemeal, reactive, and isolated way, causing little or nothing to change in response to chronic and systemic conflicts, low-level hostilities, easily anticipatable disputes and the observable escalation of interpersonal hostilities—except when they turn into full-blown crises, large-scale disruptions, or impose intolerable costs.

It is difficult to halt the downward spiral of unresolved conflicts in organizations, disabling them and leaving their relationships in tatters. Yet working preventatively to imagine, design, and implement dispute resolution systems, strategies, and procedures can enrich organizations, not only by providing mechanisms for avoiding unnecessary disruptions and preventing conflict, but institutionalizing dispute resolution practices and encouraging everyone to learn from conflicts.

The wisest course of action is to design and implement systems, structures, processes, relationships, and cultures that prevent paralyzing impasses, unnecessary costs, petty personal squabbles, and large-scale systemic dysfunctions in unresolved conflicts from occurring at all.

Designing systems for conflict prevention, resolution, and transformation on an organizational scale may seem daunting. Yet while people often behave badly in conflict and cannot reach resolution, let alone prevention or transformation, the possibility of profound personal and organizational learning and growth is *always* present in *every* conflict we encounter. As Henry David Thoreau wrote, "If you have built castles in the air, your work need not be lost; that is where they should be. Now put the foundations under them."

The Costs of Conflict

If we count the *real* costs of conflict and calculate the amount of time, energy, and money we routinely spend on unresolved disputes, it is nearly always far in excess of the amount it would have taken to sit down with a third party and work out solutions. In short, it takes us a minuscule amount of time to resolve disputes, compared with the amount of time it takes to *not* resolve them. Here are a few direct quotes from managers and staff who gave us examples of what their conflicts cost them:

- "I'm so furious! Why can't he understand what I'm trying to tell him!" A supervisor complained bitterly when a manager reporting to him did not do as he asked and decided to fire him. We discovered that the supervisor had not actually *told* the manager exactly what he wanted, assumed he understood what was needed, and did not want to appear to be micromanaging. Instead, he communicated poorly, became angry when he felt misunderstood, nearly terminated the manager, and cost the organization an enormous amount of time, energy, and money to fix the problem.
- "I made it very clear to him that I didn't want him to flirt with me, though I couldn't say so directly because I didn't want to be rude." A woman who filed a sexual harassment lawsuit against her boss told us in mediation this was why she had not asked him to stop. When we spoke with her boss he said he thought she enjoyed his shoulder massages and flirtatious comments,

and said, "If she had just told me, I would have stopped immediately." The price they and the organization paid for her lack of communication and his failure to read her nonverbal signals ran over several million dollars, without counting emotional costs and damaged careers.

- "I'm leaving because there are too many people in this organization who won't carry their own weight or do their fair share of the work and no one will call them on it." This statement came from a company director who was frustrated to the point of resigning because he could not find a way to talk about the group's unspoken agreement that "I won't call you on your shortcomings if you don't call me on mine." If we had not helped him find a constructive way to discuss the problem, he would have left, costing the company a highly valued director and the expense of finding and training a qualified replacement.
- "She must be from some village in India and I can't make any sense of how in the hell she makes decisions. She just doesn't belong here." This comment was made by the manager of a multinational corporation with employees who spanned ten countries and three continents after firing the employee. He'd had no training in diversity or prejudice reduction, and the company lost millions of dollars in legal fees, human resource time, humiliating publicity, dissatisfied customers, and disgruntled staff—all as a result of not spending time and money to train everyone in cross-cultural communication.

We picked these comments because they seem relatively minor and commonplace, yet in each case they triggered serious, costly conflicts because people were unable to communicate, or were afraid of the consequences if they did. And each of these individuals, coworkers, and organizations paid an enormous price for their unwillingness to tell each other the truth and for their lack of skill in resolving disputes before they escalated.

If we could calculate the total amount of time, energy, money, and resources that are routinely wasted on unresolved workplace conflicts—the intimacies lost; the relationships destroyed; the decreased productivity due to gossip, rumors, absenteeism, stress-related illnesses, and poor morale; the disruptions, turnover, grievances, and lawsuits; the accidents and workers' compensation cases based on stress and injuries resulting from conflict—the total would be staggering. On top of these is the hidden amounts squandered in lost potential for growth and learning, and missed possibilities for improved relationships, increased sales, and personal and organizational transformation.

A survey conducted several years ago by the American Management Association among 116 chief executive officers, 76 vice presidents, and 66 middle managers revealed that they were spending at least *24 percent* of their time resolving conflicts. They felt that conflict resolution had become more important over the past ten years, and was equal to or more important than strategic planning, communication, motivation, and decision making.

In many organizations, the amount of managerial time devoted to unresolved conflicts is greater than 24 percent, particularly when minor, low-intensity disputes are included. If we add up all the time that managers spend listening to complaints, countering rumors, delivering corrective feedback, disciplining employees for conflict-related behaviors, monitoring compliance, and searching for solutions, managerial time dedicated to resolving conflicts can easily increase to 50 percent or higher. If we multiply this figure times the number of managers and the average manager's salary, the true organizational cost of unresolved conflict becomes immense.

On the other hand, when chronic conflicts are resolved, organizations usually experience, among other results: improved productivity; increased morale; reduced waste; innovative solutions; revitalization; better alignment with vision, mission, and values; more targeted strategic planning; expanded participation; more effective communications; increased synergy and teamwork; streamlined processes; enhanced organizational learning and increased trust.

Many organizations have discovered that by expanding their existing conflict resolution programs they can substantially reduce litigation expenses and realize significant cost savings. Here are some examples cited by Karl Slaikeu and Ralph Hasson in *Controlling the Costs of Conflict:*

- In the first year of comparison, Brown and Root reported an 80 percent reduction in outside litigation expenses by introducing a systemic approach to collaboration and conflict resolution regarding employment issues.
- Motorola Corporation reported a reduction in outside litigation expenses of up to 75 percent per year over six years by using a systemic approach to conflict management in its legal

department and including a mediation clause in contracts with suppliers.

- National Cash Register Corporation reported a reduction in outside litigation expenses of 50 percent and a drop in its number of pending lawsuits from 263 to 28 between 1984 and 1993 following the systemic use of alternative dispute resolution.
- The U.S. Air Force reported that by taking a collaborative approach to conflict management in a construction project, it completed the project 144 days ahead of schedule and $12 million under budget.
- The U.S. Defense Mapping Agency reported that systemic conflict management reduced the cost of resolving a particular set of employment disputes by forty-two hundred hours.
- The U.S. Air Force estimated a savings of 50 percent per claim in one hundred equal employment opportunity complaints using mediation.

If we add the savings that are achieved by reducing gossip and rumors, stress-related sick leave, conflict-induced absences and tardiness, reassignment and retraining costs incurred as a result of staff quitting over unresolved conflicts, human resources and executive salaries devoted to employee discipline and discharge, and similar expenses related to unresolved conflicts, the figures become astronomical.

One study of sixteen hundred employees reveals greater detail regarding the price commonly paid by organizations in lost productivity:

- Twenty-two percent of employees said they decreased their work efforts as a result of conflict.
- Over fifty percent reported they lost work time because they worried about whether the instigator of the conflict would do it again.
- Twelve percent reported they changed jobs to get away from the instigator.

There are even greater, incalculable costs to unresolved conflict in terms of lost opportunities to learn, improve, and evolve. As organizations face increasing demands for rapid change, conflicts accumulate along the fault lines that lie hidden within their structures, systems, processes, relationships, and cultures. These conflicts point directly to what is not working inside the organization. Resolving these conflicts, on the other hand, often reveals new opportunities for growth and breakthrough innovations in structures, systems, processes, and cultures.

Why Systems Design

With increased globalization, it is common for executives, managers, and staff to span diverse continents, languages, and cultures, and encounter enormous social, economic, and political differences. The challenge of communicating effectively and preventing misunderstandings and conflicts then becomes an increasing priority because the potential costs, damage to the economic bottom line, and deteriorating job satisfaction can lead to loss of important opportunities and organizational dissolution.

Indeed, conflicts are often simply the sound made by the cracks in a system, the first indication of the birth of a new paradigm, a warning light that is signaling an imminent breakdown, a path to organizational improvement, and the initial stage of evolution to a higher order of conflict. The opportunity costs of leaving conflicts unresolved can therefore be measured indirectly in our failure to adapt, evolve, improve, and survive.

Most conflicts are viewed as interpersonal, or someone's fault, or a "personality clash," causing their deeper meanings to be missed. Yet as these conflicts accumulate, a point arrives when what seemed unique and personal is suddenly revealed as common, widespread, and omnipresent in the organization—in other words, as the by-product of a chronically dysfunctional organizational structure, system, process, or culture. These larger issues often get ignored, hidden, or avoided, even when hundreds or thousands experience the identical conflict.

Chronic conflicts may also be a sign that an organizational structure, system, process, or culture is unable to reform or repair itself, and has erected lines of denial, defense, counterattack, and compensatory rationalization to avoid any resolution that could involve fundamental change.

As these defenses to resolution aggregate, they produce growing insecurities, fears that the entire structure will collapse, and heightened resistance, even to minor modifications that could trigger an avalanche of disputes. As the fear of systemic meltdown increases, even those in favor of change may retreat and seek to preserve or roll back the status quo, hoping to deflect any changes in the existing system by focusing on less important issues.

Designing Organizational Systems

Few organizations have designed adequate structures, systems, processes, or cultures to encourage prevention, or even listening to and resolving disputes. Few promote collaborative negotiation, mediation, or similar skills, and choose instead to wait until unacceptable losses have occurred.

As a result, conflicts are often pigeonholed as isolated events, or as "someone else's problem," or the fault of individuals, or beyond the reach of organizational policy, or already within the expertise of people inside the organization to solve. Sometimes conflicts are considered solved when the solutions do not go deep enough to reach underlying issues or dismantle the systems that gave rise to them. As a result, conflicts become chronic and return over and over again to generate new problems.

What is needed instead are complex, collaborative, self-correcting conflict resolution structures, systems, processes, and cultures that are designed to prevent and resolve *all* disputes within the organization and offer a rich array of diverse alternatives that motivate everyone to prevent and resolve disputes, and to learn from them.

Based on ideas first propounded by William Ury, Stephen Goldberg, and Jeanne Brett, "conflict resolution systems design" asks organizations to analyze their disputes, discover their chronic and repeating causes, and regard conflict not as an isolated incident, but as a *system* that can be addressed in more than one way.

Conflict resolution systems design principles consider organizations as wholes, with *integrated* systems rather than discrete procedures. When an organization takes a systems design approach, it responds not only to single disputes, but to the *streams* of chronic conflict that flow continually inside them.

This approach encourages early evaluation and monitoring, informal problem solving, mediation, and de-escalation throughout the life of the conflict. It allows different people to work on the problem from multiple, diverse perspectives. It employs alternate methodologies in search of synergistic results, and encourages organizational learning and personal skill building.

Conflict resolution systems design prioritizes interest-based alternatives, emphasizing informal problem solving, mediation, and collaborative negotiation—while including rights and power-based systems as backups, and arranging them from lower to higher cost.

Interest-based resolution systems are more complex and innovative than power- or rights-based systems, and offer multiple opportunities for dialogue and learning. Their goal is not victory over opponents, but improved communications, processes, and relationships. Everyone in an organization can assist in designing interest-based conflict resolution systems. The initial steps in designing such systems include

- Analyzing the sources of chronic conflict, including the structures, systems, processes, relationships, and cultures that cause or exacerbate conflicts. It examines the communications, strategies, change processes, values, morale, and styles that often trigger disputes. Sometimes it means conducting a "conflict audit" to assess the chronic sources of conflict, including their locations, causes, and sometimes the individuals identified with them.
- Identifying the core cultural norms and ideas, expectations and assumptions, traditional approaches, and informal mechanisms already in place for resolving conflict, and supplementing them with enriched, complex, self-correcting alternatives to emphasize prevention and focus on interests, rather than rights- or power-based solutions.
- Expanding the number and kind of resolution alternative available both internally and externally, and arranging these procedures from low to high cost.
- Offering a full range of options from process improvements to peer mediation, with low-cost rights- and power-based backups such as binding arbitration, plus "loopbacks" to informal problem solving and collaborative negotiation.
- Encouraging consultation, facilitation, dialogue, coaching, and mentoring during the process with feedback and evaluation afterwards, aimed at altering behavioral patterns that discourage widespread use of dispute resolution procedures.
- Providing whatever training, motivation, skills, support, and resources are needed to make these procedures work, improving everyone's understanding of conflict resolution options,

clarifying how they succeed and fail, and continually improving their design.

The object of these conflict resolution systems design processes is to develop avenues and mechanisms that are tailored to unique organizational needs, resolve both isolated individual conflicts and chronic multiparty disputes, allow conflicts to be prevented and resolved, and stimulate personal and organizational growth, insight, change, and learning, leading to improved operations. The most commonly used procedures in the system design "arsenal" include

- Informal problem solving
- Peer counseling, coaching, and mentoring
- Team building
- Strategic planning
- Informal problem solving
- Facilitated meetings
- Collaborative negotiation
- Supportive confrontation
- Restorative justice techniques
- Circles and group meetings
- Large-group interventions
- Participatory feedback and evaluation
- Public dialogue and open forums
- Peer and professional mediation
- Ombudsman offices
- Internal appeals boards
- Review boards
- Binding and nonbinding arbitration

Here are eight illustrations drawn from our experience of how different organizations have used the systems design process to promote mediation and create preventative alternatives.

1. After a string of costly jury verdicts, a Fortune 100 corporation decided to develop a comprehensive systems approach to conflict resolution. We worked with human resources staff to design

an employee problem resolution procedure that led conflicting employees through a multistep process. Both parties in the conflict were assigned an "executive advisor" from outside their business unit to informally coach and advocate for them and meet confidentially to mediate the dispute. If this failed, the dispute went to a "consensus review board" that could bind the company. If these processes failed, the issue moved to arbitration that was also binding on the company.

2. A technology corporation confronted with angry clients and chronic conflicts between staff members and business partners conducted a conflict audit that revealed disgruntled information systems users, skeptical senior managers, low morale among staff who did not believe they could implement the new systems, and vendors who had no confidence that bills would be paid. At a staff retreat, they analyzed this information and reached consensus on a conflict resolution plan that began with an open dialogue with user groups. The dialogue sessions resulted in several creative ideas for implementing improved customer service, a better delivery system, and a more powerful technology architecture. Volunteers from both constituencies were trained in peer co-mediation, and immediately began resolving employee and vendor disputes with high rates of success, leading to an overall increase in morale and motivation.

3. A conflict audit at a large manufacturing company revealed multiple disputes between line workers at one of its plants. Angry outbursts, competition between team members, and threats of physical attack were disrupting operations. We worked with human resources to identify, analyze, categorize, and prioritize the sources of conflict, revealing how disputes were reinforced by their organizational culture. A small, integrated systems design team was selected to identify conflict predictors, preventive measures, safety nets, outlets for constructive expression of differences, procedures for resolution, and methods for making them effective. Their study led them to dramatically reduce the risks and costs of conflict, mediate disputes before legal costs accumulated, provide a fair forum for resolution outside the courts, and create a learning culture regarding workplace conflicts.

4. Similar results were achieved at a large utility company where a court-based consent decree forced the creation of a conflict

resolution system to handle employee complaints, particularly regarding allegations of racial discrimination. We worked with a human resources team to design a comprehensive conflict resolution system that relied heavily on informal problem solving, dialogue, and mediation by human resources staff. Line managers were trained in its use, resulting in a large-scale reduction of hostilities and litigated cases, and a significant improvement in racial relations.

5. A large corporation reorganized its staff into self-managing teams. As managers became team leaders and a largely bookkeeping and accounting staff began managing themselves, they became more service-oriented and adept at strategic planning. As these changes unfolded, conflicts arose within, between, and among teams based on miscommunications, false expectations and assumptions, inconsistencies in implementing team values, lack of equity between team members in pulling their weight, old managerial behaviors, resistance to change, and role confusions. Using systems design principles, the teams created new governance structures for themselves and the organization, communications systems with in-house customers, clear organizational roles and responsibilities, fast-forming teams to solve important problems, peer mediation training, a peer coaching program, and an orientation program for new managers and staff. They developed innovative strategies to address the systemic sources of their disputes and conducted ongoing, open, honest dialogue sessions regarding inconsistencies in the team process, resulting in dramatic improvements in morale and productivity.
6. A regulation negotiation process was initiated between city staff and neighborhood organizations to help diverse community constituencies reach consensus and avoid destructive battles over zoning regulations and public policies that had a direct impact on their lives. This design process brought civil servants and city planners together with the merchants, residents, community organizations, activists, and homeowners who had fought bitterly with each other for years. In the course of a few meetings over several months, we helped them produce a vision for the future of their neighborhoods, informal problem-solving processes for resolving future disputes, and a consensus-based proposed ordinance that was recommended to the city council and adopted unanimously.

7. Similar results were achieved in a citywide "homeless task force" that brought hostile opposing parties to complete consensus on a comprehensive set of recommendations for public action. We assisted them in designing a collaborative negotiation, problem-solving, and dispute resolution process in which those who disagreed most strongly about an issue were assigned to a team to jointly research the issue, brainstorm and collaboratively negotiate potential solutions, and return to the task force with consensus or a set of prioritized recommendations. Large-group facilitation and sidebar mediations were used to reduce personalization and refocus on problem solving.
8. An international nonprofit with a mission to provide health care services for pregnant women and newborn babies in rural African and Latin American communities was riddled with conflicts between paid staff and volunteer professionals. Disputes over the quality of delivery services, allocation of funds, and competing demands from clients had a dramatic effect on their mission. A team from the board of directors met with each staff member and key volunteers to reveal the source of the problem and create a system that would end their conflicts. They found that most volunteers had a great deal in common with the clients, yet paid staff were Caucasian, highly educated, and middle-class, rarely visited service delivery centers in Africa and Latin America, and were viewed as having limited firsthand knowledge of the needs, preferences, and pain of the women being served. Both groups felt misunderstood, isolated, unappreciated, and unable to communicate with each other. We led a team of staff and volunteers in designing a system that provided conflict coaching, joint staff-volunteer teams, and peer mediation, in which the coaches became mediators. If that did not work, a conflict review committee with client members would make a decision. Staff and volunteers were trained in mediation, communication, and conflict coaching.

Similar processes have been used to assist conflict-ridden schools, colleges, and university departments; nonprofit organizations; partnerships and family businesses; and community, political, and public interest groups in resolving their disputes using conflict resolution systems design principles, and in developing diverse processes, techniques, methods, and skills that were *at least* as complex as the issues they wanted to address.

In each of these diverse organizations and environments, conflict resolution systems design proved to be a powerful method—not just for preventing, mediating, and resolving conflicts, but also for learning and improving skills, developing internal cohesion and leadership, and using these skills to improve collaboration, democracy, morale, and their capacity for successful self-management.

In each of the organizational initiatives described above, our goal was to develop interest-based systems that would strengthen the organization's ability to respond preventively and proactively to disputes. Adoption of these initiatives reflected the willingness of leaders, managers, and employees to risk trying something new and commit to prevention and mediation, rather than avoidance, resistance, grievances, reduced morale, litigation, and costly cleanups.

Conduct a Conflict Audit

We often hear managers argue that conflict resolution and mediation take too much time and cost too much, or complain that they have too many important things to do to spend time resolving disputes. In response, we ask them to identify in some detail how much time and money they and their organization are wasting on conflict, and how little it often takes to set things right.

When we calculate a "conflict resolution bottom-line," we discover that the costs of conflict include not only attorneys fees and human resources salaries, but the amount of time people spend getting upset, distracted, and sick; the time dissipated in gossiping, spreading rumors, and discussing the conflict; the time wasted in miscommunications, lost opportunities for collaboration, and broken relationships; the alienation of customers and valuable employees; and the training and learning costs of replacing employees.

We have worked collaboratively in a number of organizations to assess the costs of poor communication, adversarial negotiation, and unresolved conflicts using a device we call a *conflict audit*. Conflict audits can be prepared independently by external consultants, or collaboratively by a consultant working with a team of volunteers. The audit consists of gathering objective data, including the numbers, costs, and time involved in

- Attorney and human resource budgets
- Terminations
- Disciplinary actions

- Grievances and labor-management relations
- Customer service complaints
- Conflicts and disagreements of all kinds
- Disputes with other organizations, including regulatory agencies
- Stress-related illnesses
- Workers' compensation claims attributable to conflict
- Employee turnover and training costs
- Similar conflict-related data

In addition, the audit includes designing *subjective* questions regarding the cost of conflict, including its effect on morale, motivation, customer retention, reputation, and similar intangible items. These questions attempt to identify and measure the time, energy, and money spent on conflicts and miscommunications, and put a price tag on them.

You can conduct a rough conflict audit in your own organization simply by estimating the number of hours employees and managers spend each week miscommunicating or engaging in conflict, then multiplying that figure by the number of staff and their salaries.

Ask yourself and others: What are the full consequences of our lack of listening? How many customers, valued employees, fresh ideas, and creative insights have we lost as a result of conflict and miscommunication? How much have these losses cost? What would be it reasonable to do in response in order to stop paying that price? Whatever figure you derive will surely be shocking and enormous.

To conduct a more detailed audit, convene a cross-functional team with members from every department and level within the organization. The main tasks of the audit team are to identify potentially useful sources of information, develop questions that reveal the true cost of unresolved conflict, gather and summarize the information, work with conflict resolution professionals to design a comprehensive systemwide response, reach consensus-based recommendations on what changes to make, and develop a collaborative process for disseminating the findings and recommendations. Here are some illustrative questions you can use to design a conflict audit:

- How much does the organization spend on lawyers, litigation, and human resources efforts related to conflict?
- How much time does the average manager or employee spend each week trying to prevent, manage, or resolve disputes? What

is the salary of each? Multiplied by how many managers or employees?

- What are the costs of stress-related illness and conflict-related turnovers?
- How much employee time is spent spreading or countering rumors and gossip, including lost productivity and reduced collaboration due to conflict?
- What is the cost of conflict in reduced staff morale and motivation, estimated in time, salaries, and the likely cost of broken relationships?
- How many conflicts recur because they are never fully resolved? What are the costs associated with these reoccurrences?
- What customers, creativity, and opportunities have been lost due to conflict? What figures can be associated with these losses?
- How might the organization's success be different if it had not experienced these conflicts? How might that cost be estimated?
- What are the core values of the organization regarding conflict? Are they being observed? If not, what has it cost the organization?
- What are the main messages sent by the organizational culture regarding conflict? What is their impact on the cost of conflict?
- Are negative conflict behaviors being rewarded? How? What is the cost of rewarding them?
- How do leaders and managers typically respond to conflicts? What is their pattern of response costing the organization? How might they respond better?
- Have employees been trained in conflict resolution? What would it cost to do so?
- What do people do when they have conflicts? Where do they go for help? How helpful are they? What would it cost to make them more effective?
- Is there an internal mediation process? Who is allowed and encouraged to use it? Who isn't? What do they do instead? How much does that alternative cost by comparison?
- How often is the process used? Do employees know about it? How could information about the process be improved?

- How satisfied are employees with existing resolution processes? What would it cost to make them more satisfactory? What will it cost if the organization fails to improve these processes?
- How skilled are managers in conflict resolution? How much has their lack of skill cost the organization? What would it cost to improve their skills?
- What obstacles hinder the use of existing resolution processes? How much does this "hindering" cost? How can employees be motivated to use them?
- What skills do employees and managers need to resolve conflicts successfully? How can they be developed? What will it cost not to?
- What other systems or cultural changes would reduce or help resolve conflicts? How much would they cost?

These are a few of the hundreds of possible questions you can use to find out what conflict is costing your organization and what can be done to reduce them.

Shifting the Culture to Support Conflict Resolution Systems

Many organizations have conflict cultures that generate rules, processes, rewards, and sanctions for responding to conflicts. These cultures often discourage honest communications, suppress intense emotions, avoid mediation, and minimize risky, truthful, and authentic dialogue. They do so to protect existing processes and relationships from unnecessary disruptions and unanticipated changes, and present a positive public image that is very different from how people actually behave.

The smiling public faces of these dysfunctional cultures mask unhappy, repressive, conflict-avoidant realities. Indeed, it is rare in many organizations that employees feel completely free to openly and honestly discuss their conflicts and thus get the help they need.

While these restrictive and avoidant cultures *seem* necessary for success or survival, they add layers of dysfunction, disillusionment, demoralization, and despair to the lives of those who work in them, adding unnecessary costs and reducing effectiveness. It does not matter how elegant or effective conflict resolution systems are, without a cultural shift they will not work.

All organizational cultures generate unspoken, informal rules for deciding when it is safe to be honest, empathetic, and collaborative in conflict, and when it could cost someone's job. In some organizations, these informal rules produce incongruent, dishonest, and unethical cultures that encourage secrecy, silence in the presence of covert behaviors, and rewards for adversarial behaviors that discourage employees from resolving their disputes.

On the other hand, these same repressive cultures can be transformed by encouraging honesty, empathy, and collaboration; identifying and calling attention to negative and covert behaviors; clarifying shared values, encouraging managers and employees to act ethically and responsibly in their conflicts, and discouraging the dysfunctional behaviors they generate.

When individuals attempt to change their organizational cultures and increase support for conflict resolution, they often discover an element of risk associated with their efforts. Culture change requires a concerted, conscious effort on the part of internal allies at all levels in the organization. It requires people who are willing to stand up and be counted, and support the development of new norms and behaviors.

For example, the leaders of a facilities management department in a Fortune 100 corporation wanted to shift their culture from one of secrecy, fragmentation, isolation, competition, and conflict-avoidance to one of openness, information sharing, teamwork, cross-functional collaboration, and conflict resolution.

The leadership team met to define the characteristics of the new culture they wanted to create, identify the elements that needed to change, and communicate the new expectations, behaviors, and rules to supervisors, who had the job of communicating them to teams of employees so they could implement the new culture. One member of the leadership team sent this e-mail following their meeting:

> After seeing the Leadership Team members interact and then the Supervisory Team discuss the proposed changes, I saw a clear difference. The Supervisors are far more driven, collaborative and compassionate about what they are doing. I sense this has a lot to do with their commitment and desire to break out of the old mode of doing things. It is my perception that the Leadership Team, at this point, is not as developed and could have a hampering effect on the Supervisory Team's growth.

He got it exactly right, and an identical dynamic was taking place between supervisors and line employees. Cultural transformation requires a leadership team with clear vision and a strong commitment to making their own behaviors congruent with the new culture of openness, collaboration, and conflict resolution. Yet, for cultural change to succeed and become sustainable, everyone in the organization needs to own the changes, participate in defining them, and be willing to implement them in ways that are consistent with what they intend to create.

In this organization, a strong sense of ownership of cultural changes was needed, not only by the leadership team and the supervisors, but also by hourly staff, craftspeople, custodial employees, engineers, and secretaries. If they had been left out of the process or failed to agree with and support the new behaviors, the leadership team's plans, no matter how brilliant, would have sunk without a trace.

The leadership team soon realized that their initial efforts were being invisibly guided by an old culture that encouraged hierarchy, bureaucracy, and autocracy, and rewarded conflict avoidance, competitiveness, isolation, passivity, and aggressive competition, leading to fear of change and tension between departments.

They proceeded to institute an honest, empathetic, and collaborative approach that included everyone and encouraged them to participate in transforming their culture. Together they agreed to implement a conflict resolution system and design a change process that would

- Eliminate unnecessary boundaries between people, departments, and teams
- Transform preconceived standards of how they should act and treat each other, especially in conflict
- Recognize baggage from the past and eliminate it
- Allow people to work together, argue, and still go to lunch with those on the other side
- Focus on specifics and not communicate too broadly
- Build better communications to eliminate mixed messages and competition
- Build trust
- Not go around roadblocks or ignore them, but stop to do something about them

- Realize that things can change and eliminate negative attitudes
- Recognize what each person brings and value it
- Unify the division into one group
- Take conflicts to an ombudsman for resolution
- Mediate disputes and get trained in how to do it
- Have fun!

Organizational cultures are *holographic,* causing every piece to contain and reproduce the whole. This makes it impossible to change one element in an organizational culture without simultaneously changing an entire matrix of mutually reinforcing behaviors that interact with each other and give the culture its overall character. This aspect of organizational culture allows the whole to be transformed by strategically altering even minor, seemingly unimportant or unrelated parts.

Steps in Changing Conflict Cultures

In a study of hundreds of organizational change efforts that failed, Richard Pascale, Mark Millemann, and Linda Gioja found that the primary reason why otherwise important change initiatives did not succeed was the failure to identify, analyze, and transform organizational culture. The study identified four principal elements in organizational culture that had blocked or minimized the effectiveness of the change process:

1. *Power and vision:* Do people believe they have the power to create change in the organization and in their work? Is there a clear, compelling vision for the future that they have created or endorse? Do people mostly collaborate or compete with one another?
2. *Identity and relationships:* With whom do people identify in the organization? Do they identify with their teams, functional work units, professions, or the organization as a whole? Does the organization value relationships? Do people empathize with those who are different?
3. *Communication, negotiation, and conflict:* What behaviors do people engage in when they experience conflict? How do others respond? Is conflict swept under the rug or discussed openly? How do conflicts finally get resolved? How do people communicate? How do they negotiate with each other? How

honest, empathetic, and collaborative are they in solving problems and resolving conflicts?

4. *Learning and assessment:* How does the organization learn and change? How do people respond to new information that doesn't fit existing paradigms? How honest are they in assessing problems, offering feedback, and communicating their critiques?

Each of these elements in organizational culture are interrelated, so that cultures in which conflict is suppressed or avoided are likely to be those in which people feel powerless, have not created a compelling vision, identify only with their allies and friends, do not resolve their conflicts, and regard learning as secondary to winning.

If you want to be successful in transforming the way conflicts are resolved by using conflict resolution systems design, it is important to understand how to change the conflict culture in ways that reinforce your efforts. But how can you shift an adversarial conflict culture to encourage greater honesty, empathy, and collaboration? Here are five steps you can take to shift the culture of conflict in your organization:

1. Invite everyone in the organization to participate in a systems design and culture change process.
2. Ask questions regarding the old culture, how it responds to conflicts and punishes or rewards honesty, empathy, informal problem solving, collaborative negotiation, and mediation.
3. Brainstorm elements of the new culture that might encourage conflict prevention, resolution, and transformation.
4. Clarify the new norms, expectations, behaviors, and rewards that will support the new culture.
5. Agree on how to introduce and support it.

One easy way to begin is to form a cross-functional team to conduct a "conflict culture analysis" in which the old culture is examined and critiqued, and new elements are identified and accepted. Here are some initial questions to assist you in analyzing the old culture and defining the new one:

- What are the unspoken rules in the culture regarding conflict?
- How are these rules learned, communicated, and changed?
- When are these behaviors considered appropriate or inappropriate?

- What do people *do* when there are problems or conflicts?
- Which problems or conflicts are swept under the rug?
- Which conflict behaviors are rewarded? Which are punished? How?
- What topics can and cannot be discussed openly? What topics are argued over?
- When is it considered inappropriate to negotiate or resolve conflicts?
- How do people finally end up resolving their conflicts?
- How are intense emotions expressed and responded to?
- How do people respond to difficulties, glitches, and failures?
- What messages regarding conflict do leaders communicate in responding to their own conflicts?
- What do people believe about their power to change their own conflict behaviors and those of others?
- What stories do people tell about conflict? How might these stories be told differently?

Once people understand what their culture is communicating implicitly, it becomes possible to reach agreement on a set of shared values that will define the new culture. Employees may decide, for example, that their culture should encourage participation and open discussion, or increase everyone's ability to be honest about their conflicts, or be more receptive to feedback, or do more to encourage trust.

Seeking immediate changes will be highly useful, but conflict cultures run deep and require long-term efforts to fully transform. A successful long-term strategy for transforming these cultures can be created by finding ways of acknowledging and supporting those who have already begun to be more honest, empathetic, and collaborative, and using the systems design process to develop ways of encouraging others to do the same.

Part of the long-range change process includes consistent implementation and practice of new cultural behaviors, eliciting ongoing feedback, and regularly and publicly monitoring the change process to make certain it is congruent with desired changes. It is particularly important for those who consider themselves leaders or change agents to model the values they seek to instill in others, especially when responding to their own conflicts.

Finally, redesigning structures, systems, processes, relationships, and cultures necessarily includes redesigning the rewards and punishments, evaluations and assessments that encourage people to revert to old cultural behaviors, cause them to blindly defend the old culture, see the new culture as idealistic or impossible to implement, or rationalize destructive and apathetic behaviors.

If you want to create meaningful and lasting changes in the conflict culture of your organization, you will need to develop considerable clarity about what most needs to change and collaboratively create a sharp, compelling vision of what you want to bring into the new culture. Most important, you will need a strong commitment to practicing honesty, empathy, and compassion as these changes are identified, agreed upon, shifted, and implemented.

Reaching Closure

There is a fundamental difference between suppressing or avoiding conflict and intervening to stop it. Similarly, there is a difference between stopping a conflict and settling it; settling it and resolving it; resolving it and reaching closure, including forgiveness and reconciliation. Reaching closure means ending it so there is little or nothing left over.

To reach closure, most people need to feel they have been listened to respectfully and have been able to communicate their experiences and emotions. They need to feel that they have said everything that was weighing them down and expressed whatever was necessary to get the conflict off their chest so it could be over.

To fully communicate everything you think and feel as a result of your conflict, let it go, not hold anything back, and reach closure, there are four steps you will have to complete.

1. Be willing to acknowledge your own role in the conflict. This is the element of *honesty*.
2. Be willing to recognize your opponent as a human being. This is the element of *empathy*.
3. Forgive your opponent and yourself. This is the element of *letting go*.
4. Do something to make sure others do not experience the same conflict. This is the element of *prevention*.

You can take the first step in moving toward closure by telling your opponent what you need to discuss for the conflict to be over for you.

You can ask your opponent if there is anything she needs to say for it to be over for her. It is important not to reescalate the conflict in doing so. Therefore, instead of saying, "This is what you did to me," which will only trigger counter-accusations and defenses and initiate a cycle of recrimination, say: "This is what I learned from the conflict." Or "This is what I need to do in the future to protect myself from behaviors that are too difficult for me to handle."

The second step consists of recognizing your opponent as a real person who is entitled to respect and acknowledgment. It should be possible for you to say *something* positive about your opponent, even if it is simply to thank him or her for meeting and talking with you about your shared problem. If you are unable to think of anything positive to say, you are probably not emotionally ready for closure. Indeed, this step is a good test to determine how far you have come in ending your conflict.

Try saying, "I know it took courage to come here today and face a difficult conversation with me, and I want to thank you for doing that." Or you can acknowledge your opponent for teaching you important lessons about how to handle similar disputes in the future, or talk about what you are doing to improve your skills in conflict resolution.

Try acknowledging your opponent in areas where you would most like to encourage growth or learning. You can, for example, praise him for facing problems squarely, listening to you empathetically, communicating honestly, being willing to compromise, sticking with the process even when it was difficult, being open and forthcoming about the issues, offering useful feedback or food for thought, being principled or assertive, reaching a number of agreements, or being willing to commit to a course of action that could end the conflict.

The third step requires you to identify what you need to do or say to let go of the conflict completely and find a constructive way of doing so. In preparation, ask yourself: If I end the conflict and do not reach closure, what issues or feelings will be left unresolved? What will happen as a result? What price will I pay? What do I need to do or say to reach closure? What can I say about my role in the conflict or resolution process? What have I learned about conflict and myself through my efforts to resolve it?

Forgiveness is something you do for yourself. It is releasing yourself from the burden of your own false expectations, or as writer Anne Lamott put it, "giving up all hope of having a better past." It is separating the person from the problem and being hard on the problem and at the same time soft on the person. It does *not* mean forgiving and forgetting, but remembering what happened and how you felt, then imagining what the other person may have experienced and how he or she may have felt.

Although it sounds counterintuitive, it is useful in reaching forgiveness to identify all the reasons for *not* forgiving your opponent, and all the expectations you had that she did not meet. Afterward, you can choose either to release yourself from each of those reasons and expectations, or honestly estimate what it will cost you, personally and organizationally, to hold on to them.

It is then helpful to design and execute a ritual or ceremony of release, as a signal through action that the conflict is really over for you. Mini-rituals and ceremonies can consolidate closure, even if they consist only of shaking hands or agreeing to let bygones be bygones. Try to think of creative ceremonies to end your disputes and return to collegiality.

We mediated a conflict in which two coworkers personally insulted each other repeatedly over five years in staff meetings and private conversations. To end their dispute, they agreed to jointly appear on the agenda at the next staff meeting and tell everyone how they had resolved their conflict and what they learned from each other and the mediation process.

The fourth step in reaching closure is also the final strategy in resolving conflicts at work, which is to search for the most important lessons in your conflict and use that information to design conflict resolution systems that will prevent future disputes, or resolve them more quickly and easily the next time they occur.

It is possible to initiate a prevention or systems design process simply by asking each person to identify one thing their leader, manager, coworkers, or the organization as a whole might have done to prevent the conflict, or make it less costly or easier to handle. After brainstorming a list of what might have been done differently, ask, "What should happen to this list?" The correct answer is to take it *together* to someone who can make sure it does not happen again and support organizational learning.

We encourage you to search for other creative ways of completing your conflict that communicate the heart of what you experienced and do not want to experience again. We encourage you to seek closure, and give it and the resolution process at least as much energy, insight, courage, perseverance, and commitment as you have given to your conflict.

Conclusion

As we come to the end of our exploration of these ten strategies, we hope they will encourage you to resolve your conflicts and move from impasse to settlement, resolution, and transformation. Perhaps you have resolved your conflicts or made them easier to handle, or perhaps they remain unresolved. In any case, we hope you have learned that conflict is a rich source of learning, growth, and improvement, in both your personal and working life.

As individuals, organizations, cultures, societies, and nations, our challenge is to learn from our conflicts so we can better communicate with our opponents and resist engaging in aggressive and defensive responses, whether in the form of small-scale disputes at work, or large-scale international conflicts like wars that destroy lives.

Conflicts of all sizes and kinds can all be reduced by welcoming differences, disagreements, and criticisms; by celebrating dissent and disagreement as gifts that lead to improvement; and by recognizing that every conflict without exception can lead to improved relationships, learning, transformation, and transcendence.

As individuals, organizations, and societies, we are only just beginning to recognize that innovation and collaboration flourish *precisely* in the midst of conflict and, as a result, are increasingly rejecting the win-lose limitations reinforced by conflict-averse, adversarial cultures.

If we can learn to experience our conflicts as journeys rather than wars, as challenges rather than burdens, and as opportunities for growth and improvement, we may actually begin to anticipate with pleasure the next chance we have to transform our conflicts into satisfying communications, creative and paradoxical problem solving, collaborative negotiations, and better relationships.

As we find more and more ways to approach our conflicts constructively, we perceive deeper levels of conflict that need to be analyzed and addressed, and make deeper levels of resolution possible. We hope we have shown how opportunities for learning and growth emerge in conflict resolution, and encourage you to keep your openness and capacity for learning alive as your conflicts swell, dissolve, soar, stall, and vanish in a puff of smoke.

We encourage you to find resting places, lookouts, safe harbors, coaches, and guides to help you along your way, as you reflect on your experiences and search for the knowledge you need to grow and become more skillful. Finally, we encourage you to share what you learn with others, including your opponents, to multiply your successes and deepen your understanding.

As you locate these opportunities in your conflicts, relax, and move toward and through them, do not ignore your limitations, weaknesses, mistakes, and contributions to impasse. Noticing these obstacles will *automatically* create the possibility of learning how to transcend them. And who could be better at highlighting these possibilities than the one whose difficult behaviors encourage you to think your conflict is about *them* and not at all about you? In this way, we are all indebted to our opponents for teaching us to become better human beings.

The path is not easy and, as the poet Anne Sexton wrote, "Sometimes it is necessary to be a hero just to be an ordinary, decent human being." We hope we have encouraged and supported you in embarking on your own heroic path of self-discovery, learning, and transformation, and we wish you *great* conflicts!

Good luck!

THE AUTHORS

KENNETH CLOKE, J.D., L.L.M., Ph.D., has been the director of the Center for Dispute Resolution in Santa Monica for thirty years and is a mediator, arbitrator, consultant, and trainer. He specializes in resolving complex multiparty conflicts, including organizational, workplace, and labor-management disputes; discrimination and sexual harassment complaints; marital, divorce, and family conflicts; and environmental and public policy issues. He is an internationally acclaimed speaker on conflict resolution and an adjunct faculty member at Pepperdine University School of Law, University of Amsterdam's ADR Institute, Saybrook University, and Southern Methodist University. He is president and founder of Mediators Beyond Borders.

He is the author of *Mediating Dangerously: The Frontiers of Conflict Resolution; Mediation, Revenge and the Magic of Forgiveness; The Crossroads of Conflict: A Journey into the Heart of Dispute Resolution;* and *Conflict Revolution: Mediating Evil, War, Injustice and Terrorism.* He is coauthor with Joan Goldsmith of *Resolving Personal and Organizational Conflict: Stories of Transformation and Forgiveness; Thank God It's Monday! 14 Values We Need to Humanize the Way We Work; The End of Management and the Rise of Organizational Democracy*, which was selected as the best book on leadership in Germany in 2002 by the German *Financial Times*; and *The Art of Waking People Up: Cultivating Awareness and Authenticity at Work.*

JOAN GOLDSMITH, M.A., Doctor of Humane Letters, is an organizational consultant, mediator, coach, and educator for forty years, specializing in leadership development, organizational effectiveness, conflict resolution, and team building. She has contributed to organizational change in Fortune 100 companies, government agencies, and nonprofit organizations in the United States, Europe, Asia, Africa, and Latin America. She specializes in resolving team miscommunications, gender-based conflicts, public policy disputes, and conflict coaching.

She is a former faculty member at Harvard University, Antioch University, and UCLA, and is a founder of Cambridge College. She is the creator of several innovative programs for women, including "Women Leaders: Creating Ourselves at the Crossroads," and "Women Writers: Finding One's Voice." She has worked as a mediator, facilitator, and trainer in conflict resolution in public, private, and nonprofit organizations. In addition to her five books coauthored with Kenneth Cloke, she is coauthor with Warren Bennis of *Learning to Lead: A Workbook on Becoming a Leader*.

INDEX

A

E

F

I

N

O

Q

R

S

Y